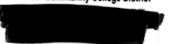

CLYMER®

POLARIS

WATER VEHICLES SHOP MANUAL
1992-1995

The World's Finest Publisher of Mechanical How-To Manuals

INTERTEC PUBLISHING

P.O. Box 12901, Overland Park, Kansas 66282-2901

Copyright ©1996 Intertec Publishing

FIRST EDITION
First Printing September, 1996
Second Printing August, 1999

Printed in U.S.A.

CLYMER and colophon are registered trademarks of Intertec Publishing.

ISBN: 0-89287-672-7

Library of Congress: 96-77869

Technical photography by Mark Jacobs.

Technical illustrations by Mike St. Clair.

Polaris watercraft for technical photographs provided by Larry Day.

Cover photo courtesy of Kinney Jones.

Intertec Book Division

President Raymond E. Maloney
Vice President, Book Division Ted Marcus

The following books and guides are published by Intertec Publishing.

Contents

Quick Reference Data

APPROXIMATE REFILL CAPACITY

Oil injection reservoir		
SL650 & SL750	3.3 L	3.5 qt.
SLT750	4.7 L	5 qt.
Fuel tank		
SL650 & SL750	37.1 L	9.8 gal.
SLT750	41.6 L	11 gal.

MAINTENANCE TIGHTENING TORQUES

	N·m	ft.-lb.
Carburetor mounting	21.7	16
Cylinder head	24.4	18
Cylinder base	38	28
Crankcase		
8 mm	21.7	16
10 mm	35.2	26
Drive coupler	216.9	160
Engine to mount plate	61	45
Exhaust manifold	21.7	16
Flywheel screw	74.6	55
Flywheel housing	8.81	78 in.-lb.
Impeller	135.6	100
Intake manifold	8.81	78 in.-lb.
Plastic air intake	2.26	20 in.-lb.
Steering cable adjusting nuts		
1992-1994 (rear)	40.7	30
1995-on (front)	40.7	30
Water outlet manifold	8.81	78 in.-lb.
Other fasteners		
5 mm	5.1-5.9	45-52 in.-lb.
6 mm	7.5-8.8	66-78 in.-lb.
8 mm	17.6-21.7	13-16
10 mm	35.2-40.7	26-30
12 mm	54.2-59.7	40-44

SPARK PLUGS

	NGK type	Champion type	Gap mm (in.)
1992-1993 models	BR8ES	RN-3C	0.7 (0.028)
1994-on	BPR7ES	–	0.7 (0.028)

IGNITION TIMING

Year and model	CDI box identification	Ignition timing @ 3,000 rpm (BTDC) degrees	mm	in.
1992				
SL 650 B924058				
Early *	F8T16271	22.5-25.5	3.54	0.139
Late **	F8T16272	22.5-25.5	3.54	0.139
1993				
SL 650 B934058	F8T16273	16.5-19.5	2.01	0.079
SL 750 B934070	F8T16273	14.5-17.5	1.59	0.063
1994				
SL 650 B944058	F8T16274 (65W95)	16-20	2.01	0.079
SL 750 B944070	F8T32071 (75W95)	22-26	3.54	0.139
SLT 750 B944170	F8T32071 (75W95)	22-26	3.54	0.139
1995				
SL 650 B954058	F8T16274 (65W95)	16-20	2.01	0.079
SL650 Std. B954358	F8T16274 (65W95)	16-20	2.01	0.079
SL 750 B954070	F8T32071 (75W95)	22-26	3.54	0.139
SLT 750 B954170	F8T32071 (75W95)	22-26	3.54	0.139

* Early models with large harmonic balancer.
** Serial No.PLE04039F292 and later models.

CHARGING/IGNITION COILS RESISTANCE

	Resistance
Alternator coil (red/purple to yellow)	0.6 ohms
High tension coils	
Primary winding (black to black/white)	0.6 ohms
Secondary winding (black to spark plug wire)*	3.3 K ohms
Plug cap	5.0 K ohms
Ignition exciter coil (red/white to green/red)	490 ohms
Ignition pulser coil (blue/red to red/white)	90 ohms
Ignition trigger coil (white/yellow to black)	220 ohms

* With the spark plug cap removed. Coil secondary resistance should not be tested with the spark plug cap installed.

STARTER MOTOR SPECIFICATIONS

Resistance between	
Commutator segments	less than 0.3 ohms
Input terminal and insulated brushes	less than 0.3 ohms
Brushes	
Minimum length	7.9 mm (5/16 in.)

CARBURETOR SPECIFICATIONS

1992 SL650	Mikuni - Super BN
Size	38 mm with 34 mm venturi
Idle speed in water	1,300 rpm
Low speed screw	1 3/8 turns open
High speed screw	
Magneto end carb.	3/8 turn open
Center carb.	
Early models	1/8 turn open
Later models (June-on)	3/8 turn open
Rear carburetor	1/4 turn open
Pop off pressure	
Early models	25-30 psi (172-207 kPa)
Later models	10-18 psi (69-124 kPa)
Pilot jet	
Early models	#85
Later models (June-on)	#80
Main jet	#80

1993 SL650	Mikuni - Super BN
Size	38 mm with 34 mm venturi
Idle speed in water	1,300 rpm
Low speed screw	1/4 turn open
High speed screw	
Magneto end carburetor	7/8 turn open
Center carburetor	3/8 turn open
Rear carburetor	5/8 turn open
Pop off pressure	10-18 psi (69-124 kPa)
Pilot jet	#77.5
Main jet	#77.5

1993 SL750	Mikuni - Super BN
Size	38 mm with 34 mm venturi
Idle speed in water	1,200-1,300 rpm
Low speed screw	1/2 turn open
High speed screw	
Magneto end carburetor	7/8 turn open
Center carburetor	1/2 turn open
Rear carburetor	5/8 turn open
Pop off pressure	10-18 psi (69-124 kPa)
Pilot jet	#72.5
Main jet	#77.5

1994 SL650 (engine serial No. 94-0001 to 94-02011)	
Carburetor type	Mikuni - Super BN
Size	38 mm with 34 mm venturi
Idle speed in water	1,250-1,350 rpm
Low speed screw	1 1/4 turns open
High speed screw	
Magneto end carburetor	3/4 turn open
Center carburetor	1/4 turn open
Rear carburetor	1/2 turn open
Pop off pressure	10-18 psi (69-124 kPa)
Pilot jet	#75
Main jet	#95

(continued)

1994 SL650 (engine serial No. 94-02011 and up)

Carburetor type	Mikuni - Super BN
Size	38 mm with 34 mm venturi
Idle speed in water	1,250-1,350 rpm
Low speed screw	1 turn open
High speed screw	
Magneto end carburetor	7/8 turn open
Center carburetor	1/2 turn open
Rear carburetor	3/4 turn open
Pop off pressure	10-18 psi (69-124 kPa)
Pilot jet	#75
Main jet	#90

1994 SL750 and SLT750

Carburetor type	Mikuni - Super BN
Size	38 mm with 34 mm venturi
Idle speed in water	1,200-1,300 rpm
Low speed screw	1/2 turn open
High speed screw	
Magneto end carburetor	1 1/4 turns open
Center carburetor	3/8 turn open
Rear carburetor	7/8 turn open
Pop off pressure	10-18 psi (69-124 kPa)
Pilot jet	#75
Main jet	#90

1995 650 STD and SL650

Carburetor type	Mikuni - Super BN
Size	38 mm with 34 mm venturi
Idle speed in water	1,200-1,300 rpm
Low speed screw	1 1/8 turns open
High speed screw	
Magneto end carburetor	1 1/4 turns open
Center carburetor	1/4 turn open
Rear carburetor	7/8 turn open
Pop off pressure	10-18 psi (69-124 kPa)
Pilot jet	#77.5
Main jet	#87.5

1995 650 STD and SL650

Carburetor type	Mikuni - Super BN
Size	38 mm with 34 mm venturi
Idle speed in water	1,200-1,300 rpm
Low speed screw	1 1/8 turns open
High speed screw	
Magneto end carburetor	1 1/4 turns open
Center carburetor	1/4 turn open
Rear carburetor	7/8 turn open
Pop off pressure	10-18 psi (69-124 kPa)
Pilot jet	#77.5
Main jet	#87.5

(continued)

CARBURETOR SPECIFICATIONS (continued)

1995 750 SL and SLT750

Carburetor type	Mikuni - Super BN
Size	38 mm with 34 mm venturi
Idle speed in water	1,200-1,300 rpm
Low speed screw	1/2 turn open
High speed screw	
Magneto end carburetor	1 turn open
Center carburetor	1/2 turn open
Rear carburetor	3/4 turn open
Pop off pressure	10-18 psi (69-124 kPa)
Pilot jet	#75
Main jet	#90

OIL INJECTION PUMP SPECIFICATIONS

Oil pump driveshaft end play	0.3-0.6 mm (0.012-0.024 in.)
Oil reservoir capacity	
All SL 650 and SL 750 models	3.3 L (3.5 qt.)
SLT 750 models	4.7 L (5 qt.)
Oil control link rod	
Length, 1995-on	162.6-164.1 mm (6.40-6.46 in.)

SERVICE CLEARANCES

	Desired mm (in.)	Wear limit mm (in.)
Pump impeller to wear ring	0.05-0.20 (0.002-0.008)	0.51 (0.020)
Driveshaft		
Runout *	–	0.13 (0.005)
Driveshaft end play **	–	2.5-5.1 (0.1-0.2)

* Support driveshaft near ends and measure runout near the center behind the bushing and seal journal.
** With new bumpers installed in both ends of the driveshaft.

CLYMER®

POLARIS

WATER VEHICLES SHOP MANUAL
1992-1995

Chapter One

General Information

This Clymer shop manual covers the 1992-1995 Polaris Personal Watercraft. The text provides complete information on maintenance, tune-up, repair and overhaul. Hundreds of photos and drawings guide you through every job. This book includes all of the information you need to know to keep your Polaris running right.

A shop manual is a reference. You want to be able to find information fast. As in all Clymer books, this one is designed with you in mind. All chapters are thumb tabbed. Important items are extensively indexed at the rear of the book. All procedures, tables and illustrations in this manual are for the reader who may be working on the watercraft or using this manual for the first time. The most frequently used specifications and capacities are summarized in the *Quick Reference Data* pages at the front of the book.

Keep the book handy in your tool box. It will help you to better understand how the watercraft operates, lower repair and maintenance costs and generally improve your satisfaction with your Polaris personal watercraft.

MANUAL ORGANIZATION

All dimensions and capacities are expressed in English units, familiar to U.S. mechanics, as well as in metric units. This chapter discusses equipment and tools useful both for preventative maintenance and troubleshooting.

Chapter Two provides methods and suggestions for quick and accurate diagnosis and repair of problems. Troubleshooting procedures discuss typical symptoms and logical methods to pinpoint the trouble.

Chapter Three explains all periodic lubrication and routine maintenance necessary to keep the watercraft operating at peak performance. Chapter Three also includes recommended tune-up procedures, eliminating the need to constantly consult chapters on the various assemblies.

Subsequent chapters describe specific systems such as the engine, fuel system, exhaust system, electrical system, and drive system. Each chapter provides disassembly, repair, and assembly procedures in simple step-by-step form. If a repair is impractical for a home mechanic, it is indicated as such. It is usually faster and less expensive to take such repairs to a dealership or competent repair shop. Specifications concerning a particular system are included at the end of the appropriate chapter.

Some of the procedures in this manual specify special tools. In most cases, the tool is illustrated either in actual use or alone. Well equipped mechanics may find they can substitute similar tools already on hand or can fabricate their own.

Table 1 lists model number coverage. General dimensions are listed in **Table 2**. **Table 3** lists the weight and capacity.

Metric and U.S. standards are used throughout this manual. U.S. to metric conversion is given in **Table 4**.

Critical torque specifications are found in table form at the end of each chapter (as required). The general torque specifications listed in **Table 5** can be used when a torque specification is not listed for a specific component or assembly.

A list of general technical abbreviations is given in **Table 6**.

Metric tap drill sizes can be found in **Table 7**.

Tables 1-7 are found at the end of this chapter.

NOTES, CAUTIONS AND WARNINGS

The terms NOTE, CAUTION and WARNING have specific meanings in this manual. A NOTE provides additional information to make a step or procedure easier or clearer. Disregarding a NOTE could cause inconvenience, but would not cause damage or personal injury.

A CAUTION emphasizes an area where equipment damage could occur. Disregarding a CAUTION could cause permanent mechanical damage; however, personal injury is unlikely.

A WARNING emphasizes an area where personal injury or even death could result from negligence. Mechanical damage may also occur. WARNINGS are to be taken *seriously*. In some cases, serious injury and death has resulted from disregarding similar warnings.

SERVICE HINTS

Most of the service procedures covered are straight-forward and can be performed by anyone reasonably handy with tools. It is suggested, however, that you consider your own capabilities carefully before attempting any operation involving major disassembly.

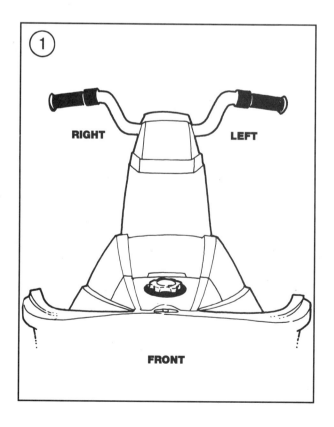

1. "Front," as used in this manual, refers to the front of the watercraft; the front of any component is the end closest to the front of the watercraft. The "left" and "right" sides refer to the position of the parts as viewed by the operator sitting on the watercraft facing forward. For example, the throttle control is on the right side. These rules are simple, but confusion can cause a major inconvenience during service. See **Figure 1**.

2. When disassembling any engine or drive component, mark the parts for location and mark all parts which mate together. Small parts, such as bolts, can be identified by placing them in plastic sandwich bags (**Figure 2**). Seal the bags and label them with masking tape and a marking pen. When reassembly will take place immediately, an accepted practice is to place nuts and bolts in a cupcake tin or egg carton in the order of disassembly.

3. Protect finished surfaces from physical damage or corrosion. Keep gasoline and harsh solvents off plastic and painted surfaces.

4. Use penetrating oil on frozen or tight bolts, then strike the bolt head a few times with a hammer and punch (use a screwdriver on screws). Avoid the use of heat where possible, as it can warp, melt or affect the temper of parts. Heat also ruins finishes, especially paint and plastics.

5. No parts removed or installed (other than bushings and bearings) in the procedures given in this manual should require unusual force during disassembly or assembly. If a part is difficult to remove or install, find out why before proceeding.

6. Cover all openings after removing parts or components to prevent dirt, small tools or other contamination from falling in.

7. Read each procedure *completely* while looking at the actual parts before starting a job. Make sure you *thoroughly* understand what is to be done and then carefully follow the procedure, step by step.

8. The recommendation is occasionally made to refer service or maintenance to a Polaris dealership or a specialist in a particular field. In these cases, the work will be done more quickly and economically than if you performed the job yourself.

9. In procedural steps, the term "replace" means to discard a defective part and replace it with a new or exchange unit. "Overhaul" means to remove, disassemble, inspect, measure, repair or replace defective parts, reassemble and install major systems or parts.

10. Some operations require the use of a hydraulic press. It is wiser to have these operations performed by a shop equipped for such work, rather than to try to do the job yourself with makeshift equipment that may damage your machine.

11. Repairs go much faster and easier if your machine is clean before you begin work. There are many special cleaners on the market for washing the engine and related parts. Follow the manufacturer's directions on the container for the best results. Clean all oily or greasy parts with cleaning solvent as you remove them.

> *WARNING*
> *Never use gasoline as a cleaning agent. It presents an extreme fire hazard. Be sure to work in a well-ventilated area when using cleaning solvent. Keep a fire extinguisher, rated for gasoline fires, handy in any case.*

12. Much of the labor charge for repairs made at a dealership are for the time involved during

the removal, disassembly, assembly, and reinstallation of other parts to reach the defective part. It is frequently possible to perform the preliminary operations yourself, then take the defective unit to the dealership for repair at considerable savings.

13. If special tools are required, make arrangements to get them before you start. It is frustrating and time-consuming to get partly into a job and then be unable to complete it.

14. Make diagrams (take a video or Polaroid picture) wherever similar-appearing parts are found. You may think you can remember where everything came from—but mistakes are costly. There is also the possibility that you may be sidetracked and not return to work for days or even weeks—in which the time carefully laid out parts may have become disturbed.

15. When assembling parts, be sure all shims and washers are replaced exactly as they came out.

16. Whenever a rotating part butts against a stationary part, look for a shim or washer.

17. Use new gaskets if there is any doubt about the condition of the old ones. A thin coat of silicone sealant on non-pressure type gaskets may help them seal more effectively. If it is necessary to make a cover gasket and you do not have a suitable old gasket to use as a guide, you can use the outline of the cover and gasket material to make a new gasket. Apply engine oil to the cover gasket surface. Then place the cover on the new gasket material and apply pressure with your hands. The oil will leave a very accurate outline on the gasket material that can be cut around.

CAUTION
When purchasing gasket material to make a gasket, measure the thickness of the old gasket (at an uncompressed point) and purchase gasket material with the same approximate thickness.

18. Heavy grease can be used to hold small parts in place if they tend to fall out during assembly.

Be sure to keep grease and oil away from electrical components.

19. A carburetor is best cleaned by disassembling it and cleaning the parts in hot soap and water. Never soak gaskets and rubber parts in commercial carburetor cleaners. Never use wire to clean out jets and air passages, because they are easily damaged. Use compressed air to blow out the carburetor only if the diaphragm has been removed first.

20. Take your time and do the job right. Do not forget that a newly rebuilt engine must be broken-in just like a new one.

ENGINE OPERATION

Figure 3 explains how a typical 2-stroke engine works. This is helpful when troubleshooting or repairing the engine.

MODEL NUMBER

Polaris uses a series of numbers (**Figure 4**) to identify the year, hull design and engine type. Refer to **Table 1** for a listing of the models numbers. The Model Number and the Hull Identification Number are both located on a plate attached to the rear of the hull (**Figure 5**, typical).

ENGINE IDENTIFICATION NUMBER

Each engine is given a unique identification number that may be used for registration. The engine identification number is located on the water outlet manifold as shown at A, **Figure 6**. The engine identification number should be recorded and stored in a safe place to help the owner identify the unit if it is stolen. The engine identification number is also stamped into the crankcase, under the exhaust manifold at B, **Figure 6**.

③

2-STROKE OPERATING PRINCIPLES

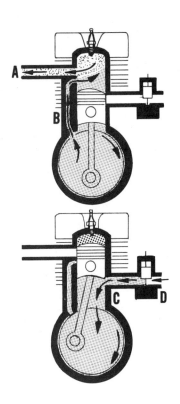
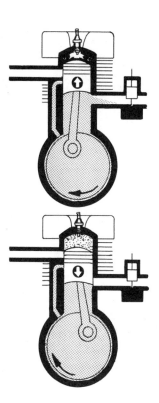

The crankshaft in this discussion is rotating in a clockwise direction.

As the piston travels downward, it uncovers the exhaust port (A) allowing the exhaust gases, which are under pressure, to leave the cylinder. A fresh fuel/air charge, which has been compressed slightly, travels from the crankcase into the cylinder through the transfer port (B). Since this charge enters under pressure, it also helps to push out the exhaust gases.

While the crankshaft continues to rotate, the piston moves upward, covering the transfer port (B) and exhaust port (A). The piston is now compressing the new fuel/air mixture and creating a low pressure area in the crankcase at the same time. As the piston continues to travel, it uncovers the intake port (C). A fresh fuel/air charge, from the carburetor (D), is drawn into the crankcase through the intake port, because of the low pressure within it.

Now, as the piston almost reaches the top of its travel, the spark plug fires, thus igniting the compressed fuel/air mixture. The piston continues to top dead center (TDC) and is pushed downward by the expanding gases.

As the piston travels down, the exhaust gases leave the cylinder and the complete cycle starts all over again.

HULL IDENTIFICATION NUMBER

Each watercraft is given a unique hull identification number that may be used for registration. The model number and the hull identification number are both located on a plate attached to the rear of the hull (**Figure 5**, typical). The hull identification number should be recorded and stored in a safe place to help the owner identify the craft if it is stolen. A second identification is attached to the hull in front of the engine (**Figure 7**, typical).

PARTS REPLACEMENT

Polaris may make changes during a model year. Some may be minor, while others may be relatively major. When ordering parts from a dealership or other parts distributor, always order by the year designation, model number, hull identification number and engine identification number. Write all of these numbers down and store them in a safe place in case they are needed for identification. Copy the numbers and take them with you when ordering parts. You should also take the old part if possible. Compare the new parts with the old parts before purchasing them. If the old and new parts are different, ask the parts manager to explain the difference to you. **Table 1** lists the model numbers and identifying colors.

> *CAUTION*
> *Use caution when servicing a craft or engine if either serial number plate is missing. It is more difficult to identify the specific parts to install. It may also indicate that the craft or engine has been stolen.*

CLEARING A SUBMERGED WATERCRAFT

If the watercraft is submerged, water may get into the engine, the oil tank (reservoir) and the fuel tank. To prevent corrosion and serious damage to the engine, the following steps must be taken before trying to restart the engine.

> *CAUTION*
> *Do not force the engine if it does not turn over. This may be an indication of internal damage or hydraulic lock. If the cylinder is filled with fluid (hydraulic locked), forcing can bend the connecting rod or crack the cylinder, head or piston.*

> *WARNING*
> *Keep your hands away from the jet pump while cranking the engine.*

> *CAUTION*
> *To prevent corrosion damage inside the engine, accomplish this clearing procedure as soon as possible after submerging the watercraft.*

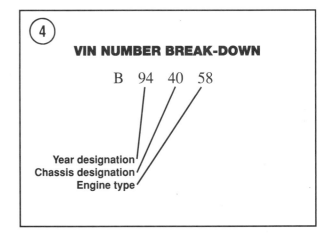

④

VIN NUMBER BREAK-DOWN

B   94   40   58

Year designation
Chassis designation
Engine type

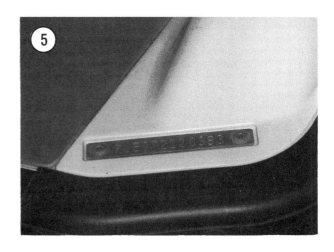

⑤

1. Beach the craft.

2. Remove the seat and engine cover.

3. Turn the fuel valve OFF.

4. Check the oil tank for water contamination. If necessary, syphon out the contaminated oil and fill with fresh oil.

5. Check the fuel tank for water contamination. Drain and refill the tank with fresh gasoline, if necessary.

6. If there is water in the bilge, drain it, then dry the compartment with a sponge and cloths.

7. Remove the spark plugs and ground their leads to the engine to prevent damage to the CDI ignition system.

CAUTION
Do not force the engine if it does not turn over. This may be an indication of internal damage and forcing can cause additional damage.

8. Crank the engine with the starter for 10 seconds, then stop and allow the starter to cool for 30 seconds. Repeat this cycle as required to force water from the cylinders.

9. Repeat Step 8 to force water out through the spark plug holes. Repeat until water no longer exits from the spark plug holes.

10. If the spark plugs are wet, spray them with electrical cleaner (if available), then dry the plugs before reinstalling them.

11. Spray a lubricant into the spark plug holes and crank the engine as described in Step 8.

12. Reinstall the spark plugs.

13. Install the seat and engine cover.

14. Launch the craft.

15. Turn the fuel ON.

16. Reinstall the tether switch and try to start the engine.

17A. If the engine starts, run it for at least 10 minutes at slow speed, before returning it to normal operation.

17B. If the engine will not start, proceed as follows.

    a. Remove and inspect the spark plugs.

    b. If the firing tips are covered with water, repeat Steps 7-16. If the plugs continue to be fouled by water, there may be water in the fuel system. Check the fuel system and remove the contaminated fuel as necessary. Refer to Chapter Six.

    c. If the firing tips of the plugs are covered with gasoline (flooded), attach a test plug and check to be sure that the spark plugs are firing. Check for damaged ignition or other electrical components.

18. Restart the engine and operate it for about 10 minutes, then stop the engine and beach the craft.

19. Remove the seat and engine cover.

20. Unbolt and remove the intake silencer and carburetor spark arrestor from the carburetors.

21. Spray a rust preventative, into the carburetor while cranking the engine with the starter.

CAUTION
Do not leave any part of the spark arrestor or intake silencer off. Be sure that all parts are correctly assembled and not changed in any way. Reworked parts, installation of incorrect parts or removal of parts may seriously damage the engine.

22. Reassemble the spark arrestor and intake silencer.

TORQUE SPECIFICATIONS

Torque specifications throughout this manual are given in Newton meters (N·m) and foot pounds (ft.-lb.). Newton meters have been adopted in place of kilogram meters (kgm) in accordance with the International Modernized Metric System. Many tool manufacturers offer torque wrenches calibrated in both Newton meters and foot pounds.

Early torque wrenches calibrated in kilogram meters can be used by performing a simple conversion. All you have to do is move the decimal point one place to the right. For example: 4.7 kgm = 47 N·m. This conversion is accurate enough for mechanical work even though the exact mathematical conversion is 46.09 N·m.

SAFETY FIRST

Professional mechanics can work for years and never sustain a serious injury. If you observe a few rules of common sense and safety, you can enjoy many safe hours servicing your own machine. If you ignore these rules you can hurt yourself or damage the equipment.

1. Never use gasoline as a cleaning solvent.
2. Never smoke or use a torch in the vicinity of flammable liquids, such as cleaning solvent, in an open container.
3. If welding or brazing is required on the machine, remove the fuel tank to a safe distance, at least 50 ft. (15 m) away.

4. Use the proper sized wrenches to avoid damage to fasteners and injury to yourself.
5. When loosening a tight or stuck nut, be guided by what would happen if the wrench should slip. Be careful; protect yourself accordingly.
6. If replacing a fastener, make sure to use one with the same measurements and strength as the old one. Incorrect or mismatched fasteners can result in physical damage and possible personal injury. Beware of fastener kits that are filled with cheap and poorly made nuts, bolts, washers and cotter pins. Refer to *Fasteners* in this chapter for additional information.
7. Keep all hand and power tools in good condition. Wipe greasy and oily tools after using them. They are difficult to hold and can cause injury. Replace or repair worn or damaged tools.
8. Keep your work area clean and uncluttered.
9. Wear safety goggles during all operations involving drilling, grinding, the use of a cold chisel or *anytime* you feel unsure about the safety of your eyes. Safety goggles should also be worn anytime solvent or compressed air is used to clean parts.
10. Keep an approved fire extinguisher (**Figure 8**) nearby. Be sure it is rated for gasoline (Class B) and electrical (Class C) fires.
11. When drying bearings or other rotating parts using compressed air, never allow the air jet to rotate the bearing or part. The air jet is capable

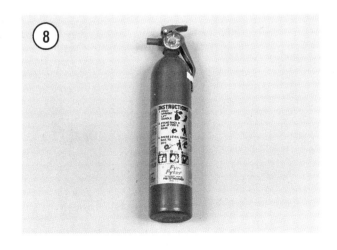

of rotating them at speeds far in excess of those for which the bearings were designed. The bearing or rotating part is very likely to disintegrate and cause serious injury and damage. To prevent injury and bearing damage when using compressed air, hold both the inner and outer bearing races (**Figure 9**) by hand.

EXPENDABLE SUPPLIES

Certain expendable supplies (**Figure 10**) are required during maintenance and repair work. These include grease, oil, gasket cement, wiping

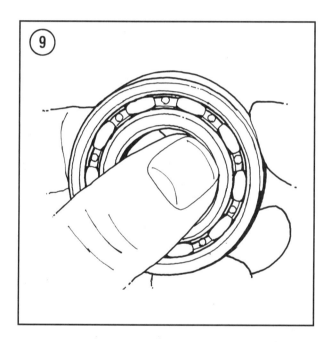

cloths and cleaning solvent. Ask your dealership for the special locking compounds, special lubricants or other products which may be suggested by the manufacturer for maintenance or repair. Cleaning solvents may be available from watercraft dealerships or some hardware stores.

> *WARNING*
> *Having a stack of clean shop cloths on hand is important when performing engine work. Most local fire codes require that used shop cloths be stored in a sealed, metal container with a self-closing lid until they can be washed or discarded.*

> *WARNING*
> *Even mild solvents and other chemicals can be absorbed into your skin while cleaning parts. Health hazards ranging from mild discomfort to major infections can often be avoided by using a pair of petroleum-resistant gloves. These can be purchased from industrial supply houses or many hardware stores.*

BASIC HAND TOOLS

Many of the procedures in this manual can be carried out with simple hand tools and test equipment familiar to the home mechanic. Keep your tools clean and in a tool box. Keep them organized with related tools stored together. After using a tool, wipe off dirt and grease with a clean cloth, then return the tool to its correct place.

Top quality tools are essential; they are also more economical in the long run. If you are now starting to build your tool collection, avoid "advertised specials" featured at some parts houses, discount stores and chain drug stores. These are usually poor grade tools that can be sold cheaply and that is exactly what they are—*cheap*. They are usually made of inferior material, and are thick, heavy and clumsy. Their rough finish makes them difficult to clean and they usually don't last very long. If it is ever your misfortune to use such tools, you will probably find out that

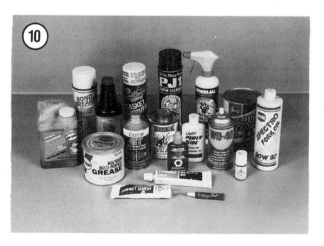

the wrenches do not fit the heads of bolts and nuts correctly and will often damage the fastener.

Quality tools are made of alloy steel and are heat treated for greater strength. They are lighter and better balanced than cheap ones. Their surface is smooth, making them a pleasure to work with and easy to clean. The initial cost of good quality tools may be more but they are less expensive in the long run. Don't try to buy everything in all sizes in the beginning; do it a little at a time until you have the necessary tools.

The following tools are required to perform virtually any repair job. Each tool is described and the recommended size given for starting a tool collection. Additional tools and some duplicates may be added as you become familiar with the craft. Polaris personal watercraft are built with metric and U.S. standard fasteners—so if you are starting your collection now, you must buy both sizes.

Screwdrivers

The screwdriver is a very basic tool, but if used improperly it will do more damage than good. The slot on a screw has a definite dimension and shape. A screwdriver must be selected to conform with that shape. Use a small screwdriver for small screws and a large one for large screws or the screw head will be damaged.

Two basic types of screwdrivers are required: common (flat-blade) screwdrivers (**Figure 11**) and Phillips screwdrivers (**Figure 12**).

Screwdrivers are available in sets which often include an assortment of common and Phillips blades. If you buy them individually, buy at least the following:

   a. Common screwdriver—5/16 × 6 in. blade.
   b. Common screwdriver—3/8 × 12 in. blade.
   c. Phillips screwdriver—size 2 tip, 6 in. blade.

Use screwdrivers only for driving screws. Never use a screwdriver for prying or chiseling metal. Do not try to remove a Phillips or Allen head screw with a common screwdriver (unless the screw has a combination head that will accept either type); you can damage the head so that even the proper tool will be unable to remove it.

Always keep the tip of a common screwdriver in good condition. **Figure 13** shows how to grind the tip to the proper shape if it becomes damaged. Note the symmetrical sides of the tip.

Pliers

Pliers come in a wide range of types and sizes. Pliers are useful for holding, cutting, bending and crimping. They should never be used to cut hardened objects or to turn bolts or nuts. **Figure 14** shows several pliers useful in watercraft repair.

Each type of pliers has a specialized function. Slip-joint pliers are used mainly for holding things and for bending. Needlenose pliers are used to hold or bend small objects. Groove-joint

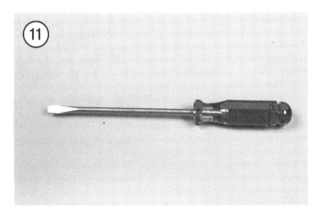

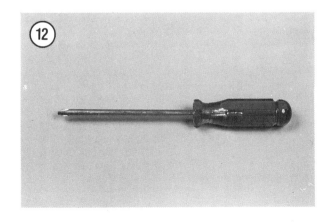

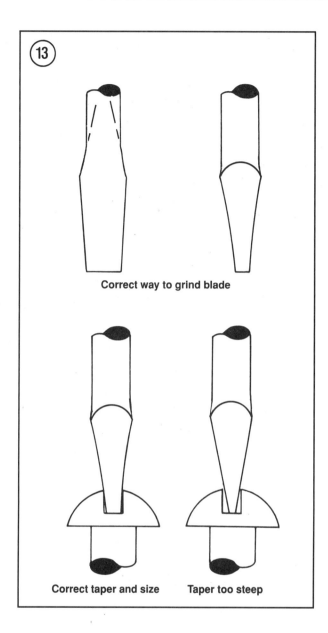

Correct way to grind blade

Correct taper and size   Taper too steep

pliers (commonly referred to as channel locks) can be adjusted to hold various sizes of objects such as pipe or tubing. There are many more types of pliers, but the ones described are the most suitable for common repairs.

CAUTION
Pliers should not be used for loosening or tightening nuts or bolts. The pliers sharp teeth will cut into the corners of the nut or bolt and damage the fastener.

CAUTION
If it is necessary to use slip-joint pliers to hold an object with a finished surface that can be easily damaged, wrap the object with tape or cardboard for protection.

Locking Pliers

Locking pliers, commonly referred to as vise-grip pliers (**Figure 15**), hold objects very tightly like a vise. Because locking pliers exert more force than regular pliers, their sharp jaws can permanently scar any object that is held. In addition, when locking pliers are locked in position, they can crush or deform thin wall material. Locking pliers are available in many types for specific tasks.

Snap Ring (Circlip) Pliers

Snap ring pliers (**Figure 16**) are made for removing and installing snap rings and should

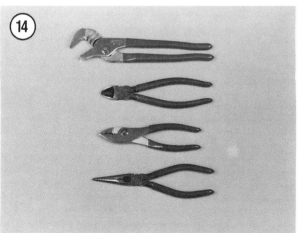

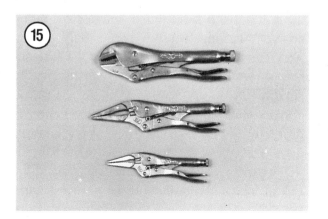

not be used for any other purpose. External pliers (spreading or expanding) are used for removing snap rings from the outside of a shaft or other similar part. Internal snap rings are located inside a tube, gear or housing and require pliers that squeeze the ends of the snap ring together so that the snap ring can be removed.

Box-end, Open-end and Combination Wrenches

Box-end and open-end wrenches (**Figure 17**) are available in sets or separately in a variety of sizes. The number stamped on open and box-end wrenches refers to the distance between 2 parallel flats of a nut or bolt head. Combination wrenches have box-end wrench on one end and an open-end wrench of the same size on the other end. The wrench size is stamped near the center of combination wrenches.

A box-end wrench generally grips all 6 corners of a fastener for a very secure grip. However, the fastener must have overhead access to use a box-end wrench. Box-end wrenches are available in 6-point or 12-point styles. A 6-point wrench provides superior holding ability, compared to a 12-point wrench, but requires a greater swinging radius. A 12-point wrench is more suitable when working in a confined area.

Open-end wrenches are speedy and work best in areas with limited overhead access. Their wide jaws make them unsuitable for situations where the bolt or nut is sunken in a well or close to the edge of a casting. These wrenches only grip on two flats of a fastener so if either the fastener head or wrench jaws are worn, the wrench may slip off.

No matter what style of wrench you choose, proper use is important to prevent personal injury. When using any wrench, get in the habit of pulling the wrench toward you. This reduces the risk of injuring your hand if the wrench should slip. If you have to push the wrench away from

you to loosen or tighten a fastener, open and push with the palm of your hand. This technique gets your fingers and knuckles out of the way should the wrench slip. Before using a wrench, always consider what could happen if the wrench slips or if the fastener breaks.

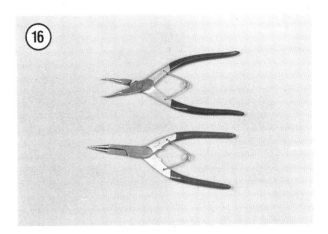

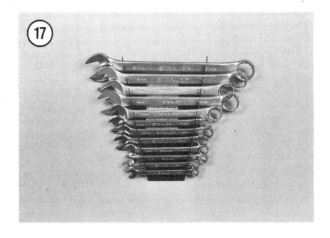

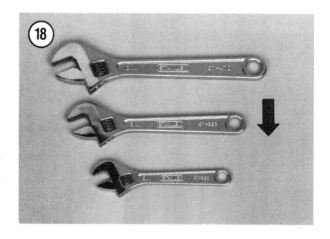

Adjustable Wrenches

An adjustable wrench (sometimes called a Crescent wrench) can be adjusted to fit nearly any nut or bolt head which has clear access around its entire perimeter. Adjustable wrenches (**Figure 18**) are best used as a backup wrench to keep a large nut or bolt from turning while the other fitting is being loosened or tightened with a proper wrench.

Adjustable wrenches have only two gripping surfaces and one is designed to move. The large physical size of adjustable wrenches limits where they can be used. The adjustable feature also makes this type of wrench more apt to slip, damaging the fastener or part and possibly injuring your hand.

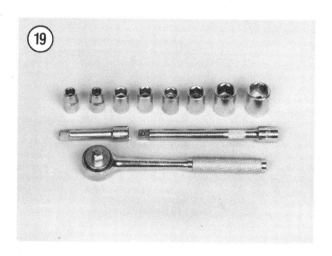

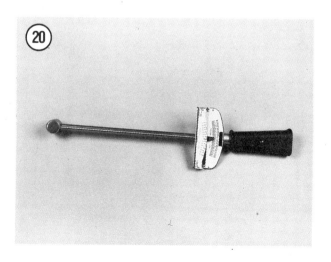

These wrenches are directional; the solid jaw must be the one transmitting the force. Apply force in the direction indicated by the arrow in **Figure 18**. If you use the adjustable jaw to transmit the force, it may loosen allowing the wrench to slip off.

Adjustable wrenches come in several sizes but a 6 or 8 in. size is recommended as an all-purpose wrench.

Socket Wrenches

This type of wrench is undoubtedly the fastest, safest and most convenient to use. Sockets which attach to a ratchet handle are available with 6-point or 12-point openings and 1/4, 3/8, 1/2 and 3/4 in. drives (**Figure 19**). The drive size indicates the size of the square hole which mates with the ratchet handle.

Torque Wrench

A torque wrench (**Figure 20**) is used with a socket to measure how tightly a nut or bolt is installed. They come in a wide price range and with 1/4, 3/8, or 1/2 in. square drive. The drive size indicates the size of the square drive which mates with the socket.

Impact Driver

This tool makes removal of tight fasteners easy and reduces the chance for damage to bolts and screw slots. Impact drivers and interchangeable bits (**Figure 21**) are available from most large hardware and motorcycle dealerships. Sockets can also be used with some hand impact drivers; however, make sure the socket is designed for impact use. Regular hand type sockets may shatter if used to loosen a tight fastener with an impact driver.

Hammers

The correct hammer (**Figure 22**) is necessary for certain repairs. A hammer with a face (or head) of rubber or plastic or the soft-faced hammer that is filled with lead shot is sometimes necessary during engine disassembly. *Never* use a metal-faced hammer on engine or pump parts, as severe damage will result in most cases. You can produce the same amount of force with a soft-faced hammer. A metal-faced hammer, however, is required when using a hand impact driver or cold chisel.

PRECISION MEASURING TOOLS

Measurement is an important part of service. When performing many of the service procedures in this manual, you will be required to make a number of measurements. These include basic checks such as engine compression (**Figure 23**) and spark plug gap (**Figure 24**). As you become involved in engine disassembly and service, measurements will be required to determine the condition of the piston and cylinder bore, crankshaft runout and so on. The type of measurement and the degree of accuracy will dictate which tool is required.

Precision measuring tools are expensive. If this is your first experience at engine service, it may be more worthwhile to have the checks made at a dealership. However, as your skills and enthusiasm increase for doing your own service work, you may want to begin purchasing some of these specialized tools. The following is a description of the measuring tools required in order to perform service described in this manual.

Feeler Gauge

Feeler gauges are available in sets of various sizes (**Figure 25**). The gauge is made of either a piece of a flat or round hardened steel of a specified thickness. Wire gauges are used to

measure spark plug gap. Flat gauges are used for most other measurements.

Vernier Caliper

This tool (**Figure 26**) is invaluable when reading inside, outside and depth measurements with close precision. Common uses of a vernier cali-

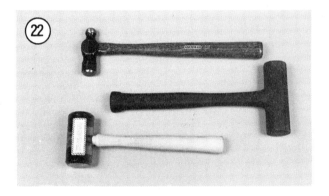

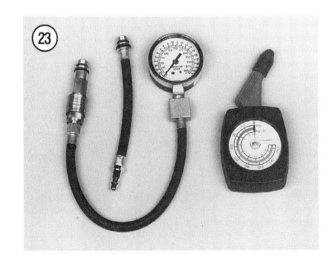

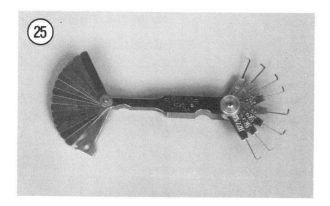

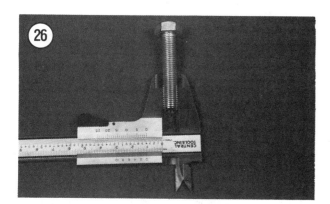

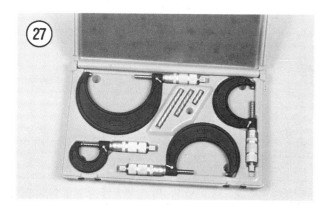

per are measuring the length of springs, the thickness of shims, or the depth of a bearing bore.

Outside Micrometers

An outside micrometer (**Figure 27**) is one of the most reliable instruments for precision measurement. Outside micrometers are required to measure precisely piston diameter, piston pin diameter, crankshaft journal and crankpin diameter. Used with a telescopic gauge, an outside micrometer can be used to measure cylinder bore size and to determine cylinder taper and out-of-round. Outside micrometers are delicate instruments; if dropped on the floor, they most certainly will be knocked out of calibration. Always handle and use micrometers carefully to ensure accuracy. Store micrometers in their padded case when not in use to prevent damage.

Dial Indicator

Dial indicators (**Figure 28**) are precision tools used to check differences in machined surfaces, such as the runout of a crankshaft or driveshaft. A dial indicator may also be used to locate the piston at a specific position for checking ignition timing. Select a dial indicator with a continuous dial (**Figure 29**). Several different mounting types are available, including a magnetic stand that attaches to iron surfaces, a clamp that can be attached to various components, and a spark plug adapter that locates the probe of the dial indicator through the spark plug hole of the cylinder head. See *Magnetic Stand* in this chapter. The various mounts are required for specific measuring requirements. The text will indicate the type of mounting necessary.

Degree Wheel

A degree wheel (**Figure 30**) is a specific tool used to measure parts of a circle and angles. A degree wheel is used to accurately position the engine crankshaft to determine the exact timing of the ignition or port opening. A degree wheel can be ordered through most parts suppliers.

Compression Gauge

An engine with low compression cannot be properly tuned and will not develop full power. A compression gauge (**Figure 31**) measures the amount of pressure present in the engine's combustion chamber during the compression/power stroke. Compression readings can be interpreted to pinpoint specific engine mechanical problems. The gauge shown (**Figure 31**) has a flexible stem with an extension. Although compression gauges with press-in rubber tips are available, a gauge with screw-in adapters are generally more accurate and easier to use. See Chapter Three for instruction regarding the use of a compression gauge and interpretation of test results.

Strobe Timing Light

This instrument is used to check ignition timing. By flashing a light at the precise instant the spark plug fires, the position of the timing mark can be seen. The flashing light makes the moving mark appear to stand still so that it can be viewed in relation to the stationary mark.

Suitable lights range from inexpensive neon bulb types (**Figure 32**) to powerful xenon strobe lights. A light with an inductive pickup is recommended to eliminate any possible damage to ignition wiring. The timing light should be attached and used according to the instructions provided by the manufacturer of the timing light.

Multimeter or VOM

A VOM (volt and ohm meter [**Figure 33**]) is a valuable tool for all electrical system troubleshooting. The voltmeter application is used to indicate the voltage applied or available to vari-

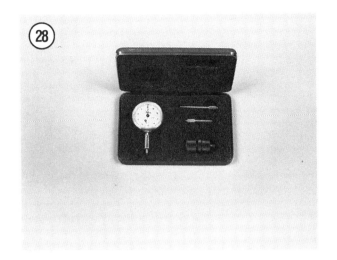

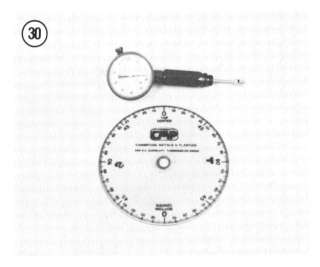

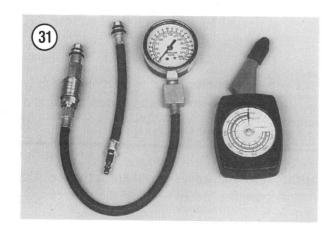

ous components. The ohmmeter is used to check for continuity and to measure resistance. Two types of multimeters are commonly available, analog and digital. Analog meters have a moving needle with marked bands indicating the volt, ohm and amperage scales. The digital meter (DVOM) is ideally suited for troubleshooting because it is easy to read, more accurate than analog, contains internal overload protection, is auto-ranging (analog meters must be calibrated each time the scale is changed) and has automatic polarity compensation.

Screw Pitch Gauge

A screw pitch gauge (**Figure 34**) determines the thread pitch of threaded fasteners. The gauge is made up of a number of thin plates. Each plate has a thread shape cut on one edge to match one thread pitch. When using a screw pitch gauge to determine a thread pitch size, try to fit different blade sizes onto the bolt thread until both threads match exactly.

Magnetic Stand

A magnetic stand (**Figure 35**) is used to securely hold a dial indicator when checking the runout of a round object or when checking the end play of a shaft.

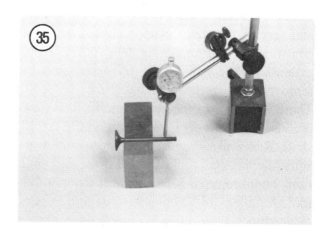

V-Blocks

V-blocks (**Figure 36**) are precision ground blocks that are used to hold a round object when checking its runout or condition.

Surface Plate

A surface plate (**Figure 37**) is used to check the flatness of parts. While industrial quality surface plates are quite expensive, the home mechanic can improvise. A piece of thick, flat metal or plate glass can sometimes be used as a surface plate. The quality of the surface plate will affect the accuracy of the measurement. The surface plate can have a piece of fine grit paper on its surface to assist cleaning and smoothing a flat surface. The machined surfaces of the cylinder head, crankcase, and other close fitting parts may require a very good quality surface plate to smooth nicked or damaged surfaces.

> *NOTE*
> *Check with a local machine shop, fabricating shop or school offering a machine shop course for the availability of a metal plate that can be resurfaced and used as a surface plate.*

Flywheel Puller

A flywheel puller (**Figure 38**) is required whenever it is necessary to remove the flywheel and service the stator plate assembly or when adjusting the ignition timing. In addition, if disassembling the engine, the flywheel must be removed before the crankcases can be split. There is no satisfactory substitute for this tool, because the flywheel is a taper fit on the crankshaft. Removal using makeshift tools often results in crankshaft and flywheel damage. Don't think about removing the flywheel without this tool. A puller can be ordered through a Polaris dealership.

SPECIAL TOOLS

This section describes special tools that may be unique to Polaris personal watercraft and engine service and repair. These tools are often a valuable asset even if used infrequently and most can be ordered through your Polaris dealership. It is often necessary to know the specific pump or engine model to select the correct special tools.

Engine/Pump Alignment Tool

A special alignment tool (part No. 2871343) is available from Polaris to help align the engine crankshaft with the pump shaft. Description of the use of this tool is included in Chapter Four.

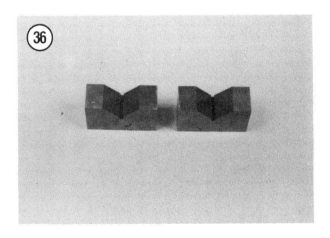

Rear Coupling Tool

A special splined tool (part No. 2871037) is available from Polaris dealerships to help remove the rear drive coupling from the rear of the engine's crankshaft. This tool looks much like the tool for removing the pump impeller, but the rear coupling tool has two rows of knurling to assist in identification. The splines for the pump impeller are different from those in the rear coupling. Description of the use of this tool is included in Chapter Four. Do not use an impact wrench when using this tool to either remove or install the rear coupling.

Pump Impeller Tool

A special splined tool (part No. 2871036) is available from Polaris to help remove the pump impeller from the stub shaft in the jet pump housing. This tool looks much like the tool for removing the rear coupling from the engine, but the pump impeller tool has one row of knurling for identification. The splines for the pump impeller are different from those in the engine's rear coupling. Description of the use of this tool is

included in Chapter Five. Do not use an impact wrench when using this tool to either remove or install the pump impeller.

MECHANIC'S TIPS

Removing Frozen Nuts and Screws

If a fastener rusts and cannot be removed, several methods may be used to loosen it. First, apply penetrating oil such as Liquid Wrench or WD-40 (available at hardware or auto supply stores). Apply it liberally and let it penetrate for 10-15 minutes, then tap the fastener several times with a small hammer. Do not hit it hard enough to cause damage. Reapply the penetrating oil if necessary. Using an *Impact Driver* as described in this chapter will often loosen a stuck bolt or screw.

> *CAUTION*
> *Do not pound on screwdrivers unless the steel shank of the tool extends all the way through the handle. Pounding on a plastic handled screwdriver is a sure way to destroy the tool.*

For frozen screws, apply additional penetrating oil as described, insert a screwdriver in the slot and tap the top of the screwdriver with a hammer. This loosens the rust so the screw can be removed. If the screw head is too damaged to use this method, grip the head with locking pliers and twist the screw out.

Avoid applying heat unless specifically instructed, as it may melt, warp or remove the temper from parts.

Removing Broken Screws or Bolts

If the head breaks off a screw or bolt, several methods are available to remove the remaining portion. If a large portion of the remainder projects out, try gripping it with locking pliers. If the projecting portion is too small, file it to fit a wrench or cut a slot in it to fit a screwdriver. See **Figure 39**.

If the head breaks off flush, use a screw extractor. To do this, centerpunch as close as possible to the exact center of the remaining part of the screw or bolt. Drill a small hole in the screw and tap the extractor into the hole. Back the screw out with a wrench on the extractor. See **Figure 40**.

Remedying Stripped Threads

Damaged threads can often be repaired by running a tap (for internal threads on nuts) or die

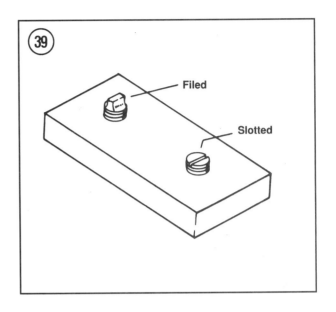

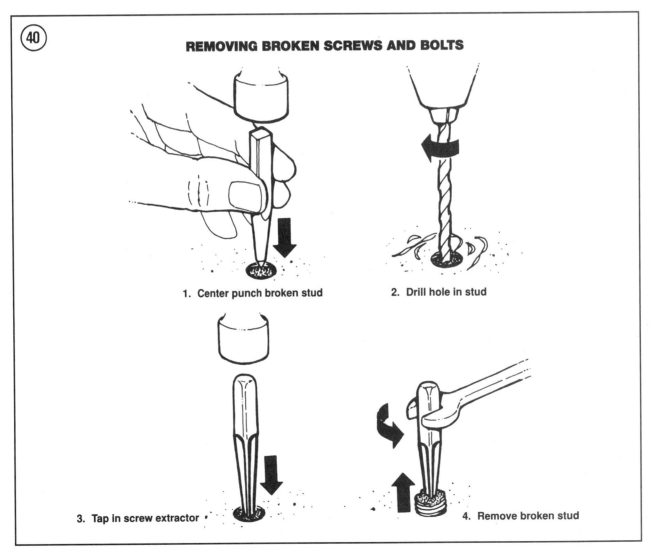

REMOVING BROKEN SCREWS AND BOLTS

1. Center punch broken stud

2. Drill hole in stud

3. Tap in screw extractor

4. Remove broken stud

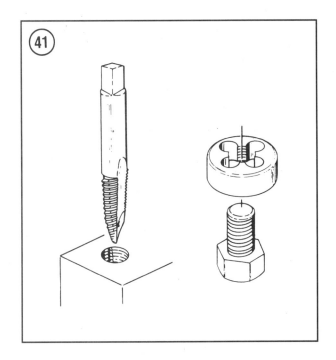

(for external threads on bolts) through the threads. See **Figure 41**. Use a spark plug tap to clean or repair spark plug threads.

NOTE
*Tap and dies can be purchased individually or in a set as shown in **Figure 42**.*

If an internal thread is damaged, it may be necessary to install a Helicoil (**Figure 43**) or some other type of thread insert. Follow the manufacturer's instructions when installing their insert.

If necessary drill and tap a hole, refer to **Table 7** for metric tap drill sizes.

Removing Broken or Damaged Studs

If some threads of a stud are damaged, but some threads remain (**Figure 44**, typical), the old stud can be removed as follows. A tube of Loctite 271 (red), 2 nuts, 2 wrenches and a new stud are required during this procedure.

1. Thread 2 nuts onto the damaged stud (**Figure 45**), then tighten the 2 nuts against each other so that they are locked.

NOTE
If the threads on the damaged stud do not allow installation of the 2 nuts, you may be able to remove the stud with locking pliers.

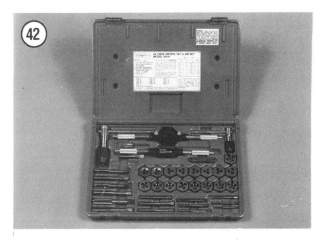

2. Turn the bottom nut counterclockwise (**Figure 46**) and unscrew the stud.

3. Clean the threads with solvent or electrical contact cleaner and allow to dry thoroughly.

4. Install 2 nuts on the top half of the new stud as in Step 1. Make sure they are locked securely.

5. Coat the bottom half of a new stud with Loctite 271 (red).

6. Turn the top nut clockwise and thread the new stud securely.

7. Remove the nuts and repeat for each stud as required.

8. Allow threadlocking compound to cure fully before returning the unit to service. Follow the instructions on the threadlock container.

Ball Bearing Replacement

Ball bearings (**Figure 47**) are used throughout the engine and chassis to reduce power loss, excess heat and noise resulting from friction. Because ball bearings are precision made parts, they must be maintained by proper lubrication and maintenance. If a bearing is damaged, it must be replaced immediately. However, when installing a new bearing, care should be taken to prevent damage to the new bearing. While bearing replacement is described in the individual chapters where applicable, use the following as a guideline.

NOTE
Unless otherwise specified, install bearings with their manufacturer's mark or number facing outward.

Removal

While bearings are normally removed only if damaged, there may be times when it is necessary to remove a bearing that is in good condition. However, improper bearing removal will damage the bearing and maybe the shaft or case

half. Observe the following when removing bearings.

1. When using a puller to remove a bearing from a shaft, care must be taken that the shaft is not damaged. Always place a spacer (**Figure 48**) between the end of the shaft and the puller screw. In addition, place the puller arms next to the inner bearing race.

2. When using a hammer to remove a bearing from a shaft, do not strike the hammer directly against the shaft. Instead, support the bearing

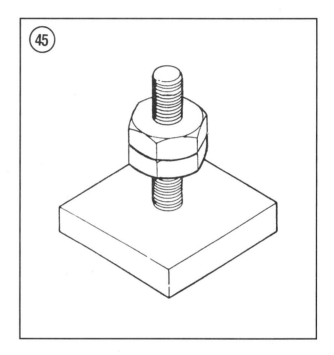
(45)

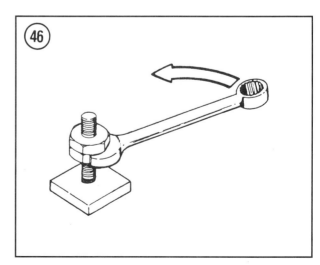
(46)

1

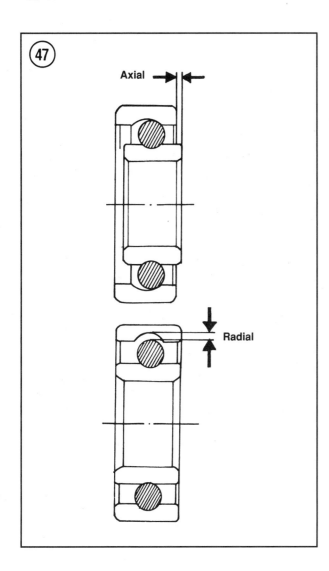

races with wooden blocks (**Figure 49**) and use a brass or aluminum rod between the hammer and shaft.

> *WARNING*
> *Failure to use proper precautions will probably result in damaged parts and may cause injury.*

3. The ideal method to remove a bearing is using a hydraulic press. However, certain procedures must be followed or damage may occur to the bearing, shaft or housing. Observe the following when using a press:

    a. Always support the inner and outer bearing races with the proper size wooden or aluminum spacer (**Figure 50**). If only the outer race is supported, the balls and/or the inner race will be damaged.

    b. Always make sure the press ram aligns with the center of the shaft. If the ram is not centered, it may damage the bearing and/or shaft.

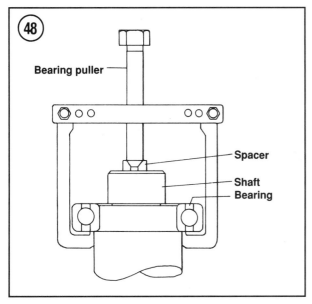

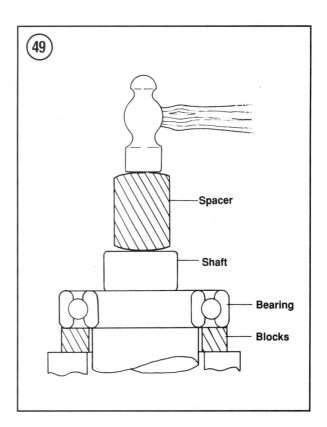

c. The moment the shaft is free of the bearing, it will drop to the floor. Secure or hold the shaft to prevent it from falling.

Installation

Refer to the following when installing bearings.

1. When installing a bearing in a housing, pressure must be applied to the *outer* bearing race (**Figure 51**). When installing a bearing on a shaft, pressure must be applied to the *inner* bearing race.

2. When installing a bearing as described in Step 1, some type of driver is required. Never strike the bearing directly with a hammer or the bearing will be damaged. When installing a bearing, a piece of pipe or a socket with an outer diameter that matches the bearing race is required. **Figure 52** shows the correct way to use a socket and hammer to install a bearing.

3. Step 1 describes how to install a bearing in a case half and over a shaft. However, when installing over a shaft and into a housing at the same time, a snug fit is required for both outer and inner bearing races. In this situation, a spacer must be installed underneath the driver tool so that pressure is applied evenly across *both* races. If the outer race is not supported as shown in **Figure 53** the balls will push against the outer bearing race and damage it.

Shrink Fit

1. *Installing a bearing over a shaft*: When a tight fit is required, the bearing inside diameter is smaller than the shaft. In this case, simply driving the bearing on the shaft may cause bearing damage. Instead, heat the bearing before installation. Note the following:

a. Secure the shaft so that it can be ready for bearing installation.

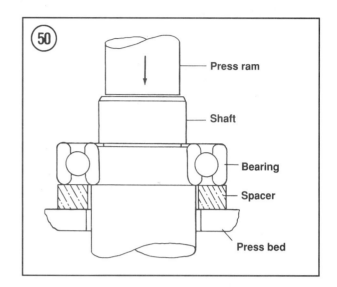

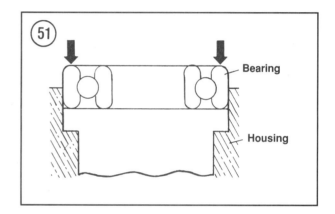

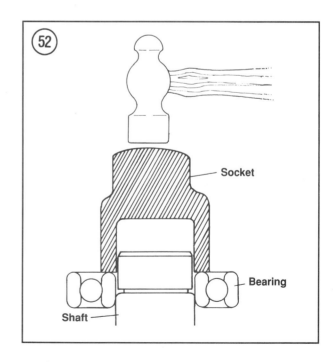

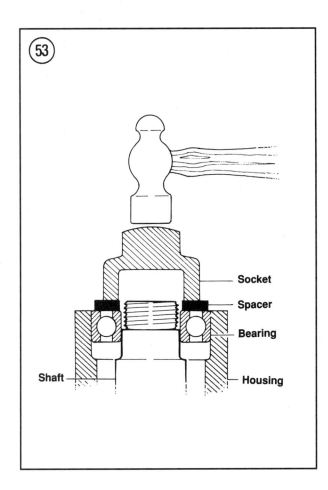

Socket

Spacer

Bearing

Shaft

Housing

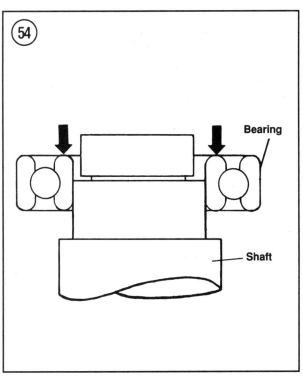

Bearing

Shaft

b. Clean the bearing surface on the shaft of all residue. Remove burrs with a file or sandpaper.

c. Fill a suitable pot or beaker with clean mineral oil. Place a thermometer (rated higher than 120° C [248° F]) in the oil. Support the thermometer so that it does not rest on the bottom or side of the pot.

d. Secure the bearing with a piece of heavy wire bent to hold it in the pot. Hang the bearing in the pot so that it does not touch the bottom or sides of the pot.

e. Turn the heat on and monitor the thermometer. When the oil temperature rises to approximately 120° C (248° F), remove the bearing from the pot and quickly install it. If necessary, place a socket against the inner bearing race (**Figure 54**) and tap the bearing into place. As the bearing chills, it will tighten on the shaft so you must work quickly when installing it. Make sure the bearing is installed all the way.

2. *Installing a bearing in a housing*: Bearings are generally installed in a housing with a slight interference fit. Driving the bearing into the housing using normal methods may damage the housing or cause bearing damage. Instead, heat the housing before the bearing is installed. Note the following:

CAUTION
Before heating the housing in this procedure to remove the bearings, wash it thoroughly with detergent and water. Rinse and rewash the housing as required to remove all traces of oil and other chemical deposits.

a. Heat the housing to about 100° C (212° F) in an oven or on a hot plate. An easy way to determine if it is at the proper temperature is to place tiny drops of water on the housing; if they sizzle and evaporate immediately, the temperature is correct. Heat only one housing at a time.

CAUTION
Do not heat the housing with a torch (propane or acetylene)—never bring a flame into contact with the bearing or housing. The direct heat will destroy the case hardening of the bearing and will likely warp the housing.

b. Remove the housing from the oven or hot plate. Hold onto the housing with a kitchen pot holder, heavy gloves, or heavy shop cloths—*it is hot.*

NOTE
A suitable size socket and extension works well to remove and install bearings.

c. Hold the housing with the bearing side down and tap the bearing out. Repeat for all bearings in the housing.

d. While heating the housing, place the new bearings in a freezer if possible. Chilling them slightly reduces their overall diameter while the hot housing assembly is slightly larger due to heat expansion. This makes installation much easier.

NOTE
Always install bearings with their manufacturer's mark or number facing outward unless the text directs otherwise.

e. While the housing is still hot, install the new bearing(s) into the housing. Install the bearings by hand, if possible. If necessary, lightly tap the bearing(s) into the housing with a socket placed on the outer bearing race. *Do not* install new bearings by driving on the inner bearing race. Install the bearing(s) until it seats completely.

Oil Seals

Oil seals (**Figure 55**) are used to prevent leakage of oil, grease or combustion gasses from between a housing and shaft. Using an improper procedure to remove a seal can damage the hous-

ing or the shaft. Improper installation can damage the seal. Note the following:

a. Prying is generally the easiest and most effective method to remove a seal from a housing. However, always place a rag underneath the pry tool to prevent damage to the housing.

b. Pack a low-temperature grease in the seal lips before the seal is installed.

c. Install oil seals (unless specified otherwise) so that their manufacturer's numbers or marks face out.

NOTE
A socket of the correct size can often be used as a seal driver. Select a socket that fits the seal's outer diameter properly and clears any protruding shafts.

d. Install oil seals with a seal driver placed against the outside of the seal. Make sure the seal is driven squarely into the housing. Never install a seal by hitting directly against the top of the seal with a hammer.

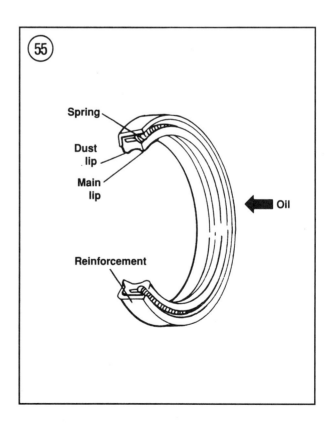

55

Spring

Dust lip

Main lip

Oil

Reinforcement

LUBRICANTS

Periodic lubrication helps ensure long life for any type of equipment. The *type* of lubricant used is just as important as the lubrication service itself. The following paragraphs describe the most often used types of lubricants. Be sure to follow the manufacturer's recommendations for lubricant application.

Generally, all liquid lubricants are called "oil." They may be mineral-based (including petroleum bases), natural-based (vegetable and animal bases), synthetic-based or emulsions (mixtures). "Grease" is an oil to which a thickening base has been added so that the end product is semi-solid. Grease is often classified by the type of thickener added; lithium soap is commonly used.

Engine Oil

2-stroke engine oil

> *CAUTION*
> *Oil designed for use in a 4-stroke is different from oil designed for use in a 2-stroke engine. All models covered in this manual are equipped with a 2-stroke engine which should use only 2-stroke oil.*

Lubrication for 2-stroke engines is provided by oil mixed with the fuel or by oil injected into the fuel/air mixture. The 2-stroke engines included in this manual are equipped with an oil injection system.

Engine oil must have several special qualities to work well in 2-stroke engines. The oil must flow freely in cold temperatures, lubricate the engine sufficiently, burn easily during combustion, it can't leave behind excessive deposits and it must be appropriate for the high operating temperatures associated with 2-stroke engines. Refer to *Engine Lubrication* in Chapter Three.

Grease

Grease is graded by the National Lubricating Grease Institute (NLGI) and assigned a number according to the consistency of the grease. The grades range from No. 000 to No. 6, with No. 6 being the most solid. A typical multipurpose grease is NLGI No. 2. For specific applications, equipment manufacturers may require grease with an additive such as molybdenum disulfide (MOS2).

> *NOTE*
> *Use marine grease wherever grease is required on the watercraft. The greases recommended by Polaris are listed in Chapter Three.*

RTV GASKET SEALANT

Room temperature vulcanizing (RTV) sealant is used on some pre-formed gaskets and to seal some components. RTV is a silicone gel supplied in tubes and can be purchased in a number of different colors. Loctite Superflex ULTRA BLUE is one type of RTV sealer recommended for use on Polaris watercraft.

Moisture in the air causes RTV to cure. Always place the cap on the tube as soon as possible when using RTV. RTV has a shelf life of one year and will not cure properly once the shelf life has expired. Check the expiration date on RTV tubes before using and keep partially used tubes tightly sealed.

Applying RTV Sealant

Clean all gasket residue from mating surfaces. Surfaces must be clean and free of oil and dirt. Remove all RTV gasket material from blind attaching holes, as it can cause a hydraulic effect and prevent the bolt from being fully installed.

Apply RTV sealant in a continuous bead 2-3 mm (0.08-0.12 in.) thick. Circle all mounting holes unless otherwise specified. Join the mating parts and tighten the retaining fasteners within 10 minutes after application.

THREADLOCKING COMPOUND

Because of the watercraft's often extreme operating conditions, a threadlocking compound (**Figure 56**) is required to help secure many of its fasteners. A threadlocking compound locks fasteners against vibration loosening and also seals against leaks. Loctite 242 (blue) and 271 (red) are recommended for many threadlocking requirements described in this manual.

Loctite 242 (blue) is a medium strength threadlocking compound for general purpose use. Component disassembly can be performed with normal hand tools. Loctite 271 (red) is a high strength threadlocker that is normally used on studs or critical fasteners. Heat or special tools, such as a press or puller, may be required for component disassembly.

Applying Threadlocking Compound

Surfaces must be clean and free of oil and dirt. If a threadlocking compound was previously applied to the component, this residue must also be removed.

Shake the Loctite container thoroughly and apply to both parts. Assemble parts and/or tighten fasteners.

GASKET REMOVER

Stubborn gaskets can present a problem during engine service as they can take a long time to remove. In addition, there is the added problem of secondary damage occurring to the gasket mating surfaces from the careless use of a gasket scraping tool. To quickly and safely remove stubborn gaskets, use a spray gasket remover. Spray gasket remover can be purchased from automotive parts houses. Following its manufacturer's directions for use.

Table 1 POLARIS MODEL NUMBERS

Year and model	Model number	Base color	Accent colors
1992			
SL 650	B924058	White	Hot Pink, blue, gray
1993			
SL 650	B934058	White	Hot pink, blue, gray
SL 750	B934070	White	Hot pink, blue, gray
1994			
SL 650	B944058	White	Rubine red, purple
SL 750	B944070	White	Rubine red, black
SLT 750	B944170	White	Caribbean blue, magenta
1995			
SL650 Std.	B954358	White	Purple velvet, rubine red
SL 650	B954058	White	Purple velvet, rubine red
SL 750	B954070	White	Purple velvet, rubine red
SLT 750	B954170	Caribbean blue	Purple velvet, caribbean blue

The first two numeric digits in the model number indicate the model year designation.

Year designation
92 - 1992
93 - 1993
94 - 1994
95 - 1995

The third and fourth numeric digits indicate the hull design.

Hull designation
40 - Modified V, Sheet Molded Compound
41 - Full V, Polyester/Fiberglass/Foam composite
43 - Modified V, Sheet Molded Compound

The fifth and sixth numeric digits indicate the engine used.

Engine designation
58 - EC65PW, 647 cc
70 - EC75PW, 744 cc

Table 2 GENERAL DIMENSIONS

Year and Model	Length		Width		Height	
	cm	in.	cm	in.	cm	in.
1992						
SL 650 B924058	268	105.5	114.3	45	95.2	37.5
1993						
SL 650 B934058	268	105.5	114.3	45	95.2	37.5
SL 750 B934070	268	105.5	114.3	45	95.2	37.5
1994						
SL 650 B944058	268	105.35	113.9	44.86	95.2	37.5
SL 750 B944070	268	105.35	113.9	44.86	95.2	37.5
SLT 750 B944170	305.6	120.3	120.1	47.3	94.0	37.0
1995						
SL 650 B954058	268	105.5	114.3	45	95.2	37.5
SL650 Std. B954358	268	105.5	114.3	45	95.2	37.5
SL 750 B954070	268	105.5	114.3	45	95.2	37.5
SLT 750 B954170	305.6	120.3	120.1	47.3	94.0	37.0

Table 3 WEIGHT AND CAPACITY

Year and Model	Dry weight		Weight capacity		Capacity people
	kg	lb.	kg	lb.	
1992					
SL 650	231.3	510	181.4	400	2
1993					
SL 650	224.5	495	181.4	400	2
SL 750	226.3	499	181.4	400	2
1994					
SL 650	224.5	495	181.4	400	2
SL 750	226.3	499	181.4	400	2
SLT 750	240.4	530	226.8	500	3
1995					
SL 650	224.5	495	181.4	400	2
SL650 Std.	224.5	495	181.4	400	2
SL 750	226.3	499	181.4	400	2
SLT 750	240.4	530	226.8	500	3

Table 4 DECIMAL AND METRIC EQUIVALENTS

Fractions	Decimal in.	Metric mm	Fractions	Decimal in.	Metric mm
1/64	0.015625	0.39688	33/64	0.515625	13.09687
1/32	0.03125	0.79375	17/32	0.53125	13.49375
3/64	0.046875	1.19062	35/64	0.546875	13.89062
1/16	0.0625	1.58750	9/16	0.5625	14.28750
5/64	0.078125	1.98437	37/64	0.578125	14.68437
3/32	0.09375	2.38125	19/32	0.59375	15.08125
7/64	0.109375	2.77812	39/64	0.609375	15.47812
1/8	0.125	3.1750	5/8	0.625	15.87500
9/64	0.140625	3.57187	41/64	0.640625	16.27187
5/32	0.15625	3.57187	21/32	0.65625	16.66875
11/64	0.171875	4.36562	43/64	0.671875	17.06562
3/16	0.1875	4.76250	11/16	0.6875	17.46250
13/64	0.203125	5.15937	45/64	0.703125	17.85937
7/32	0.21875	5.55625	23/32	0.71875	18.25625
15/64	0.234375	5.95312	47/64	0.734375	18.65312
1/4	0.250	6.35000	3/4	0.750	19.05000
17/64	2.265625	6.74687	49/64	0.765625	19.44687
9/32	0.28125	7.14375	25/32	0.78125	19.84375
19/64	0.296875	7.54062	51/64	0.796875	20.24062
5/16	0.3125	7.93750	13/16	0.8125	20.63750
21/64	0.328125	8.33437	53/64	0.828125	21.03437
11/32	0.34375	8.73125	27/32	0.84375	21.43125
23/64	0.359375	9.121812	55/64	0.859375	21.82812
3/8	0.375	9.52500	7/8	0.875	22.22500
25/64	0.390625	9.92187	57/64	0.890625	22.62187
13/32	0.40625	10.31875	29/32	0.90625	23.01875
27/64	0.421875	10.71562	59/64	0.921875	23.41562
7/16	0.4375	11.11250	15/16	0.9375	23.81250
29/64	0.453125	11.50937	61/64	0.953125	24.20937
15/32	0.46875	11.90625	31/32	0.96875	24.60625
31/64	0.484375	12.30312	63/64	0.984375	25.00312
1/2	0.500	12.7000	1	1.00	25.40000

Table 5 GENERAL TORQUE SPECIFICATIONS

Item	N·m	ft.-lb.
Bolt		
6 mm	6	4.3
8 mm	15	11
10 mm	30	22
12 mm	55	40
14 mm	85	61
16 mm	130	94
Nut		
6 mm	6	4.3
8 mm	15	11
10 mm	30	22
12 mm	55	40
14 mm	85	61
16 mm	130	94

Table 6 TECHNICAL ABBREVIATIONS

ABDC	After bottom dead center
ATDC	After top dead center
BBDC	Before bottom dead center
BDC	Bottom dead center
BTDC	Before top dead center
C	Celsius (Centigrade)
cc	Cubic centimeters
cid	Cubic inch displacement
CDI	Capacitor discharge ignition
cu. in.	Cubic inches
F	Fahrenheit
ft.-lb.	Foot-pounds
gal.	Gallons
H/A	High altitude
hp	Horsepower
in.	Inches
kg	Kilogram
kg/cm2	Kilograms per square centimeter
kgm	Kilogram meters
km	Kilometer
L	Liter
m	Meter
MAG	Magneto
ml	Milliliter
mm	Millimeter
N·m	Newton-meters
oz.	Ounce
psi	Pounds per square inch
PTO	Power take off
pt.	Pint
qt.	Quart
rpm	Revolutions per minute

Table 7 METRIC TAP DRILL SIZES

Metric (mm)	Drill size	Decimal equivalent	Nearest fraction
3 × 0.50	No. 39	0.0995	3/32
3 × 0.60	3/32	0.0937	3/32
4 × 0.70	No. 30	0.1285	1/8
4 × 0.75	1/8	0.125	1/8
5 × 0.80	No. 19	0.166	11/64
5 × 0.90	No. 20	0.161	5/32
6 × 1.00	No. 9	0.196	13/64
7 × 1.00	16/64	0.234	15/64
8 × 1.00	J	0.277	9/32
8 × 1.25	17/64	0.265	17/64
9 × 1.00	5/16	0.3125	5/16
9 × 1.25	5/16	0.3125	5/16
10 × 1.25	11/32	0.3437	11/32
10 × 1.50	R	0.339	11/32
11 × 1.50	3/8	0.375	3/8
12 × 1.50	13/32	0.406	13/32
12 × 1.75	13/32	0.406	13/32

Chapter Two

Troubleshooting

Diagnosing problems is relatively simple if you use orderly procedures and keep a few basic principles in mind. The first step in any troubleshooting procedure is to define the symptoms as closely as possible, then localize the problem. Subsequent steps involve testing and analyzing those areas which could cause the symptoms. A haphazard approach may eventually solve the problem, but it can be very costly in terms of wasted time and unnecessary parts replacement.

Proper lubrication, maintenance and periodic tune-ups as described in Chapter Three will reduce the necessity for troubleshooting. Even with the best of care, however, all watercraft are prone to problems which will require troubleshooting.

Never assume anything. Do not overlook the obvious. If you are riding and the engine suddenly quits, check the easiest, most accessible problems first. Has a spark plug wire fallen loose, is the fuel shutoff valve turned on or is the fuel tank empty.

If nothing obvious turns up in a quick inspection, look a little further. Learning to recognize and describe symptoms will make repairs easier for you or a mechanic at the shop. Describe problems accurately and fully. Did the engine loose power gradually and misfire before stopping or did it stop suddenly.

After the symptoms are defined, areas which could cause the problem can be tested and analyzed. Guessing at the cause of a problem may eventually provide the solution, but it usually leads to frustration, wasted time and a series of expensive, unnecessary parts replacements.

You do not need expensive equipment or complicated test gear to determine whether you should attempt repairs at home. A few simple checks could save a large repair bill and lost time while your watercraft sits in a dealer's service department. On the other hand, be realistic and *do not attempt repairs that are beyond your abilities*. Service departments tend to charge heavily for putting together an engine that someone else has disassembled. Some shops won't even take such a job, so use common sense and don't get in over your head.

Table 1 is located at the end of this chapter.

NOTE
*There is one kind of trouble you can expect to have occasionally if you like to push your watercraft to its performance limit —***submerging***. If there is water in the engine, refer to* **Clearing a Submerged Watercraft** *in Chapter One.*

OPERATING REQUIREMENTS

An engine needs 3 basics to run properly: Correct fuel/air mixture, sufficient compression and a spark at the right time (**Figure 1**). If 1 basic requirement is missing, the engine will not run. Ignition malfunctions are a frequent cause of problems and the ignition system can be quickly and easily checked. Keep that in mind before you begin tampering with carburetor adjustments.

If the watercraft has been sitting for any length of time and refuses to start, first check and clean the spark plugs. Then check the condition of the battery to make sure it is fully charged. If these are okay, then look to the gasoline delivery system. This includes the tank, fuel shutoff valve, fuel pump and fuel line to the carburetor. Gasoline deposits may have gummed up the carburetor's fuel inlet needle, jets and small air passages. Gasoline tends to lose its potency after standing

for long periods and condensation may contaminate it with water. Drain the old fuel and try starting with a fresh tankful.

EMERGENCY TROUBLESHOOTING

If the engine is difficult to start or won't start, it does not help to drain the battery using the electric starter. Check for obvious problems even before getting out your tools. Go down the following list step by step. Do each one; you may be embarrassed to find out that the tether switch

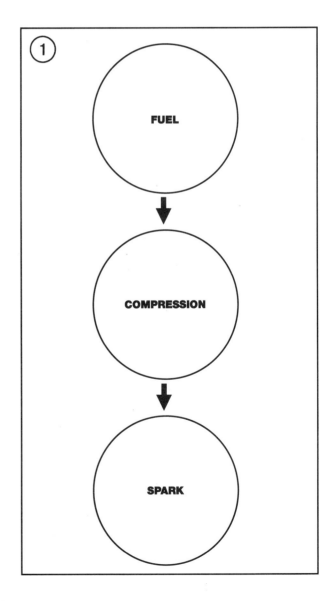

has been pulled from its switch, but it is better than draining the battery or damaging the starter.
1. Is there fuel in the tank? Open the filler cap, rock the craft and listen for fuel sloshing around.

WARNING
Do not use an open flame to check in the tank. A serious explosion and fire will probably result.

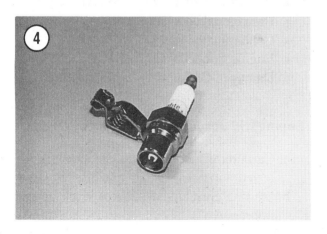

2. Is the fuel shut off (A, **Figure 2**) in the ON or RES (reserve) position?
3. Make sure the tether stop clip (**Figure 3**) is properly located under the stop switch.
4. Are the spark plug wires on tight? Push the connector on and rotate it slightly to clean the electrical connection between the spark plug and connector.
5. Is the starting enrichment (choke) knob (B, **Figure 2**) in the correct position? A warm engine may be easily flooded by choking, but some engines may not start unless the mixture is enriched. It helps to know the starting characteristics of the specific engine. Pulling the knob out enrichens the mixture. The craft should be operated with the knob pushed IN.

ENGINE STARTING

An engine that refuses to start or is difficult to start is very frustrating. More often than not, the problem is very minor and can be found with a simple and logical troubleshooting procedure.

The following items show a beginning point from which to isolate engine starting problems.

Engine Fails to Start

Perform the following spark test to determine if the ignition system is operating properly.
1. Remove the spark plugs.

NOTE
*A test plug (**Figure 4**) is a useful tool that can be quickly attached to check the ignition system. The clip makes attachment to a ground easier than a standard plug and the gap can be clearly viewed. Test plugs like the one shown are available from tool and parts suppliers that have ignition test equipment and service parts.*

2. Connect the spark plug wire to a removed spark plug (or test plug) and touch the spark plug's base to a good ground like the bare alumi-

num of the engine cylinder head. Position the plug so that you can see the electrodes.

WARNING
If it is necessary to hold the high voltage lead, do so with a pair of insulated pliers. The high voltage generated by the ignition system could produce serious shocks that could be fatal.

3. Crank the engine with the starter and observe the test plug's electrodes exposed. A fat blue spark should be evident across the electrodes.

4. If the spark is good, the problem is probably a lack of fuel, but first check the condition of the spark plugs. If the plugs is questionable, install new spark plugs of the correct type and heat range. Make sure the choke knob (B, **Figure 2**) is in the correct position. Fuel must enter the cylinder, but the cylinder must not be flooded with fuel.

5. If the spark is not good or does not occur regularly, check the following possible causes.
   a. Loose electrical connections.
   b. Broken or shorted spark plug high tension lead.
   c. Shorted engine stop switch or connecting wires.
   d. Damaged ignition high tension coil.
   e. Damaged CDI unit.

Engine Is Difficult to Start

Check for one or more of the following possible malfunctions:
   a. Fouled spark plug(s).
   b. Starting enrichment (choke) is incorrectly set.
   c. Fuel system is contaminated.
   d. Carburetor incorrectly adjusted.
   e. Poor compression.
   f. Incorrect type or damaged ignition high tension coil.
   g. CDI unit faulty or improperly grounded.

Engine Will Not Crank

Check for one or more of the following possible malfunctions:
   a. Discharged battery.
   b. Damaged electric starter or solenoid.
   c. Internal engine damage, such as seized piston or crankshaft bearings.

ENGINE PERFORMANCE

In the following checklist, it is assumed that the engine runs, but is not operating at peak performance. This will serve as a starting point from which to isolate a performance problem.

The possible causes for each malfunction are listed in a logical sequence and in order of probability.

Engine is Hard to Start or Starts and Dies

   a. Fuel tank empty or fuel tank vent is closed.
   b. Obstructed fuel line, fuel shut off valve or fuel filter.
   c. Sticking carburetor float valve.
   d. Carburetor incorrectly adjusted.
   e. Improper operation of the starting enrichment (choke) valve.
   f. Operator not allowing the engine to warm up before opening the throttle.
   g. Fouled or improperly gapped spark plugs.
   h. Ignition timing incorrect.
   i. Broken or damaged ignition coil.
   j. Damaged reed valve.
   k. Contaminated fuel.
   l. Engine flooded with fuel.
   m. Damaged CDI unit.

Engine will not Idle or Irregular Idle

   a. Carburetor incorrectly adjusted (either too lean or too rich). Usually the pilot air screw.
   b. Starting enrichment (choke) stuck or used improperly.

c. Fouled or improperly gapped spark plugs.

d. Obstructed fuel line or fuel shut off valve.

e. Vacuum leak between carburetor and cylinder.

f. Leaking compression (blown head gasket).

g. Incorrect ignition timing.

h. Low engine compression.

Engine Misfires at High Speed

a. Fouled or improperly gapped spark plugs.

b. Improper ignition timing.

c. Incorrect main jet installed.

d. Clogged carburetor jets.

e. Obstructed fuel line or fuel shut off valve.

f. Damaged ignition coil or CDI unit.

Engine Overheating

a. Obstructed cooling passages or filters. Refer to Chapter Nine.

b. Thermostat damaged.

c. Improper ignition timing.

d. Improper spark plug heat range.

e. Craft overloaded.

f. Fuel mixture too lean.

Engine Loses Power at Normal Riding Speed

a. Carburetor incorrectly adjusted.

b. Engine overheating.

c. Incorrect ignition timing.

Engine Lacks Acceleration

a. Improperly adjusted carburetor (too lean).

b. Incorrect ignition timing.

c. Damaged jet pump impeller.

Engine Backfires —Explosions in Muffler

a. Fouled or improperly gapped spark plugs.

b. Incorrect ignition timing.

c. Contaminated fuel.

d. Lean fuel mixture.

ENGINE NOISES

A change in the sound is often the first clue that the rider notices indicating that something may be wrong with the engine. Noises are difficult to differentiate and even harder to describe. Experience is needed to diagnose sounds accurately, but identifying a problem quickly may reduce the cost of repair and eliminate some inconvenience. The following are some noises that may help locate sources of trouble.

Knocking or Pinging During Acceleration

a. Poor quality or contaminated fuel.

b. Spark plugs of the wrong heat range.

c. Engine overheating.

d. Incorrect ignition timing.

Slapping or Rattling Noise at Low Speed or During Acceleration

a. May be piston slap caused by excessive clearance.

b. May be caused by broken piston skirt.

Knocking or Rapping While Slowing

May be caused by excessive (damaged) connecting rod bearing clearance.

Persistent Knocking and Vibration

May be caused by excessive (damaged) main bearing clearance.

2

Rapid On-Off Squeal

a. Compression leak around the head gasket.

b. Loose spark plug and compression leak around plug.

EXCESSIVE VIBRATION

Most reports of excessive vibration result from the engine not securely attached. Check mounting components for tightness and damage. Vibration can also be caused by an improperly aligned engine and jut pump unit. Refer to Chapter Four.

TESTING ELECTRICAL COMPONENTS

Most dealers and parts houses will not accept returns of electrical components. When testing electrical components, make sure that you perform the test procedure as described in this chapter and that your test equipment is operating properly. If a test result shows that the component is defective or close to the service limit, it is still a good idea to have the component retested by a Polaris dealer to verify the test result before purchasing a new component. The dealer may know of other components that could lead to the failure of the faulty component and suggest testing those components before installing the new part.

Accurate meters (**Figure 5**) that measure direct current (DC) voltage, alternating current (AC) voltage and resistance (ohmmeter) are needed to conduct these tests. Most multimeters are able to conduct all of these tests. Troubleshooting is only intended to trace the malfunction to a specific component. Refer to Chapter Seven for component removal, inspection and installation procedures.

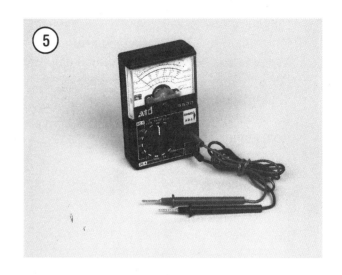

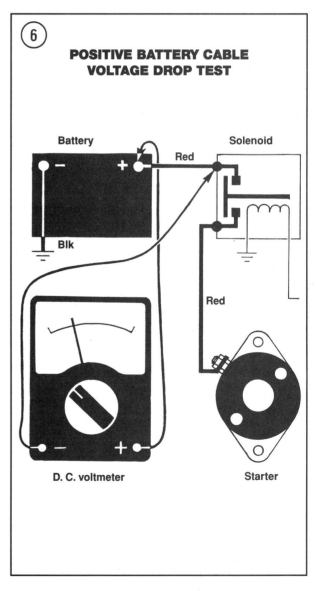

POSITIVE BATTERY CABLE VOLTAGE DROP TEST

Battery   Solenoid

Red

Blk

Red

D. C. voltmeter   Starter

STARTING SYSTEM

If a starting problem is encountered, use the following procedure to isolate the faulty component of the starting system.

1. Make sure the battery is fully charged.
2. Make sure the battery terminals and the cables are clean and attached securely.
3. Make sure that the battery cables are the proper size, are in good condition and are the correct length.
4. Make sure the fuel tank is filled with an adequate supply of fresh gasoline.
5. Make sure the spark plugs are in good condition and are gapped properly.

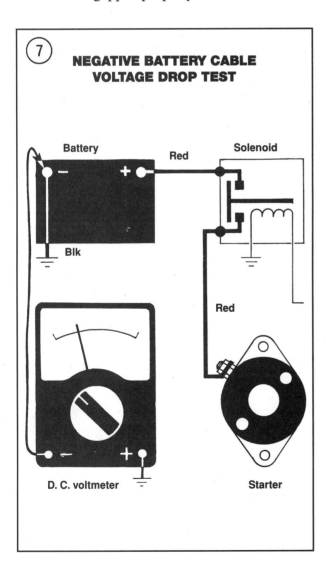

NEGATIVE BATTERY CABLE VOLTAGE DROP TEST

Battery   Red   Solenoid

Blk

Red

D. C. voltmeter   Starter

6. Make sure the ignition is properly timed as described in Chapter Three.

Battery Positive Cable Voltage Drop

A meter that measures direct current (DC) voltage is needed to conduct this test.

1. Connect the positive voltmeter lead to the positive terminal of the battery (**Figure 6**).
2. Connect the negative voltmeter lead to the positive battery connection (terminal) of the starter solenoid (**Figure 6**).
3. Crank the engine with the starter and observe the voltmeter. If the indicated voltage exceeds 0.1 volt, clean the positive battery cable connections and retest. If the indicated voltage is still excessive, replace the cable.
4. Disconnect the voltmeter leads.

Battery Negative Cable Voltage Drop

A meter that measures direct current (DC) voltage is needed to conduct this test.

1. Connect the negative voltmeter lead to the negative battery terminal (**Figure 7**).
2. Connect the positive voltmeter lead to a good engine ground (**Figure 7**).
3. Crank the engine with the starter and observe the voltmeter. If the indicated voltage exceeds 0.1 volt, clean the negative battery cable connections and retest. If the indicated voltage is still excessive, replace the cable.
4. Disconnect the voltmeter leads.

Starter Relay (Solenoid) Switch Voltage Drop

A meter that measures direct current (DC) voltage is needed to conduct this test.

1. Read this procedure through before testing. An assistant is required to help with this test.

2. Connect the positive voltmeter lead to the solenoid terminal with the positive battery connection (**Figure 8**).

3. Have an assistant press the starter button and hold it down while you connect the negative voltmeter lead to the solenoid terminal with the starter connection (**Figure 8**).

4. With the engine cranking, the voltmeter should indicate 0.1 volt or less.

CAUTION
*To prevent damage to the voltmeter, both leads from the meter should be connected to the starter relay while the starter button is pressed (engine turning over). Disconnect the leads **before** the starter button is released.*

5. Disconnect both test leads, then have your assistant release the starter button.

6. If the indicated voltage is more than 0.1 volt, replace the starter relay switch.

7. If the voltage is near 0.1 volt, but the starter does not turn, test the cable from the starter relay to the starter for continuity as described in this chapter.

Cable from Starter Relay to Starter Voltage Drop

A meter that measures direct current (DC) voltage is needed to conduct this test.

1. Read this procedure through before testing. An assistant is required to help with this test.

2. Connect the positive voltmeter lead to the starter terminal of the starter relay (solenoid) (**Figure 9**).

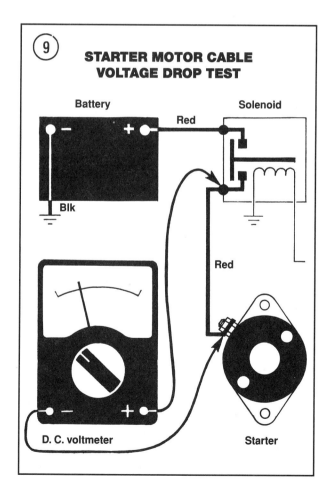

8 **STARTER RELAY VOLTAGE DROP TEST**

Battery Red Solenoid

Blk

Red

D. C. voltmeter Starter

9 **STARTER MOTOR CABLE VOLTAGE DROP TEST**

Battery Red Solenoid

Blk

Red

D. C. voltmeter Starter

3. Have an assistant press the starter button and hold it down while you connect the negative voltmeter lead to the cable terminal at the starter (**Figure 9**).

4. With the engine cranking, the voltmeter should indicate 0.1 volt or less.

5. Disconnect both test leads, then have your assistant release the starter button.

6. If the indicated voltage is more than 0.1 volt, clean both ends of the cable and their connections, then retest. If the test still indicates exces-

sive voltage drop, replace the cable from the starter relay to the starter.

Starter Relay Continuity Test

The starter relay can be tested with an ohmmeter or other continuity meter while it is mounted in the electric box.

1. Open the electric box to gain access to the starter relay.

2. Confirm the starter relay wire electrical connections with the connections shown in the wiring diagram (end of book) for your model.

3. Detach *all* of the electrical connections from the starter relay.

4. If necessary, set the ohmmeter to the R × 1 scale, then touch the test leads together to be sure the meter indicates zero.

5. Connect the ohmmeter leads to the 2 large terminals of the starter relay (solenoid). Refer to **Figure 10**.

 a. The meter should indicate no continuity (infinite resistance).

 b. If the meter shows continuity, the relay is defective and should be replaced.

6. Momentarily attach the 2 leads from a 12-volt battery to the 2 smaller terminals (**Figure 10**) while observing the ohmmeter.

7. Detach the battery leads and interpret the results as follows:

 a. If the starter relay switch clicks and the ohmmeter indicates continuity (0 ohm), the relay is good.

 b. If the starter relay does not click or if the ohmmeter continues to indicate an open circuit (high resistance), the switch is defective and must be replaced.

8. Detach and remove all test equipment.

9. Reattach the electrical leads to the starter relay. Refer to the wiring diagram for your model at the end of this book.

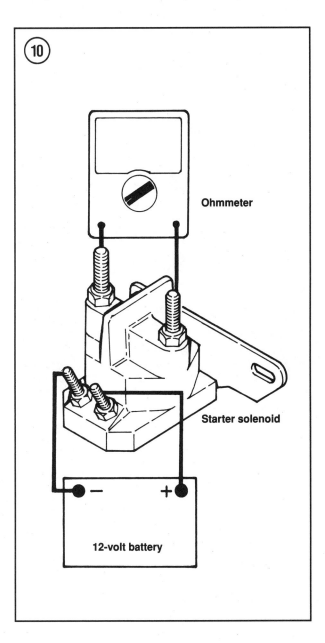

10

Ohmmeter

Starter solenoid

12-volt battery

CHARGING SYSTEM

The charging system consists of a charge coil mounted on the magneto stator plate (**Figure 11**), permanent magnets located within the flywheel rim, a rectifier to change alternating current (AC) to direct current (DC), the battery and connecting wiring. The rectifier is a solid state device that sometimes incorporates a voltage regulator that prevents overcharging the battery.

If a starting problem is encountered, use the following procedure to isolate the faulty component of the starting system.

1. Make sure the battery cables are properly attached. If the polarity is reversed, the rectifier is probably damaged.
2. Carefully inspect all wiring between the magneto base and battery for worn or cracked insulation. Also check the wiring for corroded or loose connections. Replace wiring, clean terminals or tighten loose connections as necessary.
3. Check battery condition. Clean and recharge the battery as required.

Regulated Voltage Output Test

A meter that measures direct current (DC) voltage is needed to conduct this test.

> *CAUTION*
> *Never operate the engine out of the water for more than 15 seconds (even when the engine is cold). The engine will be quickly damaged by overheating.*

1. Remove the seat and engine cover.
2. Put the craft in at least 3 ft. (0.9 m) of water.
3. Secure the watercraft to a permanent stationary object with a strong rope. Refer to **Figure 12**. Attach the rope to the rear attachment point of the craft and be sure to select an object strong enough to withstand full thrust of the watercraft.
4. Attach a tachometer to the engine following its manufacturer's directions.

> *CAUTION*
> *The electrical box must be out of the way of the driveshaft and other components that may cause damage.*

5. Release the hold down straps attaching the electrical box to the top of the battery and move the electrical box out of the way.
6. Remove the top cover from the battery.
7. Start the engine and allow it to idle. Open the throttle 2-3 times to make sure the anchor rope has no slack and is secure at both ends.
8. Connect the positive (red) lead from the voltmeter to the positive terminal of the battery.
9. Connect the negative (black) voltmeter test lead to the negative terminal of the battery.
10. Increase the engine speed to 3,000 rpm and observe the voltmeter. Slow to idle, then stop the engine after checking the voltage.

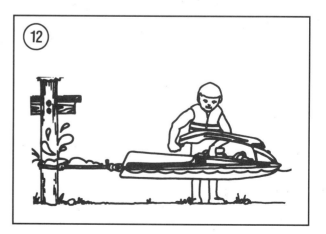

11. The correct voltage is approximately 14.5 volts DC.

12. Indicated voltage less than 14.5 may indicate:

   a. Excessive system load.

   b. Faulty regulator/rectifier.

   c. Faulty alternator. Check the alternator using the *Unregulated Charging System Output Test* as described in this chapter.

13. Indicated voltage more than 14.5 may indicate:

   a. Poor ground for the heat sink located in the electrical box.

   b. Faulty regulator/rectifier.

14. Detach and remove all test equipment.

Unregulated Charging System Output Test

A meter that measures alternating current (AC) voltage is needed to conduct this test.

CAUTION
Never operate the engine out of the water for more than 15 seconds (even when the engine is cold). The engine will be quickly damaged by overheating.

1. Put the craft in at least 3 ft. (0.9 m) of water.

2. Secure the watercraft to a permanent stationary object with a strong rope. Refer to **Figure 12**. Attach the rope to the rear attachment point of

the craft and be sure to select an object strong enough to withstand full thrust of the watercraft.

3. Start the engine and allow it to idle. Open the throttle 2-3 times to make sure the anchor rope has no slack and is secure at both ends, then stop the engine.

4. Remove the seat and engine cover.

5. Release the hold down straps attaching the electrical box to the top of the battery.

6. Turn the electrical box upside down and remove the screws attaching the two halves of the electrical box to gain access to the electrical components. Refer to **Figure 13**.

7. Confirm the wire connections with the wiring diagram (end of book) for your model.

8. Separate the yellow wire and the red/purple wire (**Figure 13**) leading from the alternator inside the electrical box.

9. Attach one lead of the AC voltmeter to the yellow wire from the alternator.

10. Attach the other test lead of the AC voltmeter to the red/purple wire.

11. Attach a tachometer to the engine following its manufacturer's directions.

12. Start the engine.

13. Increase the engine speed to 3,000 rpm and observe the AC voltmeter.

14. The AC voltmeter should indicate voltage above 20 VAC.

15. If there is no output, refer to Chapter Seven to inspect and remove the alternator stator.

16. Stop the engine and remove the test meters after tests are completed.

17. Reattach all disconnected wiring connectors.

18. Reassemble the electrical box, making sure the gasket (**Figure 14**) is in good condition.

IGNITION SYSTEM

All models are equipped with a capacitor discharge ignition (CDI) system. This section describes complete ignition troubleshooting.

This solid state system uses no contact breaker points or other moving parts. Because of the solid state design, problems with the capacitor discharge system are relatively few. Problems are usually limited to no spark, but that lack of spark might only occur when the engine is subjected to certain temperatures, loads or vibrations. It is often easier to find the cause of no spark than those with intermittent problems. If the ignition has no spark, first check for broken or damaged wires. Also make sure that the engine stop switch wires are not shorted to ground.

Test Equipment

Basic testing of the ignition and electrical system can be performed with an accurate ohmmeter. A visual inspection and tests with an ohmmeter will usually pinpoint electrical problems caused by dirty or damaged connectors, faulty or damaged wiring or electrical components that may be cracked or broken. If basic checks fail to locate the problem, take your watercraft to a Polaris dealership and have them troubleshoot the electrical system.

Precautions

Certain precautions must be taken to protect the capacitor discharge system. Instantaneous damage to semiconductors in the system will occur if the following is not observed.
1. Do not crank the engine if the CDI unit is not grounded to the engine.
2. Do not disconnect any ignition components when the engine is running or while the battery cables are connected.
3. Never connect the battery, battery charger or jumper cables with leads reversed. Reverse polarity can damage components instantly.
4. Keep all connections between the various units clean and tight. Be sure that the wiring connectors are pushed together firmly.

Troubleshooting Preparation

Refer to the wiring diagram for your model at the end of this book when performing the following.
1. Check the wiring harness for visible signs of damage.

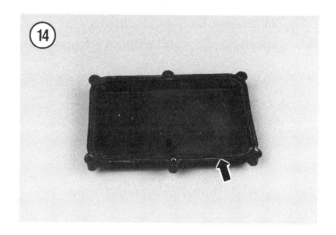

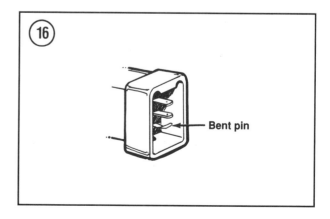

NOTE
To test the wiring harness for poor connections in Step 2, bend the molded rubber connector while checking each wire for continuity.

2. Make sure all of the connectors (**Figure 15**) are properly attached as follows:

NOTE
Never pull on the wires when separating an electrical connector. Pull only on the housing of the connector.

a. Disconnect each electrical connector in the ignition circuit. Check for bent or damaged male connector pins (**Figure 16**). A bent pin will not connect properly and will cause an open circuit.

b. Check each female connector end. Make sure the metal connector at the end of each

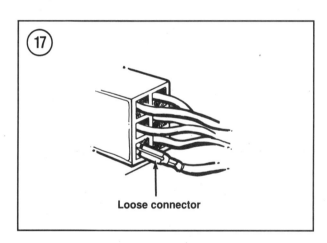

Loose connector

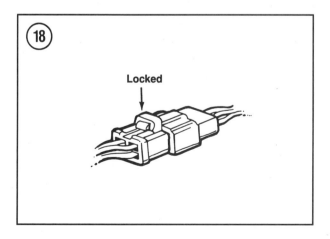

Locked

wire (**Figure 17**) is pushed all the way into the plastic connector. If not, use a small, narrow blade screwdriver to carefully push them in. Make sure you do not pinch or cut the wire. Also, make sure that you do not spread the connector.

c. Check the wires to make sure that each is properly attached to a metal connector inside the plastic connector.

d. Make sure all electrical connectors are clean and free of corrosion. If necessary, clean the connectors with an electrical contact cleaner.

e. After making sure that all of the individual connectors are in acceptable condition, push the connectors together until they click. Make sure they are fully engaged and locked together (**Figure 18**).

3. Check all electrical components for a good ground to the engine.

4. Check all wiring for short circuits or open circuits.

5. Make sure the fuel tank has an adequate supply of fresh fuel and that the oil tank is properly filled.

6. Check spark plug cable routing and be sure the cables are properly connected to spark plugs.

CAUTION
Blow away any dirt that has accumulated around the spark plug base. Dirt could fall into the cylinder when a plug is removed, causing serious engine damage.

7. Remove the spark plugs and check their condition. See Chapter Three.

8. Make the following spark test:

WARNING
During this test do not hold the spark plug, wire or connector with fingers or a serious electrical shock may result. If necessary, use a pair of insulated pliers to hold the spark plug wire.

a. Remove the spark plug.

NOTE
*A special test plug such as the one shown in **Figure 19** is available from many parts suppliers. The clip can be attached to a good engine ground.*

b. Connect the spark plug cable connector to a spark plug that is known to be good (or the test plug) and touch the base of the spark plug base to a good ground like the unpainted metal of the engine cylinder head. Position the spark plug so you can see the electrode.

c. Turn the ignition switch ON and attach the tether clip (**Figure 20**).

d. Crank the engine with the starter. A fat blue spark should be evident across the spark plug electrode. In bright light, it may be difficult to see the spark, but a good spark will be accompanied by an audible snap that can be heard.

e. If there is no spark or only a weak one, check for loose connections at the coil. If all external wiring connections are good, check the remaining components of the ignition system.

f. Turn the ignition switch OFF.

Engine Stop Switch Test

1. Make sure to attach the tether clip (**Figure 20**).

2. Separate the connector from the stop switch containing the black/yellow and black wires.

3. If necessary set the ohmmeter to the R × 1 scale, then touch the test leads together to be sure the meter indicates zero.

4. Attach one ohmmeter lead to the black/yellow pin and the other test lead to the black pin.

   a. The meter should indicate no continuity (infinite resistance).

   b. If the meter shows continuity, the switch or connecting wires are shorted. If the wires are not shorted, replace the switch (**Figure 20**).

5. Momentarily press the stop button (**Figure 20**) and observe the ohmmeter.

   a. The meter should indicate less than 0.3 ohm resistance when the button is pressed, then return to infinite resistance when it is released.

   b. If pressing the button does not complete the stop circuit, the engine will not stop when the button is pressed. Check for broken wires. Replace the switch if a broken wire is not located.

   c. If the switch does not open the circuit every time the button is released, the switch is sticking or shorted. Install a new switch (**Figure 20**).

6. Pull the tether cord (**Figure 20**) from the switch and observe the ohmmeter.

   a. The resistance should be less than 0.3 ohm.

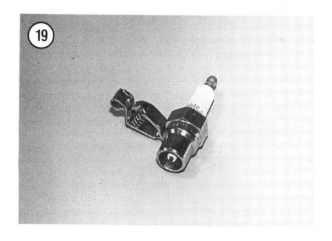

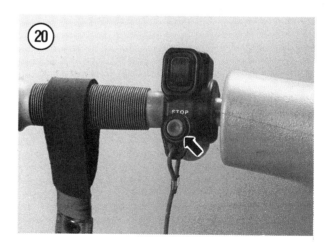

b. If detaching the tether does not complete the stop circuit, the engine will not stop in an emergency when the tether is pulled. Check for open wires. Install a new switch if an open wire is not located.

7. Install the tether cord and make sure that resistance is infinite (open).

Ignition High Tension Coil Resistance Test

An accurate ohmmeter is required to perform the following tests. Refer to **Figure 21**.

1. Locate the ignition high tension coils (A, **Figure 21**) inside the electrical box.

NOTE
The 3 coils are connected in series and each must be checked individually.

2. Disconnect the black/white primary connector from a high tension coil.

3. Check the primary resistance of each coil as follows:

a. If necessary, switch the ohmmeter to the R × 1 scale.

b. Measure resistance between the small primary terminal and the coil ground (small black wire). Refer to **Table 1** for specifications.

c. Disconnect the meter leads.

4. Check the secondary resistance of each ignition coil as follows.

a. Remove the spark plug cap (B, **Figure 21**) from the end of each high-tension cable.

b. If necessary, switch the ohmmeter to the R × 1000 scale.

c. Measure resistance between the high-tension (spark plug) cable and the coil ground (small black wire). Refer to **Table 1** for specifications.

d. Measure resistance of the spark plug cap. Refer to **Table 1** for specifications.

5. Check the ignition coil insulation for cracks or other defects that would permit moisture to enter the coil. Internal damage can be checked using additional test equipment. If condition is questioned, take the coil to a Polaris dealership for additional tests.

6. If resistance of a coil is not as specified in **Table 1**, the coil is probably faulty. Have the dealer recheck the coil to verify that the unit is faulty before buying a replacement.

NOTE
Normal resistance in both the primary and secondary (high-tension) coil windings is not a guarantee that the unit is working properly; only an operational spark test can tell if a coil is producing an adequate spark from the input voltage. A Polaris dealership may have the equipment to test the coil's output. If not, substitute a known good coil to see if it fixes the problem.

Exciter Coil Resistance Test

The ignition system is equipped with an ignition exciter coil attached to the stator plate located behind the engine flywheel.

1. Locate the red/white and green/red wires leading from under the engine flywheel to the electrical box and ignition CDI ignition module (C, **Figure 21**).

2. Separate the connectors for the red/white and green/red wires inside the electrical box near the CDI unit (C, **Figure 21**).

3. If necessary switch the ohmmeter to the R × 1 scale.

4. Attach the ohmmeter between the red/white wire and the green/red wire from the engine to check the Exciter coil.

5. Compare the reading to the specification listed in **Table 1**. If the measured resistance is not within specification, replace the Exciter coil assembly as described in Chapter Seven.

6. Attach the ohmmeter between the connector for the red/white wire and the engine ground to test for a short circuit.

7. The test in Step 6 should indicate an open circuit (infinite resistance). If not, check the connecting wires for damage or replace the coil assembly as required.

8. Reattach the connectors.

Pulser Coil Resistance Test

1. Locate the blue/red and red/white wires leading from under the engine flywheel to the electrical box and ignition CDI module (C, **Figure 21**).

2. Separate the connectors for the blue/red and red/white wires near the CDI unit (C, **Figure 21**).

3. If necessary switch the ohmmeter to the R × 1 scale.

4. Attach the ohmmeter between the blue/red wire and the red/white wire from the engine to check the pulser coil.

5. If the resistance is not within the specification listed in **Table 1**, replace the pulser coil assembly as described in Chapter Seven.

6. Attach the ohmmeter between the connector for the red/white wire and the engine ground to test for a short circuit.

7. The test in Step 6 should indicate an open circuit (infinite resistance). If not, check the connecting wires for damage or replace the coil assembly as required.

8. Reattach the connectors.

Trigger Coil Resistance Test

The trigger coil is mounted on the stator plate behind the flywheel.

1. Locate the white/yellow and black wires leading from under the engine flywheel to the electrical box and connectors near the CDI unit (C, **Figure 21**).

2. Separate the connectors.

3. If necessary switch the ohmmeter to the R × 1 scale.

4. Connect the ohmmeter to the white/yellow and black wires leading from the engine.

5. Compare the reading to the specification in **Table 1**. If the reading is not within 10% of the listed specification, replace the coil assembly as described in Chapter Seven.

6. Reattach the wire connectors and assemble the electrical box.

FUEL SYSTEM

Some owners automatically assume that the carburetor is at fault if the engine does not start or does not run properly. While fuel system problems are not uncommon, carburetor adjustment is not always the answer. In many cases,

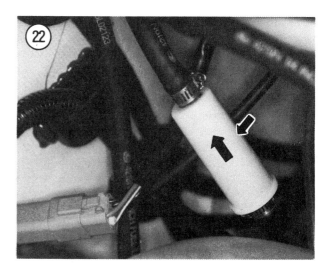

adjusting the carburetor only compounds the problem, making the engine run worse.

Fuel system troubleshooting should start at the fuel tank and work through the system, reserving the carburetor as the final point. Most fuel system problems result from an empty tank, a plugged fuel filter (**Figure 22**), malfunctioning fuel pump or contaminated fuel. **Figure 23** shows a typical fuel system. Refer to Chapter Six for a complete description of the various fuel systems used.

The carburetor choke can also present problems. A choke that is stuck open will cause hard starting. A choke that sticks closed will cause flooding that may also make starting difficult. Check the operation of the choke and adjust it if necessary.

Identifying Carburetor Conditions

The following list can be used as guide when trying to determine rich and lean carburetor conditions.

If the engine is running too rich, one or the more of the following conditions may be observed:

a. The spark plugs foul quickly.

b. The engine misfires and runs rough when under load.

c. As the throttle is opened, exhaust smoke is excessive.

d. When the throttle is fully open, the exhaust will sound dull and choked.

If the engine is running too lean, one or more of the following conditions may be evident:

a. The spark plug firing end is white or blistered in appearance.

b. The engine overheats.

c. Acceleration is slower and may hesitate while trying to accelerate.

d. Flat spots are noted during operation, much like the engine is running out of gas.

e. Engine power is reduced.

f. At full throttle, engine speed is not steady.

ENGINE

Engine problems are usually symptoms of something wrong with a support system such as the ignition, fuel or starting system. If properly maintained and serviced, the engine should experience very few problems except those caused by age and wear. The engine, however, can be quickly damaged as a secondary result of continued operation with a fuel system or ignition system problem. It is important to recognize, diagnose and repair the primary problems quickly before they cause more extensive (and expensive) damage to the engine.

Overheating and Lack of Lubrication

Many engine mechanical problems can be traced to overheating and incorrect engine lubrication. The engine creates a great deal of heat and is not designed to operate for a long at idle speed. Make sure the cooling system is not clogged with sand or the jet intake plugged with weeds or other debris.

Incorrect ignition timing or an excessively lean fuel mixture can also cause the engine to overheat. Using a spark plug of the wrong heat range can cause a hole to be burned in the piston.

Check for a clogged oil filter or incorrectly adjusted oil injection pump. Refer to Chapter Three. The engine may be extensively damaged very quickly by lack of lubrication if the correct type of oil is not delivered in the correct quantity. Check the lubrication system for crimped, cracked or detached lines or any other condition that can reduce the amount of oil delivered to the engine.

Preignition

Preignition is the premature burning of fuel and is caused by a hot spot(s) in the combustion chamber (**Figure 24**) that ignites the fuel before normal ignition occurs. Glowing deposits in the combustion chamber or very hot metal such as an overheated spark plug can ignite the fuel prematurely. Preignition is usually noticed as a power loss, but can quickly cause extensive damage to the piston, cylinder and other internal parts because of the very high temperature and excessive combustion pressure.

Detonation

Commonly called "spark knock," detonation is a violent explosion in the combustion chamber instead of the controlled burn that occurs during normal combustion. See **Figure 25**. Detonation often results in severe engine damage.

During normal combustion, the spark plug ignites the fuel/air charge. A flame front then burns from one side of the piston to the other and creates the rapid expansion of the combustion gasses that pushes the piston downward in the cylinder. During detonation, the energy created by the expanding gasses is mostly wasted because detonation usually happens prior to the normal ignition time, before the piston reaches the top of its stroke. In addition, the extreme heat and pressure created by detonation can force the combustion gasses past the piston rings instead of being converted to useful energy.

Detonation can occur even when using good quality, high-octane gasoline. Over advanced ignition timing, excessively lean fuel mixture, overheated engine or excessive compression pressure are common causes of detonation. Excessive combustion chamber deposits can cause a significant increase in compression with detonation being the result.

Detonation is often difficult to detect, because it occurs most often at high speed when engine and background noise is high. If detonation continues unnoticed, piston damage will soon result.

FUEL HOSE ROUTING

1. Check valve
2. Fuel vent hose
3. T fitting
4. Fuel vent hose
5. Expansion check valve
6. Fuel vent hose
7. Fitting
8. Vent fitting
9. Fuel vent hose
10. Fuel return hose
11. Fuel reserve hose
12. Fuel valve
13. Fuel on valve
14. Fuel hose to pump
15. Fuel filter
16. Fuel hose to pump
17. Fuel primer (1992 only)
18. Fuel hose to pump
19. Fuel pump
20. Impulse line to crankcase
21. Fuel pressure line

2

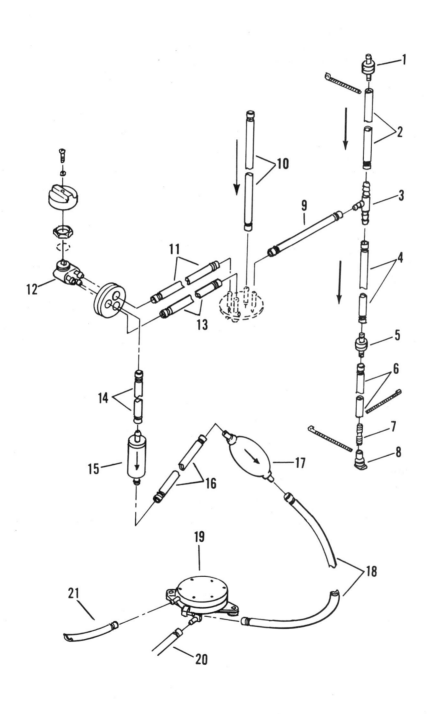

Poor Idling Performance

Rough idling may be caused by improper carburetor adjustment, incorrect timing or an ignition system malfunction. Check the carburetor pulse and vent lines for kinks or other obstructions. Check to be sure the carburetors are mounted tightly, the flange gasket is in good condition and the mounting bolts are tight.

Misfiring

Misfiring can be the result of either an ignition or fuel system component failure. A dirty or fouled spark plug can keep the engine from starting and cause misfiring throughout the rpm range. Uneven running can be caused by contaminated fuel or a fuel system malfunction, but the most common problem is easily repaired by installing a new spark plug.

Water Leakage into the Cylinder

The fastest and easiest way to check for water leakage into the cylinder(s) is to inspect the spark plugs. Water inside the combustion chamber during combustion will turn to steam and thoroughly clean the spark plug and combustion chamber. I one spark plug is clean, and the other plugs show normal deposits, water ingestion is possibly taking place in the cylinder with the clean plug.

Water ingestion can be verified by installing used spark plugs with normal deposits into each cylinder. Run the watercraft for 5-10 minutes, then stop the engine and allow it to cool. Remove and inspect the spark plugs. If one or more plugs are clean, water leakage is probably occurring.

Flat Spots

If the engine seems to die momentarily when the throttle is opened, check for dirty or incorrectly adjusted carburetor(s). A flat spot during acceleration is usually caused by a mixture that is too lean, but can also be caused by excessively rich mixture.

Power Loss

Any of a number of problems can cause a power loss and a reduction in top speed. Refer to **Figure 26**. Check the easiest problems first, but do not overlook the obvious or the more obscure possibilities. Check and adjust ignition timing as described in Chapter Three. Exhaust leakage into the engine compartment will reduce perform-

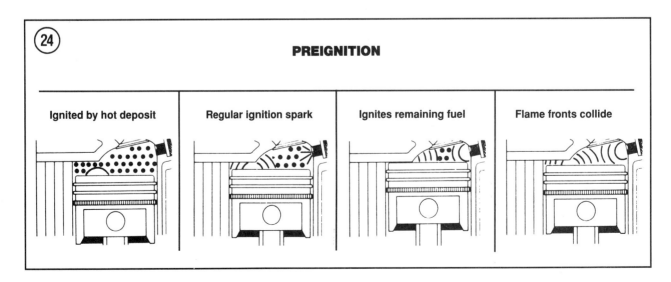

PREIGNITION

| Ignited by hot deposit | Regular ignition spark | Ignites remaining fuel | Flame fronts collide |

ance and may even prevent the engine from idling.

Mechanical problems such as piston galling, broken or stuck piston rings, leaking gaskets or other physical damage can not be corrected by turning an adjustment screw or pouring an additive into the fuel tank.

Piston Seizure

Piston seizure or galling is the transfer of metal from the piston to the cylinder bore. Friction causes piston seizure and the most common causes are lack of lubrication and overheating. Friction, galling and seizure can be caused by improper repair or assembly techniques or clearances. Be sure to follow the recommended clearances when repairing the engine and maintain the correct lubrication adjustment.

A noticeable reduction of speed may be your first sign of seizure, while immediate stoppage indicates a full lockup. A top end rattle should be considered an early sign of seizure.

When diagnosing piston seizure, inspect the pistons to help discover the cause. High cylinder temperatures normally cause seizure above the piston pin, while seizure below the piston pin is usually caused by lack of lubrication.

Excessive Vibration

Excessive vibration may be caused by a poorly running engine or a damaged driveshaft, jet pump or impeller. Vibration is often caused by loose engine mount bolts or damaged engine mountings.

2-STROKE PRESSURE TESTING

2-stroke engines are sometimes plagued by hard starting and generally poor running, for which there seems to be no cause. Checks of the fuel system, ignition and cylinder compression indicates the engine's upper end is in top shape.

What a compression check does not show is a lack of primary compression in the engine crankcase. In a 2-stroke engine, the crankcase must be alternately under pressure and vacuum. Movement of the piston up in the cylinder creates a vacuum to draw air and fuel from the carburetor into the crankcase. As the piston lowers in the cylinder, it first closes the transfer ports to seal the crankcase. Further movement of the piston compresses the fuel and air mixture trapped in the crankcase. The mixture is pressurized so that when the transfer ports open, the fresh charge of fuel and air will rush into the cylinder.

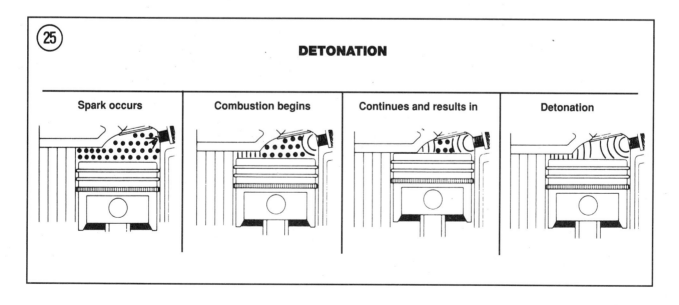

㉕ **DETONATION**

| Spark occurs | Combustion begins | Continues and results in | Detonation |

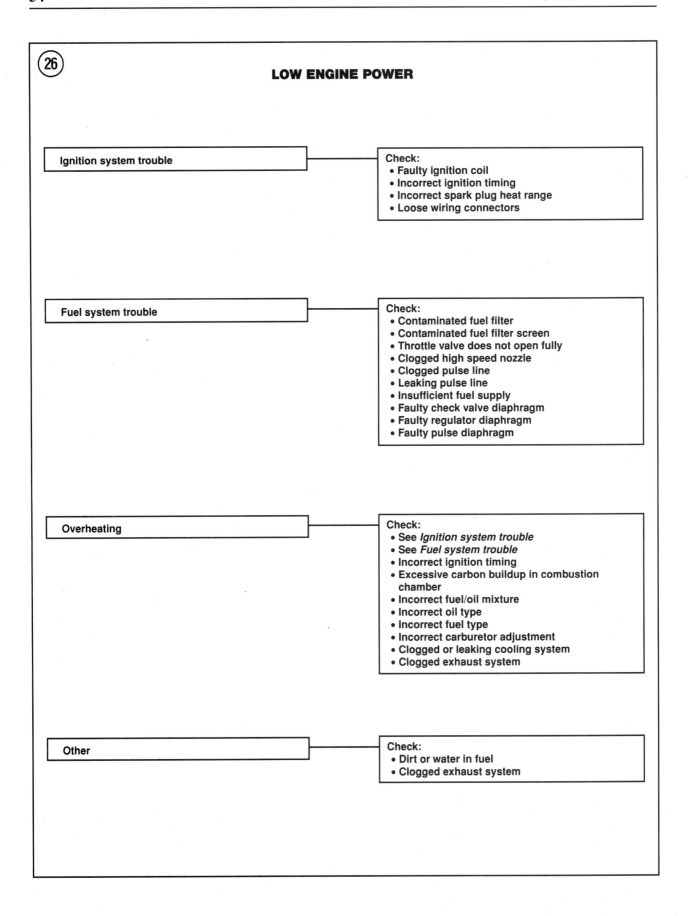

26

LOW ENGINE POWER

Ignition system trouble

Check:
- Faulty ignition coil
- Incorrect ignition timing
- Incorrect spark plug heat range
- Loose wiring connectors

Fuel system trouble

Check:
- Contaminated fuel filter
- Contaminated fuel filter screen
- Throttle valve does not open fully
- Clogged high speed nozzle
- Clogged pulse line
- Leaking pulse line
- Insufficient fuel supply
- Faulty check valve diaphragm
- Faulty regulator diaphragm
- Faulty pulse diaphragm

Overheating

Check:
- See *Ignition system trouble*
- See *Fuel system trouble*
- Incorrect ignition timing
- Excessive carbon buildup in combustion chamber
- Incorrect fuel/oil mixture
- Incorrect oil type
- Incorrect fuel type
- Incorrect carburetor adjustment
- Clogged or leaking cooling system
- Clogged exhaust system

Other

Check:
- Dirt or water in fuel
- Clogged exhaust system

NOTE
*The operational sequence of a 2-stroke engine is illustrated in Chapter One under **Engine Principles**.*

If the crankcase seals or gaskets leak, the crankcase cannot hold the pressure and vacuum necessary for the engine to run properly. Any source of leakage including cracked castings can also prevent the engine from running.

It is possible to test for and isolate (locate) crankcase leaks, but special (but simple) equipment is necessary. A typical 2-stroke pressure test kit is shown in **Figure 27**. Briefly, the test is done by sealing off all of the normal openings, then pressurizing the crankcase. If the crankcase does not hold air, a leak is indicated. A solution of mild soap and water can be used to help isolate the leak.

The following procedure describes a typical pressure test.

NOTE
The cylinders cannot be checked individually, so openings for all three cylinders must be blocked before applying pressure and testing.

1. Remove the carburetors as described in Chapter Six.

2. Install rubber plugs tightly in the intake manifold openings.

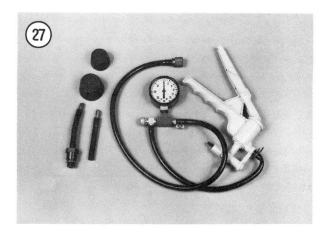

3. Remove the exhaust pipes and block off the exhaust ports using suitable adapters and fittings.

4. Plug the crankcase pulse fitting.

5. Remove one of the spark plugs and install the pressure gauge adaptor into the spark plug hole.

6. Connect the pressure pump and gauge to the pressure gauge adapter.

7. Pressurize the engine by squeezing the hand pump lever until the gauge indicates approximately 62 kPa (9 psi).

8. Observe the pressure gauge. If the engine is in good condition the pressure should not drop more than 10-14 kPa (1 1/2-2 psi) after several minutes. All points from which pressure is leaking should be located and a decision made depending upon the location and amount of leakage.

Make sure that the test equipment is not leaking before blaming the engine. If the equipment shows no sign of leaking, inspect the whole engine carefully. Large leaks can be heard. Small leaks can be located by applying a soapy solution with a small brush. Some possible points of leakage are:

a. Crankshaft seal(s).

b. Spark plug(s).

c. Cylinder head joint.

d. Cylinder base joint.

e. Reed valve base joint(s).

f. Crankcase joint.

STEERING

The steering system should operate smoothly. **Figure 28** provides a series of causes that can be useful in localizing steering problems. Service the steering assembly as described in Chapter Ten. Steering adjustment procedures are described in Chapter Three.

JET PUMP

Reduced jet thrust can occur gradually or all of a sudden and will cause cavitation, power loss or engine damage.

A gradual reduction of jet thrust can be hard to detect and is usually caused by worn jet pump components. To detect damaged components, inspect the impeller and wear ring (**Figure 29**) for scuffing and damage. Check impeller clearance as described in Chapter Five. Impeller clearance is critical to jet pump operation and vehicle performance.

NOTE
*If the bolt (**Figure 30**) at the front of the intake grate is removed, its water-tight seal will be broken. Once removed, the bolt must be thoroughly released using a marine-grade RTV sealant (1992-1993 models) or Loctite 242 (1994-on).*

The sudden loss of jet thrust is usually caused by weeds or other debris entering or clogging the jet pump's water intake area. Because the engine's cooling water is first picked up at the jet pump, a clogged pump intake can cause engine damage from overheating.

If you suspect weeds or other debris have clogged the pump intake area, clean it as follows.

1. The intake grate is accessible with the craft on most trailers, without removing it from the trailer. If it is necessary to tip the craft on its side to inspect or clean the intake, observe the following.

    a. Turn the fuel valve OFF.

    b. Remove the seat and engine cover.

    c. Remove the battery.

CAUTION
It is important to raise the right side of the craft, not the left, because if the left side is higher than the right, water can run out of the cooling system, through the exhaust ports and into the cylinders.

    d. Tip the craft by lifting the right side.

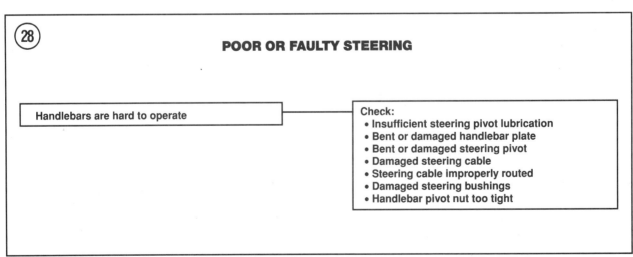

POOR OR FAULTY STEERING

| Handlebars are hard to operate | Check:
• Insufficient steering pivot lubrication
• Bent or damaged handlebar plate
• Bent or damaged steering pivot
• Damaged steering cable
• Steering cable improperly routed
• Damaged steering bushings
• Handlebar pivot nut too tight |

2A. On 1992-1993 models, hold the lock nut inside the hull (under the driveshaft) and remove the screw (**Figure 30**).

2B. On 1994-on models, remove the screw (**Figure 30**) which is threaded into a threaded insert in the hull. Coat the threads of the screw with Loctite 242 (blue) when installing it.

3. Unbolt and remove the ride plate, located to the rear of the intake grate.

4. Pull the intake grate down and forward.

5. Check the inlet for water pickup to cool the engine.

   a. On 1992-1993 models, the cooling water pickup is located near the rear of the pump housing. Also make sure that the welch

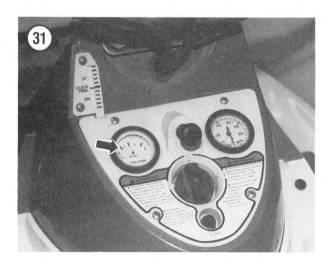

plugs on the outside of the housing are in place.

   b. On 1994-on models, the cooling water pickup is located in the (rear) extension housing. A screen covers the opening on 1995 models and this screen (part No. 543 1523) can be installed on 1994 models to reduce the possibility of debris plugging the pump.

   c. The water inlet opening must be open and clear.

6. Reassemble by reversing the disassembly procedure, observing the following.

   a. On 1992-1993 models, seal the screw (**Figure 30**) to the hull with RTV sealer.

   b. On 1994-on models, coat the threads of screw (**Figure 30**) with Loctite 242 (blue) when installing.

   c. Clean and dry the front edge of the ride plate and the mating surface of the hull so that RTV sealer will stick to the surfaces.

NOTE
*Any leak in the seal at the front of the ride plate can cause cavitation. Be sure there are no pin holes or gaps in the continuous bead of sealer. Apply sealer to cleaned surfaces **just** before installing the ride plate.*

   d. Coat the entire front edge of the ride plate with a continuous bead of RTV sealer.

   e. Coat threads of the screws attaching the ride plate with Loctite 242 (blue) before installing.

FUEL GAUGE

The fuel gauge consists of a sender unit located in the fuel tank and a gauge unit located in the console (**Figure 31**) or multi-function unit. Refer to Chapter Three for a description of the multi-function unit and to Chapter Six to service the fuel gauge sender unit in the fuel tank. Refer to Chapter Seven to remove the console mounted instrument.

Testing

1. Lift the front hatch and remove the storage basket.

2. Disconnect the wires from the sender unit (**Figure 32**, typical) located in the fuel tank.

3. Measure the resistance between the two terminals with an ohmmeter as shown in **Figure 33**.

4. Compare the resistance with the following standard specifications.

    a. When the tank sender float is fully up (tank full) resistance should be 31.5-38.5 ohms when measured at room temperature.

    b. When the tank sender float is fully down (tank empty) resistance should be 216-264 ohms when measured at room temperature.

5. If the fuel sender provides the correct resistance, but the gauge indicates an incorrect amount of fuel, proceed as follows.

    a. Check the condition of the connecting wires.

    b. Make sure the gauge located in the console is receiving the correct voltage.

    c. Install a new console mounted gauge if it is damaged.

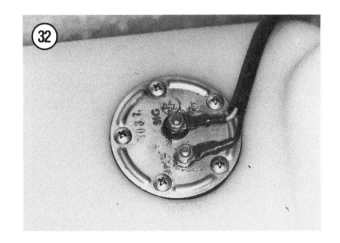

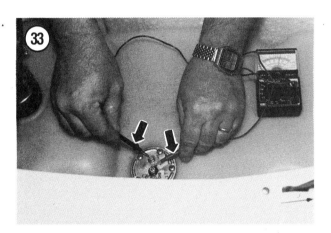

Table 1 CHARGING/IGNITION COIL RESISTANCE SPECIFICATIONS

	Resistance
Alternator coil (red/purple to yellow)	0.6 ohms
High tension coils	
Primary winding (black to black/white)	0.6 ohms
Secondary winding (black to spark plug wire)*	3,300 ohms
Plug cap	5,000 ohms
Ignition exciter coil (red/white to green/red)	490 ohms
Ignition pulser coil (blue/red to red/white)	90 ohms
Ignition trigger coil (white/yellow to black)	220 ohms
* Test with the spark plug cap removed. Coil secondary resistance should not be tested with the spark plug cap installed.	

Chapter Three

Lubrication, Maintenance, and Tune-up

Your Polaris watercraft requires periodic maintenance to operate efficiently without breaking down. This chapter covers the regular maintenance required to keep your craft in top shape. Regular, careful maintenance is the best guarantee for a trouble-free, long lasting machine. Personal watercraft are high-performance machines that demand proper lubrication, maintenance and tune-ups to maintain the high level of performance, extend engine life and extract the maximum economy of operation.

You can do your own lubrication, maintenance and tune-up if you follow the correct procedures and use common sense. Always remember that damage can result from improper tuning and

adjustment. In addition, where special tools or testers are called for during a particular maintenance or adjustment procedure, the tool should be used or you should refer service to a qualified Polaris dealership or repair shop.

The following information is based on recommendations from Polaris that will help you keep your craft operating at its peak level.

NOTE
Due to the number of models and years covered in this book, be sure to follow the correct procedure and specifications for your specific model and year. Also use the correct quantity and type of fluid as indicated in the tables.

Tables 1-8 are at the end of this chapter.

OPERATIONAL CHECKLISTS

Each of the following checklists is included to provide you with an organized comprehensive servicing procedure to maximize the amount of time your watercraft is operating at its peak.

Pre-Ride (or Daily)

Perform the checks and procedures listed in **Table 1** prior to launching the craft.

1. Visually inspect the hull for cracks or other damage. Damaged areas must be repaired before launching the craft. This inspection is especially important before unloading a craft that has been transported a long distance.

2. On 1995 models, refer to **Figure 1** and check the fuel/water separator for water. Remove and clean it if necessary.

3. Check the choke (A, **Figure 2**) and throttle (**Figure 3**) controls for proper operation. The controls should not stick or bind. The throttle lever should return to the fully closed position when released. Also check throttle movement at the carburetor. Make sure the choke returns to fully open position.

4. Turn the handlebars from side to side and check the operation of the jet pump steering nozzle (**Figure 4**). Make sure it moves from side to side corresponding to handlebar movement.

5. Open the front cover and lift out the basket (**Figure 5**).

6. Remove the seat and engine cover. Allow the hull to air out before servicing components inside.

7. Check that the fuel tank (A, **Figure 6**), oil tank (B, **Figure 6**), electrical box (A, **Figure 7**), battery (B, **Figure 7**) and other components are properly mounted. Tighten any loose bolts, nuts or hose clamps.

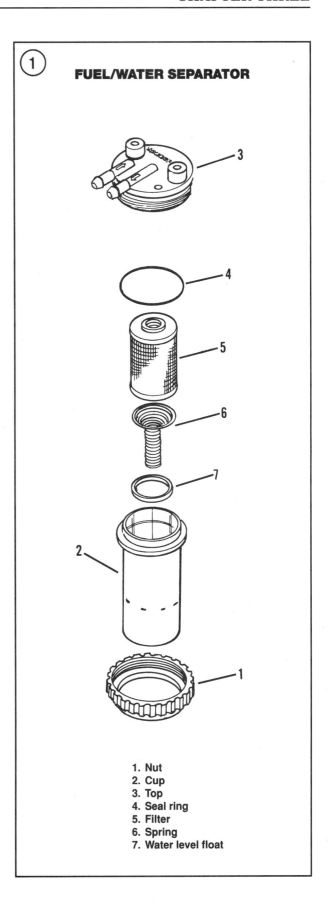

① **FUEL/WATER SEPARATOR**

1. Nut
2. Cup
3. Top
4. Seal ring
5. Filter
6. Spring
7. Water level float

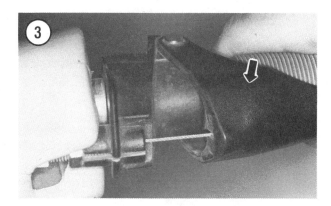

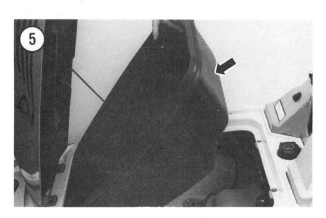

8. Check battery condition. It may be necessary to add water to the battery cells more frequently in hot weather.

9. If there is water in the bilge, remove the drain plug, dry the hull and determine the cause. Check the intake screens at the bottom of the bilge drain hoses (at the stern). The screens must not be clogged. The water trap drains (**Figure 8**) must

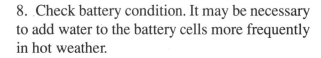

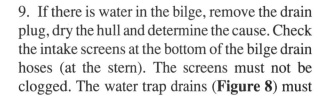

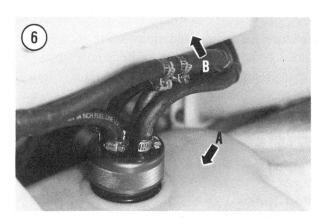

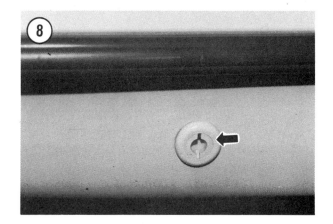

not allow water to enter (**Figure 9**). The bilge should remain dry.

10. Check that you have a fire extinguisher on board and that it is fully charged and properly stowed in the front compartment (**Figure 10**).

Each Time the Watercraft is Filled With Gasoline

1. Always check the oil level in the oil reservoir (**Figure 11**) when adding gasoline to the fuel tank. Add the proper type of oil if necessary.

2. On models with fuel/water separator (**Figure 1**), check for water and drain if present. Remove and clean the bowl if necessary. If water is frequently in the separator, it may indicate improper fuel handling or contaminated fuel.

Post-Ride

1. Turn fuel shut off valve (B, **Figure 2**) to the OFF position.

2. Remove the seat and inspect the bilge. Wipe any water remaining in the compartments under the seat.

3. If water has been above the level of the driveshaft coupler (**Figure 12**), grease the driveshaft coupler and the bearing housing.

4. Clean the hull and check for damage.

5. If the craft is operated in saltwater or especially dirty water, flush cooling system with clean freshwater at the end of each day. Refer to Chapter Nine for the flushing procedure.

End of Day Checklist

Before putting your watercraft away for the day, make sure the following procedures are completed.

1. Turn the fuel shut off valve (B, **Figure 2**) to the OFF position.

2. If the craft is operated in saltwater or especially dirty water, flush cooling system with

clean freshwater at the end of each day. Refer to Chapter Nine for the flushing procedure.

3. Clear excess water from the exhaust system by starting the engine without water running through the engine. Run the engine for no more than 10 seconds. During this short period, operate the throttle in quick bursts from idle to about 3/4 throttle. Stop the engine.

> *WARNING*
> *The exhaust gases are poisonous. Do not run the engine in a closed area. Make sure there is plenty of ventilation.*

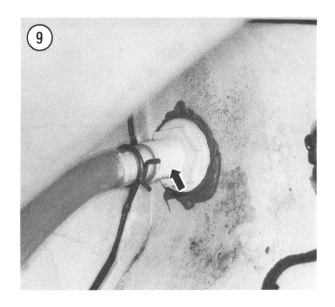

3

CAUTION
Do not run the engine for more than 10 seconds without a supply of cooling water or the rubber parts of the exhaust system will be damaged. Prolonged running without coolant will also cause serious internal engine damage. Do not operate the engine at maximum speed out of the water.

4. Rinse the outside of the craft with clean water. Clean any dirt or marine growth.

5. Lightly rinse the engine compartment with clean water. Do not use a powerful water flow or flood the area.

6. Remove water from the bilge, then dry the engine, pump and bilge areas with a clean, dry rag. Remove as much moisture from these components and compartments as possible.

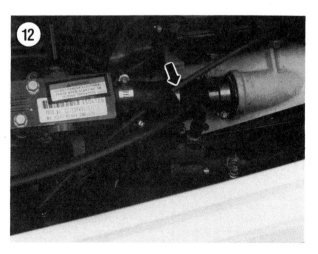

7. Spray a rust inhibitor onto all metal components to help reduce corrosion buildup.

8. If possible, leave the engine compartment partially uncovered to prevent condensation and corrosion buildup.

Break-In Procedure

Following cylinder service such as boring, honing and new rings, or major lower end work, the engine must be broken-in just as if it were new. The performance and service life of the engine depends greatly on a careful and sensible break-in.

1. For the first 10 hours of operation, run the engine at no more than 3/4 throttle. Vary engine speed as much as possible. Prolonged steady running at 1 speed, no matter how moderate, is to be avoided, as is hard acceleration.

2. To ensure adequate protection to the engine during break-in, add 500 ml (16.9 oz.) of the same oil used in the injection system to the first tank of gas. Use this oil together with the oil supplied by the injection system.

3. Throughout the break-in period, check the oil injection reservoir tank to make sure the injection system is working properly (the oil level in the tank should be diminishing).

4. After engine break-in is complete, perform the *10-Hour Inspection* as described in the following section. In addition, retighten the cylinder head nuts as described in this chapter.

NOTE
After the break-in is complete, install new spark plugs as described in this chapter.

10-Hour Inspection

After the initial 10-hours of operation, inspect the craft and perform the maintenance listed in **Table 2**. While this initial inspection may have already been performed on your machine, repeat the engine inspection whenever the engine top- or bottom-end has been overhauled or the engine removed from the hull. The initial inspection will also help a new owner become more familiar with the machine. Perform the steering inspection procedures after major service has been performed to components of that system.

Pre-Season Check-Up

Before the start of each new season, clean, inspect, service and repair the watercraft as necessary. Repairs should be made before storing or during the off season, but sometimes they are put off or the damage is not noticed until it is nearly time to use the craft. Refer to the Pre-Season check list included in **Table 1** and the following.

1. Check the fuel tank. If old gasoline remains in the tank, it must be drained. Fill the tank with clean, fresh gasoline.

2. Make sure the engine oil tank (**Figure 11**) is full. If necessary, refill it as described in this chapter.

3. If so equipped, check the fuel/water separator for the presence of water.

4. Remove the seat and engine cover.

5. Check the electrolyte level in the battery (B, **Figure 7**). See Chapter Seven for battery service. Always fill the battery with distilled water if electrolyte level is low.

6. Remove, clean and check the gap of the spark plugs as described in this chapter. Install new spark plugs if necessary.

7. Inspect and lubricate the throttle and choke cables. Operate the throttle lever (**Figure 3**) and check that it returns to the fully closed position when released. Also check throttle movement at the carburetors. Operate the choke control (A, **Figure 2**) and make sure the control does not stick or bind.

8. Check the adjustment of the carburetor mixture and idle speed.

9. Perform *General Lubrication* as described in this chapter.

10. Check the fuel filter (A, **Figure 13**) and oil filter (B, **Figure 13**). Install new filters at the beginning of each season. Install filters with the arrow molded into the side of the filter indicating the correct direction of flow.

11. Tighten the cylinder head retaining nuts as described in this chapter.

12. Check to be sure the handlebar retaining nuts (**Figure 14**) are tight. Only 3 of the 4 nuts are shown **Figure 14**.

13. Check to be sure the handlebar grips do not slip on the handlebar. Grasp each of the hand grips tightly and try to twist it on the bar. Both grips must be tight. Reglue or replace grips as described in Chapter Ten.

14. Check the steering column and bearings for wear.

15. Check the steering and jet nozzle (**Figure 4**) for proper movement. Check the steering cable

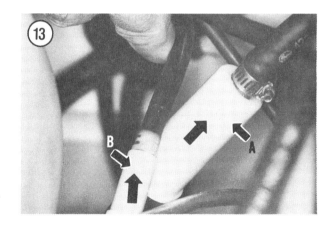

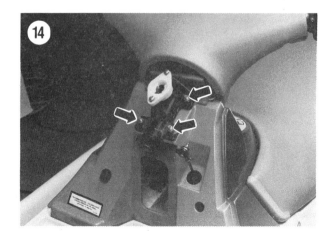

adjustment and make sure the cable is mounted securely.

16. Check all components in the engine compartment for looseness or damage. Repair or replace components as required. Some items to check for looseness are:

    a. Carburetor mounting screws.

    b. Engine mounting fasteners.

    c. Exhaust assembly.

    d. Battery mounting and cables.

17. Check all fuel and oil hoses for leakage and loose or damaged conditions. Do not operate the craft until all leaks are repaired and fuel spilled inside the hull is wiped up thoroughly.

18. Inspect the oil injection system for proper operation. Refer to Chapter Eight if additional tests or repair is necessary.

19. Remove enough oil from the oil injection reservoir to cause the low oil level tone to sound or the warning light to illuminate. Refill the reservoir if the warning operates properly. Refer to Chapter Eight if the sender is faulty or to Chapter Seven if the warning buzzer is faulty.

20. Check the electrical connections for the engine overheating signal. The sender is located in the water outlet manifold.

21. Clean and inspect water trap drains (**Figure 8** and **Figure 9**) for damage or leakage. The bilge should be dry.

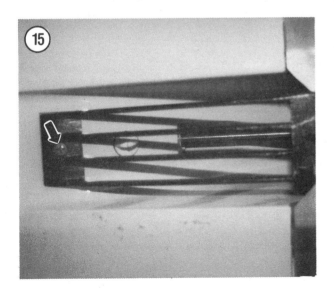

22. Check the condition of the battery and cables. The cables and terminals should be clean and the connections should be tight.

23. Look into the jet pump intake and check the condition of the pump impeller and clearance to the wear ring.

24. Grease the driveshaft couplers and bearing housing (**Figure 12**).

NOTE
*Do not turn the screw (**Figure 15**) attaching the front of the water intake grate unless it is being removed. If it is necessary to remove the screw, refer to Step 26 for assembly.*

25. Inspect the condition of the water intake grate (**Figure 15**). Make sure the grate is securely attached.

26. Check the water intake (**Figure 15**) for weeds or other obstructions that might cause the engine to overheat. If access to the inlet is restricted, proceed as follows:

    a. Turn the fuel valve OFF.

    b. Remove the battery as described in Chapter Seven.

    c. Tip the craft so that its left side is down.

CAUTION
Do not tip the craft so the left side is up. When the engine is not running, water from the exhaust system may drain into the engine's exhaust ports, then enter the cylinders causing serious engine damage.

    d. Remove any weeds or other obstructions from the water intake area. It may be necessary to remove the intake grate (**Figure 15**) so that you can clean the area thoroughly. Unbolt and remove the ride plate, located to the rear of the intake grate. On 1992-1993 models, hold the lock nut inside the hull (under the driveshaft) and remove the screw (**Figure 15**). On 1994-on models, the screw (**Figure 15**) is screwed into a threaded insert in the hull. Pull the intake grate down and forward.

NOTE
*Any leak in the seal at the front of the ride plate can cause cavitation. Be sure there are no pin holes or gaps in the continuous bead of sealer. Apply sealer to cleaned surfaces **just** before installing the ride plate.*

   e. Reinstall the grate, if removed. On 1992-1993 models, seal the screw (**Figure 15**) to the hull with RTV sealer, then tighten the grate mounting screw securely. On 1994-on models, coat the threads of screw (**Figure 15**) with Loctite 242 (blue) when installing. On all models, clean and dry the front edge of the ride plate and the mating surface of the hull so that RTV sealer will stick to the surfaces. Coat the entire front edge of the ride plate with a continuous bead of RTV sealer. Coat threads of the screws attaching the ride plate with Loctite 242 (blue) before installing.

   f. Rotate the craft so that it is upright.

   g. Reinstall the battery (Chapter Seven).

   h. Bleed the oil pump as described in Chapter Eight.

27. Check the condition of the driveshaft cover.

28. Flush the cooling system as described in Chapter Nine.

29. Inspect the rubber parts of the cooling system and install new parts if necessary.

30. Remove and inspect the cooling system thermostat. Install a new thermostat as described in Chapter Nine if necessary.

31. Remove and inspect the cooling system filters including any screens installed at the exhaust pipe. Clean or install new filters.

32. Check the engine mounts for damage. Install new mounts if damaged.

33. Check the seat latch attachment stud. The stud should be tight and should be adjusted to hold the seat firmly in place. Install the seat and engine cover, making sure that it is fastened securely.

34. After launching the craft, check the starter and start the engine. Check the stop switch and the tether switch (**Figure 16**) for proper operation by operating each in turn. Do not operate the craft if either switch fails to stop the engine instantly.

35. Check that you have a fire extinguisher on board, that it is fully charged and is properly stowed (**Figure 10**).

36. Clean the hull and inspect for cracks or other damage.

FUEL AND LUBRICATION

Use regular unleaded (87 octane or higher) gasoline to prevent engine knock and ensure proper operation. Refer to **Table 3** for fuel tank capacity.

WARNING
Serious fire hazards always exist around gasoline. Do not allow any smoking in areas where fuel is being mixed or while refueling your machine. Always have a fire extinguisher, rated for gasoline and electrical fires.

Polaris 2-stroke engines are lubricated by oil that is injected into the engine, circulates through the crankcase, and eventually enters the combus-

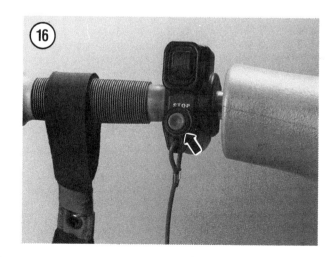

tion chamber with the fuel. The oil is eventually burned with the fuel and expelled through the exhaust. Components of the engine are lubricated by the oil that clings to the various parts as it passes through the crankcase and cylinders. The oil is never reused and the amount of oil in the reservoir will diminish as the oil is being used.

Check Oil Level

An oil injection system is used on all models. During operation, oil is automatically injected into the engine. On 1992-1994 models, a fixed-ratio oil injection system is used. On models so equipped, the system delivers oil to the engine at a fixed ratio throughout the entire engine speed range. On 1995 models, a variable ratio oil injection system is used. On these models, the oil pump control lever is connected to the throttle mechanism. The fuel/oil ratio is thereby varied according to engine speed and load conditions.

The oil reservoir (**Figure 17**) that supplies oil for the oil injection system is located ahead of the engine and can be serviced after opening the front compartment cover. The oil reservoir has a low warning signal, but visually check the oil level daily and each time the watercraft is filled with fuel. Refer to **Table 3** for oil tank capacity.

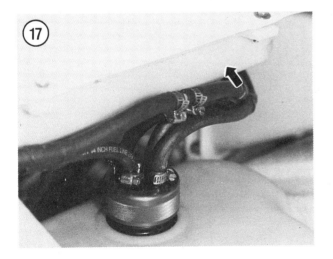

The rider will probably not notice any performance difference if lubrication stops for one or more of the cylinders, until the affected cylinder(s) are seriously damaged. It is important to make sure that the oil injection system is always properly adjusted and maintained. Oil level in the reservoir (tank) should be checked daily and each time gasoline is added to the fuel tank.

1. Position the watercraft so that it is level.

2. Open the front cover.

3. Remove the basket from the front compartment (**Figure 5**), then observe the oil level in the oil tank (**Figure 17**).

4. Unscrew the fill cap (**Figure 11**) from the oil tank, then check the level of oil through the opening.

5. Fill the oil tank with the recommended 2-stroke injection oil until the oil level is correct.

SERVICE INTERVALS

Following the service and lubrication intervals shown in **Table 1** will help ensure long service under normal operating conditions; however, if the craft is operated in extremely dirty, silty or salty water, service should be more frequent.

For convenience when maintaining your personal watercraft, most of the services listed in **Table 1** are described in this chapter although, the text may refer you to another chapter for more complete service.

Driveshaft Couplings and Bearing Housing Lubrication

Grease fittings are located on the driveshaft coupling (A, **Figure 18**) and on the bearing housing (B, **Figure 18**). Lubricate these fittings with a premium grade marine grease (part No. 2871066 or equivalent). The normal service interval is every 25 hours of operation, but the fittings should be greased whenever water in the compartment is above the level of the driveshaft. The fitting should also be lubricated more frequently if the craft is operated in saltwater. To lubricate the driveshaft couplings and the bearings in the pump housing, proceed as follows.

1. Remove the tether switch to make sure the engine cannot start.

2. Remove the seat and engine cover.

3. Disconnect the battery ground cable from the battery terminal to prevent accidental starting.

4. Loosen the clamp (C, **Figure 18**) attaching the plastic driveshaft cover, then turn the cover about 180°, so the open side is up.

5. Connect a grease gun with the appropriate type of marine grease to the fitting (A, **Figure 18**) on the coupler.

6. Pump grease into the fitting until the coupler boot just begins to expand, then remove the grease gun.

7. Connect the grease gun to the fitting (B, **Figure 18**) for lubricating the bearings in the bearing housing.

8. Pump grease into the fitting until the grease comes out around the seals.

9. Turn the driveshaft cover until the open side is down, then tighten the clamp (C, **Figure 18**) to 20-25 in.-lb. (2.8 N•m).

10. Reattach the battery ground cable.

11. Install the seat, making sure that it is fastened securely.

General Lubrication

Use Polaris Marine grease (part No. 2871066) or equivalent where grease is required. Where a rust inhibitor is called for, Use T-9 Metal Protectant (part No. 2871064) or an equivalent penetrating rust inhibitor.

1. Remove the seat and engine cover.

2. Detach the throttle cable (**Figure 19**) from the hand lever.

3. Spray a rust inhibitor along the cable and into the cable housing.

4. Reattach the throttle cable and operate the throttle lever.

5. Disconnect the choke cable from the carburetor, then spray a rust inhibitor into the cable housing.

6. Reattach the choke cable.

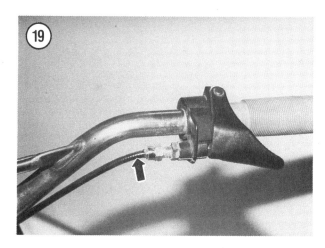

7. Pull the choke knob (**Figure 20**) out and spray the exposed part of the shaft with a rust inhibitor. Operate the choke several times to distribute the lubricant along the cable.

8. Spray the exposed part of the steering cable shaft (**Figure 21**) with a rust inhibitor.

9. Apply dielectric grease to both battery terminals and all exposed electrical connectors.

10. Lubricate carburetor and oil injection springs, shafts and cable ends with a rust inhibitor.

11. Lubricate the hinges, latches and hooks with a rust inhibitor.

PERIODIC MAINTENANCE

Inspect the following maintenance items at the intervals specified in **Tables 1-2**.

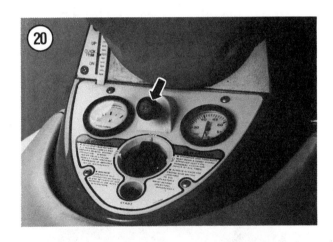

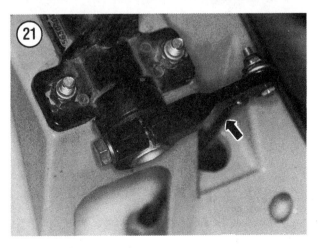

Nuts, Bolts and Other Fasteners

Visually check for loose or missing fasteners in the engine compartment, on the steering assembly and at the jet pump assembly. Replace missing fasteners with the same type, made of the same material as the original. For example, many of the fasteners used on the machine are stainless steel. Substituting a stainless steel fastener with a similar one made of carbon steel will allow corrosion buildup that may eventually result in broken fasteners and various service related problems. After checking for missing fasteners, check all of the exposed fasteners for looseness. Check with a wrench or socket. Use a torque wrench when tightening critical fasteners. Refer to the appropriate chapters in this manual for tightening torques. General torque specifications are listed in **Table 4**.

Hose Clamps

Check all of the hose clamps for tightness. Replace damaged hose clamps, as required.

Fuel System Service

Before servicing the fuel system components in the following sections, observe the following information:

> *WARNING*
> *Explosive and flammable conditions always exist around gasoline, so observe the following precautions to minimize the risk of injury.*

1. Check for the presence of raw gasoline fumes immediately after removing the engine cover. If the odor seems to be strong, there may be a fuel leak. Immediately locate and repair the leak.

2. Allow the engine compartment to air out before beginning work.

3. Disconnect the ground cable from the negative terminal of the battery before working on any fuel system component.

4. Gasoline dripping onto a hot engine component may cause a fire. Always allow the engine to cool completely before disconnecting a fuel line or removing the fuel tank.

5. Wipe up spilled gasoline immediately with dry rags. Store the rags in a suitable metal container until they can be cleaned or discarded. Do not store gas, oil or solvent soaked rags in any compartment of the hull.

6. Do not service any fuel system component while in the vicinity of open flames, sparks or while anyone is smoking. This includes natural gas appliances, such as a clothes dryer or water heater.

7. Always have a Coast Guard approved fire extinguisher close at hand when working on the engine.

8. Loosen the fuel filler cap before disconnecting any fuel line or hose to relieve any pressure in the fuel tank.

Fuel Filter

Review the WARNING listed under *Fuel System Service* in this chapter, then proceed with the following procedure. The filter is located in the fuel line between the fuel tank and the fuel pump.

1. Open the front cover and remove the basket.
2. Turn the fuel valve OFF.
3. Place a rag underneath the fuel filter (A, **Figure 22**) or the bowl of the water/fuel separator (**Figure 23**) to catch any spilled gasoline.
4A. On models with the inline filter shown at A, **Figure 22**, proceed as follows:
   a. Loosen the 2 hose clamps.
   b. Pull the filter from the fuel lines.
   c. Install a new filter with the arrow on the side pointing toward the direction of flow.
   d. Tighten the hose clamps. Do not tighten the clamps enough to cut the fuel line or collapse the ends of the filter.

4B. On models equipped with the water/fuel separator shown in **Figure 23**, service the filter as follows:
   a. Unscrew and remove the filter bowl from the housing.
   b. Remove the filter from the water/fuel separator bowl.
   c. Clean the filter bowl and dry with compressed air.
   d. Clean the filter element with compressed air (low pressure), if available.
   e. Inspect for a torn or contaminated filter element. Replace the filter if damaged or if compressed air will not clean it.
   f. Replace the bowl O-ring if worn or damaged.
   g. Install the filter bowl O-ring into the bowl groove. Make sure the O-ring seats in the groove correctly.
   h. Install the filter element into the top of the water/fuel separator housing.
   i. Install the filter bowl and thread it onto the housing. Tighten hand tight.

5. Turn the fuel valve ON and check for leaks.

> *WARNING*
> *Do not start the engine if the fuel filter leaks. Repair any leak immediately. Wipe up all spilled gasoline before installing the engine cover.*

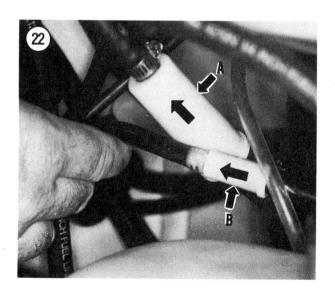

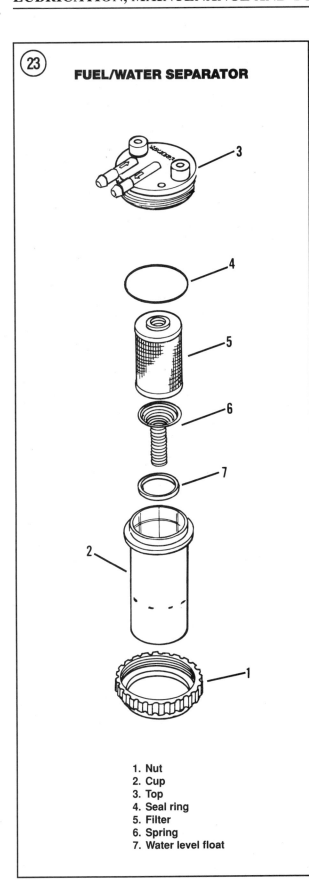

(23) **FUEL/WATER SEPARATOR**

1. Nut
2. Cup
3. Top
4. Seal ring
5. Filter
6. Spring
7. Water level float

6. Perform the *Fuel System Pressure Test* as described in Chapter Six before starting the engine.

Carburetor Adjustment

Refer to *Engine Tune-up* in this chapter.

Fuel System Pressure Test

Refer to Chapter Six.

Injection Oil Filter Inspection/Replacement

An inline oil filter (B, **Figure 22**) is installed between the oil tank and the oil pump. The oil filter will prevent contaminants from obstructing oil passages in the oil pump. Inspect the oil filter frequently for contamination or blockage. If the oil filter is contaminated or blocked, it must be replaced immediately. At the minimum, replace the oil filter once per year.

> *CAUTION*
> *A contaminated or plugged oil filter will prevent oil from reaching the engine, causing engine seizure.*

1. Place a cloth underneath the oil filter to absorb oil when the filter is removed.
2. Prepare plugs to stop oil from flowing from the detached lines.

> *NOTE*
> *The oil filter is directional and must be installed correctly. Note the placement of the oil filter in the oil system, drawing a diagram, if necessary, for reassembly.*

3. Remove the clamps from the hoses attached to each end of the filter, then detach both hoses from the filter (B, **Figure 22**).
4. Plug the lines to prevent the entrance of dirt and the loss of oil.
5. Attach both hoses to the new oil filter, making sure the filter is properly aligned in the system.

3

Secure each hose with a clamp. Tie wraps are sometimes used as clamps.

6. Bleed the oil pump as described in Chapter Eight.

7. Remove and discard the oil soaked catch cloth and clean the hull.

Battery

Check the battery electrolyte level on a periodic basis. Fill with distilled water as required. Refer to Chapter Seven for complete battery service information.

Electrical Wiring and Connectors

NOTE
It is important to seal all of the electrical connections to prevent the entrance of water. All seals must be in good condition and a corrosion resistant grease such as Nyogel (part No. 2871044) should be used when assembling. Nyogel or a similar dielectric grease designed for use on electrical connections should also be used liberally on wiring connectors. Do not attempt to use silicone sealer, other types of grease or any products that will cause corrosion. It is extremely difficult to remove corrosion and improper sealers from the connectors.

1. Remove the straps holding the electrical box to the top of the battery.

2. Lift the electrical box from the battery and remove the top cover from the battery.

3. Detach the battery ground from the negative (−) terminal of the battery.

4. Check all of the external wiring connectors (**Figure 24**) for corrosion or loose connectors.

5. Separate the connectors and inspect them for damaged or corroded contacts. Spray connectors with electrical contact cleaner and apply dielectric grease to the connectors before reattaching them.

6. Attach battery ground cable, install the battery cover and install the electrical box.

7. Attach the straps and make sure the battery and electrical box are held securely.

Electrical Box

1. Remove the straps holding the electrical box to the top of the battery.

2. Lift the electrical box from the battery and remove the top cover from the battery.

3. Detach the battery ground from the negative (−) terminal of the battery.

4. Remove the screws attaching the 2 halves of the electric box and separate the 2 halves of the box. See **Figure 25**.

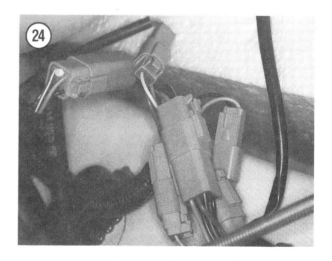

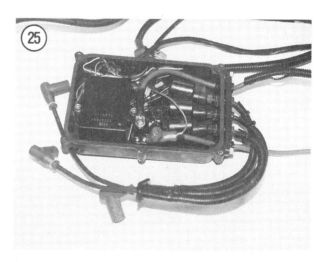

5. Inspect the inside of the electrical box for moisture. The box must be sealed and remain dry.

6. Separate the connectors and spray them with electrical contact cleaner. Apply dielectric grease to the connectors before reattaching them.

7. Inspect the high-tension electrical leads to the spark plugs for cracks or breaks in the insulation. Replace any lead that is damaged.

8. Inspect all wires that connect electrical components. Replace damaged wiring.

9. Check the manual reset circuit breaker.

10. When reassembling and installing the electrical box, observe the following:

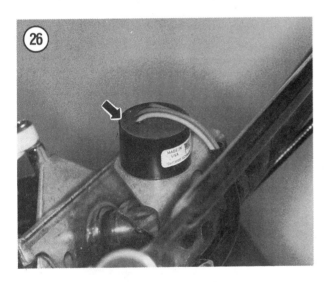

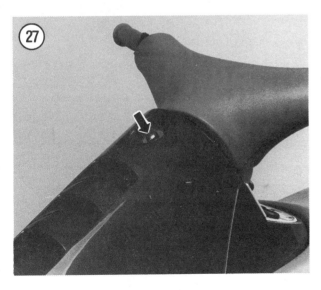

a. Be sure that all seals are in good condition and in place. It is important to make sure that water is not allowed to enter the electrical box.

b. Tighten all screws sufficiently without stripping. Repair damaged threads and replace any missing fasteners.

c. Secure the electrical box, making certain that all exposed wiring is properly routed.

Engine Stop Switch and Tether Switch

If the engine stop switch or tether switch (**Figure 16**) fails to operate properly, remove and test it as described in Chapter Two. Replace the switch if damaged. Do not operate the watercraft if these switches will not stop the engine.

Engine Start Switch and Starter Solenoid

If the engine start switch fails to energize the starter, first make sure the battery is properly charged. Test the start switch and the starter solenoid (located in the electrical box) as described in Chapter Two. Replace the switch if damaged.

Engine Overheat Warning Buzzer Check

Check the overheat warning buzzer (**Figure 26**) for proper operation. A damaged system will not warn the operator of engine overheating, resulting in engine damage. Refer to Chapter Seven. On models with a multi-function display the red WARNING LED will light and the display will flash the message "HOT."

Hatch Lock

Open the front hatch (compartment) by turning the knob (**Figure 27**) counterclockwise. The compartment is held closed by turning the knob clockwise, engaging the latch pin with the receiver (**Figure 28**). Check for loose or damaged parts.

Hull Inspection

Inspect the hull for scratches or punctures. Punctures or other types of severe damage should be repaired by a competent technician.

Steering Inspection

Move the handlebars from side to side. They should turn smoothly without sticking or roughness. If the steering is not smooth, check for a damaged steering cable or loose or damaged steering components. Refer to **Figure 29**. If the steering feels too tight or too loose, adjust or repair it as described in Chapter Ten.

Steering/Jet Pump Alignment

For proper steering, the handlebars must be aligned with the jet pump steering nozzle.
1. Place the watercraft in quiet water or on a level surface.
2. Turn the handlebars so they are straight ahead.
3. Measure from the center of one handlebar grip straight down to the floorboard. Repeat for the other side. If necessary, reposition the handlebars until measurements for both sides are the same. This is the correct straight-ahead steering position.
4. Place a straightedge across the back of the steering nozzle as shown in **Figure 30**, then measure the distance from the back of the hull to the straightedge on both sides. The distance should be the same, indicating that straightedge (and the nozzle) are parallel to the hull.

NOTE
*The cable adjusting nuts on 1992-1994 models are at the rear of the cable as shown in **Figure 31** and **Figure 32**. The*

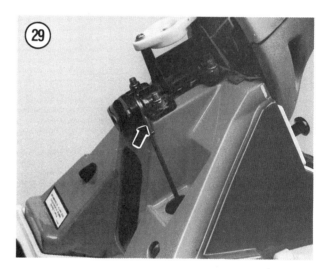

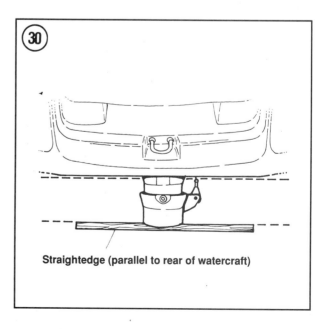

Straightedge (parallel to rear of watercraft)

cable adjusting nuts are similar, but at the front of the cable on 1995 models.

5. If the straightedge is not parallel to the hull, locate the adjusting nuts (**Figure 31** and **Figure 32**) on the steering cable. Turn the adjusting nuts until the straightedge is parallel to the hull.

6. Tighten the adjusting nuts to the torque listed in **Table 4**, then recheck the steering adjustment.

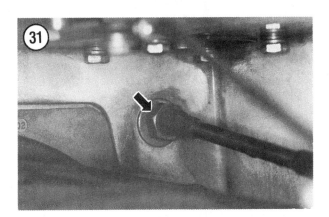

Engine Cooling System Filters and Thermostat

Filters are located at various places in the cooling system depending upon the year and model of the watercraft. It is important that these filters remain in place and remain clean. Check the filters, thermostat and pop-off valve at the intervals listed in the **Tables 1-2**. Refer to Chapter Nine for specific servicing procedures.

Intake Grate

Weeds or other obstructions in the water intake (**Figure 33**) can cause engine overheating. If you suspect weeds or other debris have clogged the pump intake area, clean it as follows.

1. The intake grate is accessible on some trailers without removing the craft from the trailer. If it is necessary to tip the craft on its side to inspect or clean the intake, observe the following:

   a. Turn the fuel valve OFF.

   b. Remove the seat and engine cover.

   c. Remove the battery.

> *CAUTION*
> *It is important to raise the right side, not the left, because if the left side is higher than the right, water can run out of the cooling system, through the exhaust ports and into the cylinders.*

   d. Tip the craft by lifting the right side, with the left side down.

2A. On 1992-1993 models, hold the locknut inside the hull (under the driveshaft) and remove the screw (**Figure 33**).

2B. On 1994-on models, remove the screw (**Figure 33**). The screw is threaded into a nut plate in the hull.

3. Unbolt and remove the ride plate, located to the rear of the intake grate.

4. Pull the intake grate down and forward.

5. Check the water inlet. The pickup opening must be open and clear.

a. On 1992-1993 models, the cooling water pickup is located near the rear of the pump housing. Also make sure that the welch plugs on the outside of the housing are in place.

b. On 1994-on models, the cooling water pickup is located in the (rear) extension housing. A screen covers the opening of 1995 models and this screen (part No. 543 1523) can be installed on 1994 models to reduce the possibility of debris plugging the pump.

6. Reassemble by reversing the disassembly procedure, observing the following:

a. On 1992-1993 models, seal the screw (**Figure 33**) to the hull with RTV sealer.

b. On 1994-on models, coat the threads of screw (**Figure 33**) with Loctite 242 (blue) when installing.

c. Clean and dry the front edge of the ride plate and the mating surface of the hull so that RTV sealer will stick to the surfaces.

> *NOTE*
> *Any leak in the seal at the front of the ride plate can cause cavitation. Be sure there are no pin holes or gaps in the continuous bead of sealer. Apply sealer to cleaned surfaces **just** before installing the ride plate.*

d. Coat the entire front edge of the ride plate with a continuous bead of RTV sealer.

e. Coat threads of the screws attaching the ride plate with Loctite 242 (blue) before installing.

Impeller

Inspect the impeller blades (**Figure 34**) for nicks, deep scratches or gouges at the intervals specified in **Table 1**. Refer to Chapter Five.

Impeller Clearance

Excessive impeller housing clearance will reduce jet thrust, lowering the craft's speed and reducing overall performance. If wear is suspected, measure the impeller housing clearance as described in Chapter Five.

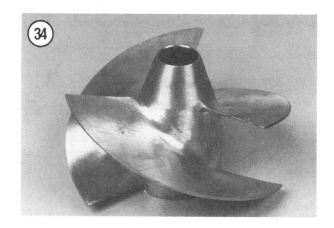

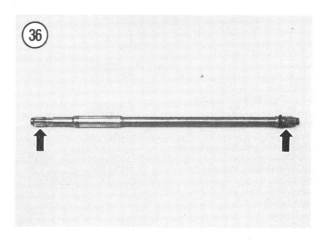

Driveshaft Boots

Inspect the driveshaft boot(s) for tearing or other damage. Refer to **Figure 35**. Refer to Chapter Five for replacement.

Driveshaft Splines

Inspect the driveshaft splines (**Figure 36**) at regular intervals for excessive wear or damage. Refer to Chapter Five for jet pump/driveshaft removal and service procedures.

Cooling System Flushing

Flush the cooling system with freshwater at the beginning of each season and every 3 months

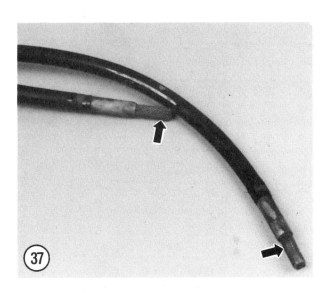

(or every 50 hours of operation) as listed in **Table 1**. If the craft is operated in salty, silty or dirty water, it is recommended to flush the cooling system at the end of every day. It is also recommended before the craft is stored for an extended period of time. Refer to Chapter Nine for the usual flushing procedure.

If the craft will be stored where there is *any* possibility of freezing, pour a biodegradable (RV) antifreeze into the system as described in Chapter Eleven. Install a flush kit (part No. 287 1034) on 1992 models not originally equipped with provisions for flushing. Refer to Chapter Nine for cooling system service.

Spark Plugs

Refer to *Engine Tune-up* in this chapter.

Bilge Syphon System Check

Bilge siphon hoses are connected to the jet pump to remove water from the hull. The hoses inside the engine compartment are fitted with an elbow, with a 1 mm (0.040 in.) orifice and the hoses are looped to the top of the engine compartment to prevent water from entering the hull while the craft is stopped. The lower ends of the bilge siphon hoses are fitted with screens (**Figure 37**) and are glued to the lower rear surfaces of the bilge. Make sure the screens are clean and properly located.

Water traps allow water to drain from the areas inside the hull, but prevent water from entering the same openings. Inspect the water trap drains (**Figure 38** and **Figure 39**) for contamination or leakage. Clean or install new drains if necessary.

Throttle Cable Adjustment

Adjust the throttle cable so the carburetor throttle valves can open completely. Check and adjust the cable adjuster as follows.

1. Lubricate the throttle cable as described in this chapter.

2. Remove the air intake silencer from the top of the carburetors and check to make sure the chokes are open.

3. Squeeze the throttle lever (**Figure 40**) to make sure it moves smoothly and does not bind. It is especially important that the throttle does not stick wide open when the throttle lever is held against the handlebar, then released. Perform this check as you move the handlebars from side to side. If the throttle lever is tight or sluggish, correct the problem before proceeding to Step 4. The throttle must operate smoothly.

4. When released, the handlebar mounted throttle control lever should have approximately 0.8-1.3 mm (0.03-0.05 in.) free play as shown in **Figure 41**. To adjust throttle lever free play, proceed as follows:

   a. Loosen the throttle cable adjuster locknut (A, **Figure 42**).

   b. Turn the adjuster (B, **Figure 42**) in or out until free play is correct.

   c. Tighten the locknut and recheck the adjustment.

5. Squeeze the throttle lever (**Figure 40**) and hold it against the handlebar. Look into the carburetors and check to see if the throttle valves are completely open. Be sure the cable is not too tight. The throttle cable should have approximately 2 mm (1/16 in.) additional play.

6. The throttle cable is attached to the front carburetor, but the center and rear carburetors should be open the same amount as the front carburetor.

   a. If the throttle valves of all carburetors are all open completely, adjustment is correct. Proceed to Step 7.

   b. If the carburetors do not open completely, the cable adjuster may be adjusted as described in Step 4.

   c. If the carburetors are not opened the same amount, the carburetors should be *synchronized* as described in this chapter.

NOTE
Even if the throttle openings appear to be the same, the throttle valves may not be synchronized. Refer to **Synchronize Carburetors and Choke** *in this chapter for procedures to check and adjust.*

7. After adjusting the throttle lever free play, turn the handlebar from side to side and repeat Step 3. Make sure the throttle lever moves

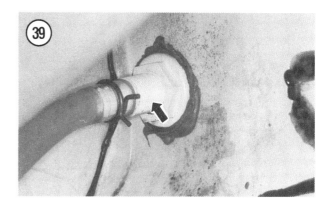

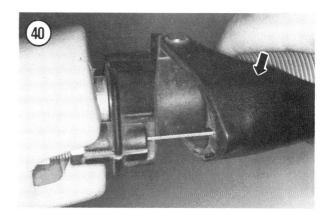

smoothly and that the cable does not bind or stick with the handlebar in any position.

> *WARNING*
> *Make sure the stop lever contacts the idle speed screw when the throttle lever is released.*

Oil Pump Control Rod (1995-On)

On 1995 and later models, a control lever that varies the amount of oil delivery is incorporated into the pump. Because the oil pump on late models controls oil flow to the engine, the pump must be matched to the carburetor throttle setting. A rod connects the pump control lever to the carburetor throttle linkage, so when the carburetor throttle lever moves, the carburetor throttle and the oil pump control move simultaneously. Minimum oil pump output will

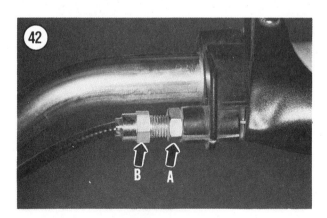

correspond to idle speed opening of the throttle valve and the wide open throttle position will move the pump control to its maximum position. The oil pump control lever on 1995 and later models is spring loaded to the maximum delivery position so if the rod becomes detached, the engine will not be damaged because of insufficient oil.

The control rod is 162.6-164.1 mm (6.40-6.46 in.) long and the ends pop into position in the levers. If detached, install a new control rod assembly. Do not reinstall the old control rod.

The amount of oil delivered by the oil pump on 1992-1994 models is fixed and changed only by changing the engine speed.

Choke Cable Adjustment

An incorrectly adjusted choke cable will cause hard starting problems when the engine is cold.
1. Remove the air intake silencer from the top of the carburetors.
2. Operate the choke knob (**Figure 20**) while watching the choke valves in the carburetors (**Figure 43**). All 3 choke valves should close when the knob is pulled out and should open completely when the knob is pushed in. The knob should move smoothly and the cable should not bind.
3. Pull the choke knob out and look into the carburetors. All 3 choke valves should be closed. Refer to **Figure 43**.
4. The choke cable is attached to the front carburetor, but the center and rear carburetors should move to full open and full close at the same time as the front carburetor.
   a. If the carburetor choke valves of all carburetors are completely closed, adjustment is correct.
   b. If the choke valves all move together, but do not close or do not open completely, the cable adjuster should be adjusted as described in Step 5.

c. If the choke valves on all 3 carburetors are not opened the same amount, *synchronize* the valves as described in this chapter.

5. If cable adjustment is necessary, loosen the set screw (**Figure 44**) in the front carburetor choke lever, reposition the cable in the lever and retighten. Recheck choke operation.

6. Reinstall the intake silencer.

Synchronize Carburetors

The throttle cable is attached to the front carburetor. Movement of the front carburetor is transmitted to the center and rear carburetors by connecting linkage.

Refer to *Throttle Cable Adjustment* in this chapter to adjust the cable attachment.

1. Remove the seat and engine cover.

2. Unbolt and remove the air intake silencer from the top of the carburetors.

> *NOTE*
> *Special test manometer (part No. 2870672), test vacuum gauge set or similar equipment is required to measure vacuum from all 3 test points at the same time.*

3. Remove the rubber caps (A, B and C, **Figure 45**) from each of the 3 carburetors and attach the hoses from the manometers or vacuum gauges.

> *NOTE*
> *On models with "Auto Cock," an external vacuum pump must be used to supply vacuum to the hose (C, **Figure 45**) to open the automatic fuel shut off valve.*

4. Attach a service tachometer (part No. 2870788 or equivalent).

5. Start the engine and adjust the idle speed to the rpm listed in the appropriate table (approximately 1200-1300 rpm). Adjust the idle speed by turning the stop screw (**Figure 46**) located on the front carburetor.

6. Observe the vacuum indicated by the gauges attached in Step 3. The vacuum for each of the 3

carburetors should be the same. Differences in vacuum indicates that the carburetor throttle valves are not synchronized.

7. Proceed as follows to synchronize the throttle openings for the center and rear carburetors to the opening of the front carburetor.

a. Turn the screw (A, **Figure 47**) located between the front and center carburetors to adjust the vacuum for the center carburetor

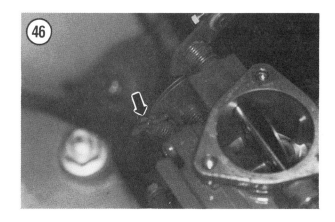

so that it is the same as the vacuum for the front carburetor.

b. Turn the screw (B, **Figure 47**) located between the center and rear carburetors to adjust the vacuum for the rear carburetor so that vacuum for all 3 carburetors is the same.

c. Check the idle speed and readjust by turning the stop screw (**Figure 46**) if necessary. If the idle speed is adjusted, recheck to be sure the vacuum remains the same for all 3 carburetors.

NOTE
*After idle speed is properly adjusted by setting the stop screw (**Figure 46**), turn the similar screw for the rear carburetor until it just touches its throttle lever. Adjustment of the idle stop for the rear carburetor helps maintain an accurate idle speed setting.*

8. Remove the vacuum gauges and reinstall the rubber plugs (A, B and C, **Figure 45**).

9. Reinstall the air intake silencer and seat.

Synchronize Carburetor Choke Valves

The choke cable is attached to the front carburetor. Movement of the front carburetor is transmitted to the center and rear carburetors by connecting linkage.

Refer to *Choke Cable Adjustment* in this chapter to adjust the cable attachment.

1. Remove the seat and engine cover.

2. Unbolt and remove the air intake silencer from the top of the carburetors.

3. Loosen 1 of the set screws in each of the 2 connectors (**Figure 48**) located between the front and center carburetors and between the center and rear carburetors.

4. Pull the choke knob out. The choke valve for the front carburetor must be completely closed.

5. Push the choke valve for the center carburetor closed, hold it closed, then tighten the set screw (**Figure 48**) in the connector located between the front and center carburetors.

6. Push the choke valve for the rear carburetor closed, hold it closed, then tighten the set screw (**Figure 48**) in the connector located between the center and rear carburetors.

7. Push the choke knob in and observe the position of the choke valves. All 3 choke valves should be completely open.

8. Pull the choke knob out and observe the choke valves, which should all be closed. If the valves are not closed, readjust as described in Steps 5-6.

9. Reinstall the air intake silencer and seat.

GENERAL INSPECTION AND MAINTENANCE

Engine Compartment

Inspect all components mounted in the engine compartment for loose, missing or damaged parts. Tighten, replace or repair components as required.

Starter Operation

If the starter fails to operate properly, troubleshoot the starting system as described in Chapter Two. If the starter motor is at fault, service it as described in Chapter Seven.

Seat Latch

Periodically check the seat latch for proper adjustment and for tight mounting. Install the latch attaching screws with Loctite 242 on the screw threads. Damage will occur if they are allowed to loosen.

The latch should engage the seat base adjuster stud in the hull and hold the seat firmly. If necessary, the stud can be repositioned by turning the 2 attaching nuts as required to tighten the seat mounting. Coat threads of the nuts with Loctite 242 or equivalent to prevent loosening.

Clips holding the front of the seat are attached to the hull with pop rivets. Repair or replace the front clips if broken, missing, damaged or loose.

Fuel Tank Cleaning

The fuel tank (A, **Figure 49**) can be removed for a thorough cleaning and inspection. Refer to Chapter Six.

Oil Tank

Inspect the oil tank (B, **Figure 49**) for damage that could cause an oil leak. Replace the tank if damaged. Refer to **Table 3** for oil tank capacity.

Multi-Function Display Operation

Some SL750 and SLT750 models are equipped with a display (**Figure 50** or **Figure 51**) that can indicate the time of day, running time, distance run, peak rpm, current engine rpm, current speed, fuel level, oil level, operating voltage, low battery voltage, high temperature warning and low fuel warning. The multi-function

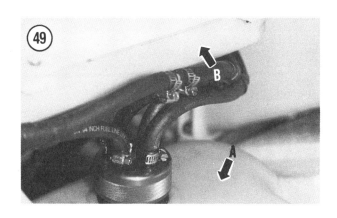

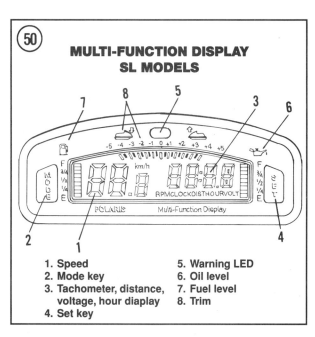

1. Speed
2. Mode key
3. Tachometer, distance, voltage, hour diaplay
4. Set key
5. Warning LED
6. Oil level
7. Fuel level
8. Trim

display automatically turns on when the engine is started and will automatically turn off after 5 minutes of inactivity. Pressing the MODE key turns the multi-function display on if it has turned off automatically.

Speed

Craft speed in 0.1 increments is the primary display that is shown in the left display (1, **Figure 50**) on SL models or in the top display on SLT models (1, **Figure 51**). Speed can be set to indicate either mph (miles per hour) or km/h (kilometers per hour). To change from one unit of measurement to the other, first press the MODE key (2, **Figure 50** or 2, **Figure 51**) as many times as necessary until the display (3, **Figure 50** or 3, **Figure 51**) is in the VOLT mode, then press the SET key (4, **Figure 50** or 4, **Figure 51**). This will change the unit of measurement

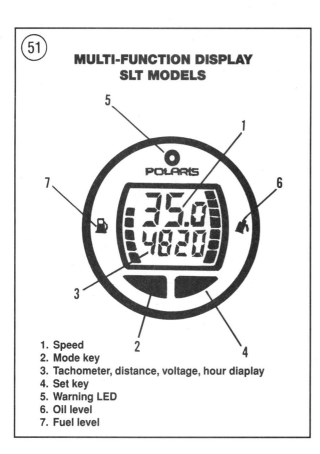

MULTI-FUNCTION DISPLAY SLT MODELS

1. Speed
2. Mode key
3. Tachometer, distance, voltage, hour diaplay
4. Set key
5. Warning LED
6. Oil level
7. Fuel level

for the speed and distance function. The pickup is located inside the jet pump intake grate area. If battery voltage is low, all speed and distance functions will be disabled until normal voltage is restored.

Total accumulated hours

The total numbers of hours accumulated is a secondary function that can be selected by operating the MODE key (2, **Figure 50** or 2, **Figure 51**). The HOUR annunciator is on when in this mode. The total hours that the engine has operated are recorded in 0.1 hour increments up to 999.9 total hours. The total number of hours is stored in memory that is not affected by disconnecting the battery.

Clock

The clock is a secondary display that can be selected by operating the MODE key (2, **Figure 50** or 2, **Figure 51**). The clock annunciator is on when in the clock mode. To set the time, first display the clock function by touching the MODE key, then hold the SET key (4, **Figure 50** or 4, **Figure 51**) down for 4 seconds. To set the time, touch the MODE key (2, **Figure 50** or 2, **Figure 51**) to select the digit, then touch the SET key (4, **Figure 50** or 4, **Figure 51**) to increase the selected digit. After setting the digits, operate the MODE key (2, **Figure 50** or 2, **Figure 51**) to start the clock. When running, the colon will flash.

Peak speed and engine rpm

To view the peak speed and the maximum engine rpm since this function was reset, press the SET key (4, **Figure 50** or 4, **Figure 51**) momentarily while the display is in the TACH mode. To reset this function, press and hold the SET key (2, **Figure 50** or 2, **Figure 51**) for 4 seconds. Refer to the *Speed* description for changing the unit of measurement.

Tachometer

The engine speed (tachometer) is a secondary function that can be selected by pressing the MODE key (2, **Figure 50** or 2, **Figure 51**). Engine speed is displayed within 10 rpm in the right display of SL models or in the lower display of SLT models. The rpm annunciator is on when in the tachometer mode.

Distance

The distance traveled since this function was last set is a secondary function that can be selected by pressing the MODE key (2, **Figure 50** or 2, **Figure 51**). The distance in 0.1 increments is shown in the left display of SL models or in the top display of SLT models. The DIST annunciator is on when in this mode. To reset this function, press and hold the SET key for 4 seconds while in the DIST mode. Distance can be set to indicate either miles or kilometers. Refer to the *Speed* description for changing the unit of measurement. If battery voltage is low, all speed and distance functions are disabled until normal voltage is restored.

Volt

Voltage from 5 to 18 volts in 0.1 volt increments is shown in the right display of SL models or in the lower display of SLT models. The volt annunciator is on when in this mode. If the voltmeter does not operate, check the 1/4 amp fuse located in the circuit board of the multi-function display. If the battery voltage is less than 10.9 volts, the display flashes "LOPR." If battery voltage is low, all speed and distance functions are disabled until normal voltage is restored.

Fuel

The quantity of fuel is indicated by the bar graph located at the left side of the display. Quantity is indicated in 1/8 tank increments. The display flashes "FUEL" and the red warning LED (5, **Figure 50** or 5, **Figure 51**) is illuminated if the fuel level is less than 1/8 tank. The low fuel warning can be disabled for 5 minutes by pressing the SET key (4, **Figure 50** or 4, **Figure 51**).

Oil

The quantity of oil is indicated by the bar graph located at the right side of the display. Quantity is indicated in 1/8 tank increments. The display flashes "OIL" and the red warning LED (5, **Figure 50** or 5, **Figure 51**) is illuminated if the oil level is less than 1/8 tank. The low oil warning can be disabled for 15 minutes by pressing the SET key.

High temp

If the engine temperature sender, located in the water outlet manifold, determines that the engine is overheated, it sends a signal to the multi-function display. The display will flash "HOT" and the warning LED (5, **Figure 50** or 5, **Figure 51**) will be illuminated. Pressing the SET key (4, **Figure 50** or 4, **Figure 51**) will disable the display for 5 minutes, but the LED will continue to glow.

Multi-Function Display Troubleshooting

If the multi-function display does not operate, inspect for the following possible causes:
   a. Check the battery terminals and attaching cables for loose or corroded connections.
   b. Check the condition of the 4 amp fuse located in the electrical box (located above the battery).

c. Verify the power (red/purple wire) and ground (black wire) connections to the multi-function display.

d. If battery voltage is low, all speed and distance functions are disabled until normal voltage is restored.

e. If the display does not indicate some features, check the sensors for that feature and connecting wires. The tan wire is from the temperature sender (in the water outlet housing); the blue wire is from the low oil sender (in the oil tank); the pink wire is from the fuel level sender (in the fuel tank); the yellow wire is from the alternator (to indicate engine rpm).

ENGINE TUNE-UP

There are a number of definitions of the term *tune-up*, but for the purposes of this book, a tune-up is general adjustment and maintenance to ensure or restore peak engine performance.

The following paragraphs discuss each phase of a proper tune-up which should be performed in the order given. Have the new parts on hand before you begin.

To perform a tune-up, you need the following tools and equipment:

a. Spark plug wrench.

b. Socket wrench and assorted sockets.

c. Phillips head screwdriver.

d. Spark plug feeler gauge and gap adjusting tool.

e. Compression gauge.

Cylinder and Cylinder Head Nuts

Tighten the cylinder head nuts once a year. Refer to Chapter Four for tightening torque and procedure.

Cylinder Compression

A cylinder cranking compression check is one of the quickest ways to check the condition of the rings, piston, cylinder and head gasket. It's a good idea to check compression at each tune-up, write it down and compare it with the reading you get at the next tune-up. This will help you spot any developing problems.

1. Warm the engine to normal operating temperature. If the craft is out of the water, a temporary cooling system must provide water to the engine. Refer to Chapter Nine.

> *CAUTION*
> *Do not run the engine for more than 10 seconds out of the water or the rubber parts of the exhaust system will be damaged. Prolonged running without coolant will cause serious engine damage. Never operate the engine at maximum speed out of water.*

2. Remove the spark plugs (**Figure 52**). Insert the plugs in the caps and ground the plugs against the cylinder head.

3. Remove the tether cord cap from its switch.

> *CAUTION*
> *If the plugs or plug wires are not grounded during the compression test, the CDI ignition could be damaged.*

4. Screw a compression gauge into 1 spark plug hole or, if you have a press-in type gauge, hold it firmly in position.

5. Hold the throttle wide open and crank the engine several revolutions until the gauge indicates the highest reading.

6. Observe the highest pressure indicated by the gauge, then record that pressure for the cylinder being tested. Refer to **Table 5** for a chart that can be used to record compression tests.

7. Press the pressure release button on the gauge and remove the gauge.

8. Repeat the test in Steps 4-7 for the remaining 2 cylinders.

9. The difference in the compression between any 2 of the cylinders should not exceed 10 percent.

10. If the compression of 1 cylinder is very low, a ring is probably stuck or broken. It is also possible that the piston is seriously damaged.

NOTE
Since the manufacturer does not list engine compression test specifications, it is important to compare the results of your current compression test with previous

(53) **SPARK PLUG CONDITIONS**

WORN OUT

NORMAL USE

CARBON FOULED

GAP BRIDGED

OVERHEATED

SUSTAIED PREIGNITION

OIL FOULED

*tests. Refer to **Table 5**. If the pressure has changed enough to notice a difference, the cause should be investigated further.*

11. Inspect, clean, regap and install the spark plugs. Install new spark plugs if necessary.

Correct Spark Plug Heat Range

The proper spark plug is very important in obtaining maximum performance and reliability. The condition of a used spark plug can often tell a trained mechanic a lot about engine condition and carburetion.

Select plugs of the heat range designed for the loads and conditions under which the craft will be operated. Operating an engine with spark plugs of the incorrect heat range can cause en-

gine damage. While often referred to as HOT or COLD plugs, the heat range is actually relative. A plug that is correct in one engine, operating in one set of conditions may be unsuitable for another engine or even the same engine operating with different conditions.

Check the spark plugs every time they are removed, but if you install spark plugs that are of a different heat range, you must check their condition often to be sure the selected range is correct. The plug should operate hot enough to burn off unwanted deposits, but not be so hot they burn the electrodes or cause preignition. A spark plug of the correct heat range will show a light tan color on the portion of the insulator within the cylinder after the plug has been in service. See **Figure 53**.

In general, the plugs recommended by Polaris (**Table 6**) should be used. If the standard plug fouls quickly, the speed is usually slow, the load is light and the temperatures are cool, try plugs with a slightly warmer heat range. If the standard plug seems to burn or if the engine seems to detonate and the craft is frequently operated at high engine speed, with heavy loads at high temperatures, try spark plugs with a slightly cooler heat range.

The reach (length) of a plug (**Figure 54**) is also important. A spark plug that is longer than the correct plug could interfere with the piston, causing permanent and severe damage. Refer to **Figure 55**.

The standard heat range spark plug for the various models is listed in **Table 6**.

Spark Plug Removal/Cleaning

1. Grasp the connector at the end of the spark plug lead and pull it from the plug. If it is stuck, twist the connector slightly to break it loose. Do not pull on the plug wire.

2. Blow away any dirt that has accumulated around the spark plug base.

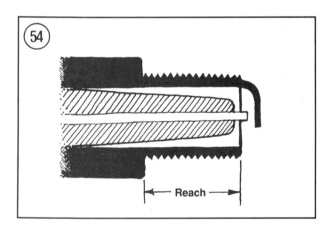

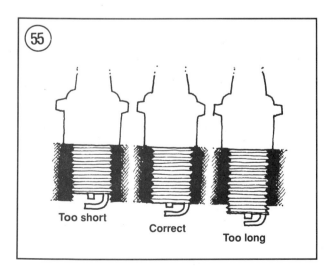

CAUTION
Dirt could fall into the cylinder when a plug is removed, causing serious engine damage.

3. Remove the spark plug with a spark plug wrench.

NOTE
If the plug is difficult to remove, apply penetrating oil around the base of the plug and let it soak in about 10-20 minutes. Be extremely careful not to damage the threads in the cylinder head by careless removal procedures.

4. Inspect the plug carefully. Look for a broken center porcelain, excessively eroded electrodes and excessive carbon or oil fouling.

NOTE
A common problem for spark plugs in a personal watercraft is water fouling. Water or a water/oil emulsion on the plug electrodes indicates water in the fuel or inside the engine. A plug with this condition should be dried with electrical contact cleaner or replaced with a clean, dry plug.

Gapping and Installing the Plug

Carefully adjust the electrode gap on new spark plugs to ensure a reliable, consistent spark. Use a special spark plug gapping tool and a wire feeler gauge.

1. Insert a wire feeler gauge between the center and side electrode (**Figure 56**). The correct gap is listed in **Table 6**. If the gap is correct, you will feel a slight drag as you pull the wire through. If there is no drag, or the gauge won't pass through, bend the side electrode with a gapping tool (**Figure 57**) to set the proper gap.

2. Apply antiseize compound to the plug threads before installing the spark plug.

NOTE
Antiseize compound can be purchased at most automotive parts stores.

3. Screw the spark plug in by hand until it seats. Very little effort is required. If force is necessary, you may have the plug cross-threaded. Unscrew it and try again.

4. Use a spark plug wrench to tighten the plug until it is very lightly seated. If you are installing a new plug, tighten the plug 1/4 to 1/2 turn after the gasket has made contact with the head. If you are reinstalling a used plug with a used gasket, tighten only 1/4 turn after the gasket has contacted the head.

NOTE
Do not overtighten the spark plug. Overtightening will over-compress the gasket and destroy its sealing ability. Overtightening may also strip the threads in the cylinder head.

5. Attach the spark plug cap to the spark plug, making sure it fits tightly on the spark plug.

CAUTION
Make sure the spark plug wire is positioned away from the exhaust pipe.

Reading Spark Plugs

The firing end of a spark plug operates in the combustion chamber, so investigating the burning patterns on the spark plug can reveal impor-

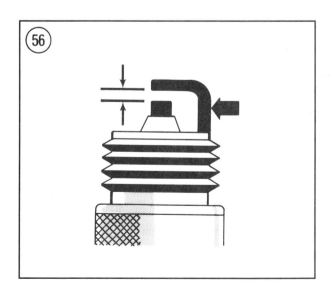

tant information about the operating condition of the engine.

Spark plug performance can also be determined by careful examination of the spark plugs. This information is only valid after performing the following steps.

1. Launch the craft and warm the engine to normal operating temperature.
2. Ride the watercraft a short distance at full throttle.

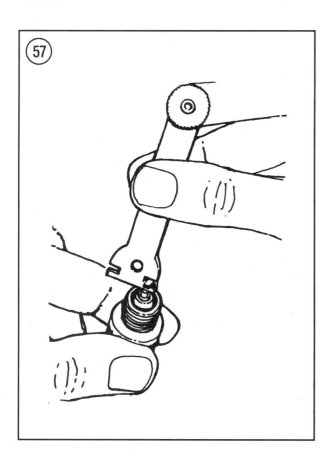

3. While running at full throttle, push on the stop switch before closing the throttle, then coast back to shore.
4. Remove the spark plugs and examine them.
5. Compare each plug to **Figure 53**, noting the following information.

Normal condition

The spark plug removed from an engine in good condition will have a light tan to gray deposit without any abnormal erosion or increased electrode gap. If the plug's condition is normal, the heat range is correct and the plug may be returned to use.

Carbon fouled

Soft, dry, sooty deposits covering the entire firing end of the plug are evidence of incomplete combustion. Even though the firing end of the plug is dry, the plug's insulation decreases. An electrical path is formed that lowers the voltage from the ignition system. Engine misfiring is often a sign of carbon fouling. Carbon fouling can be caused by one or more of the following:

  a. Too rich fuel mixture (incorrect jetting).
  b. Spark plug heat range too cold.
  c. Over-retarded ignition timing.
  d. Ignition component failure.
  e. Low engine compression.

Wet fouled

The tip of an oil fouled plug has a damp oily film over the firing end and may have a layer of carbon over the entire end of the plug. The insulator tip may be covered with a heavy layer of black carbon. The electrodes are not worn. Common causes for this condition are:

  a. Too much oil in the fuel (incorrect jetting or incorrect oil pump adjustment).

b. Wrong type of oil. Metal additives in some oil may short out the spark plug.

c. Ignition component failure.

d. Spark plug heat range too cold. If the heat range is too cold the plug will not burn off unwanted deposits.

Wet fouled spark plugs may be cleaned in an emergency, but it is better to replace them. It is important to correct the cause of fouling before the engine is returned to service.

Gap bridging

Plugs with this condition exhibit gaps shorted by combustion deposits between the electrodes. If the gap is bridged by material, but the overall condition of the plug appears OK, check for an improper (leaded) gasoline, improper type of oil, excessive carbon in combustion chamber or a clogged exhaust port and pipe. Be sure to locate and correct the cause of this condition.

Overheating

Badly worn electrodes and premature gap wear are signs of overheating. The porcelain insulator surface will be a gray or white and will usually appear to be blistered. The most common cause for this condition is using a spark plug that is the wrong heat range (too hot). If you have not recently changed to a hotter spark plug or changed the type of service such as running with a heavier load. Consider the following causes:

a. Lean fuel mixture (incorrect main jet or incorrect oil pump adjustment).

b. Ignition timing too advanced.

c. Cooling system malfunction.

d. Air leak in the engine's intake system.

e. Improper spark plug installation (overtightening).

f. No spark plug gasket.

Worn out

Hot corrosive gases formed by combustion and high voltage sparks will eventually eroded the electrodes. Spark plugs in this condition require more voltage to fire under hard acceleration. Replace the spark plugs.

Preignition

If the spark plug's electrodes are melted, preignition is almost certainly the cause. Continued operation will certainly damage the engine, so it is important to find the cause of the preignition before returning the engine into service. Check for carburetor mounting or intake manifold leaks and for over-advanced ignition timing. It is also possible that a plug of the wrong heat range (too hot) can cause this condition.

Ignition Timing

All models are equipped with a sealed, capacitor discharge ignition (CDI) that uses no breaker points. Timing with this system is usually not affected by dirt, moisture or wear.

Ignition timing is difficult to adjust with the engine installed.

Usually it is not necessary to check or change the ignition timing unless the engine is already removed for other repairs or if ignition components are removed. The timing reaches maxi-

mum advance at about 3,000 rpm. The flywheel and crankcase are not usually equipped with ignition timing marks. A 2-step ignition timing procedure is recommended. First, static timing must be confirmed and timing marks placed on the engine flywheel, if necessary. Then, dynamic timing is checked with the engine running using a timing light.

Static timing requires the use of an accurate dial indicator (part No. 2870459 or equivalent) or degree wheel. Determine top dead center (TDC) of the piston, then verify the location of any existing timing marks before making any timing adjustment.

Dynamic ignition timing requires a timing light (part No. 2870630 or equivalent). As the engine is cranked or while it is running, the light flashes each time the spark plug fires. When the light is pointed at the moving flywheel, the mark on the flywheel appears to stand still. The flywheel mark should align with the stationary timing pointer on the engine.

Refer to Chapter Seven to check and adjust the ignition timing. Ignition timing specifications are listed in **Table 7**.

Carburetor Adjustment

The following procedure describe carburetor mixture adjustments. Before changing throttle mixture settings, it is important that all 3 carburetors open and close the same amount at the same time. Refer to *Synchronize Carburetors* and *Synchronize Carburetor Choke* in this chapter to check and adjust the openings.

Initial carburetor mixture settings are for sea level conditions. If operating your craft at higher elevations, additional carburetor adjustment may be required. In all cases, use spark plug readings as the determining factor when making carburetor adjustments.

> *CAUTION*
> *The rider may not notice if 1 of the 3 carburetors is operating lean, except for a slight loss of power. The cylinder that is affected by the lean mixture may be seriously damaged by overheating before power is low enough to cause the rider to complain. It is also important to make sure the oil injection system and fuel system are properly adjusted and maintained in proper operating condition.*

> *NOTE*
> *It is difficult or impossible to adjust the idle speed and mixture correctly with the craft out of the water. More accurate adjustment is possible with the craft in quiet water about 3 ft. (0.9 m) deep. Secure the craft to a dock, a tree or other immovable object with a strong rope attached to the rear of the craft. Be sure to use an object that is strong enough to withstand the full thrust of the craft.*

When adjusting the engine's *idle speed*, note the following:

a. Refer to *Synchronize Carburetors* in this chapter to adjust the engine idle speed.

b. To increase engine idle speed, turn the idle speed screw (**Figure 58**) clockwise (IN).

c. To decrease engine idle speed, turn the idle speed screw counterclockwise (OUT).

When adjusting the *low-speed mixture*, note the following:

a. To increase fuel flow (enrichen the mixture), turn the mixture needles (**Figure 59**) counterclockwise (OUT).

b. To decrease fuel flow (lean the mixture), turn the mixture needles clockwise (IN).

When adjusting the *high speed mixture*, note the following:

a. To increase fuel flow (richen the mixture), turn the mixture needles (**Figure 60**) counterclockwise (OUT).

b. To decrease fuel flow (lean the mixture), turn the mixture needles clockwise (IN).

CAUTION
The high-speed mixture needles have covers that prevent the needles from turning too far. If the mixture cannot be properly adjusted with the caps installed, refer to the following High-speed Mixture procedure in this chapter.

Before adjusting the carburetor as described in the following sections, check throttle cable and choke cable adjustments. Also, check the throttle and choke synchronization as described earlier in this chapter. On 1995-on models, check the control rod from the carburetor to the oil injection pump. If the control rod is detached, oil delivery will increase to maximum and it will be impossible to accurately adjust the fuel mixture.

Low-speed Mixture

The low-speed mixture needle (**Figure 59**) is a needle valve that regulates fuel flow when the engine is idling. The low-speed mixture adjustment is critical to engine idle and throttle response. Each carburetor is equipped with a low-speed mixture needle and each must be adjusted.

CAUTION
Engine idle speed may be either faster or slower if the mixture is wrong, but do not attempt to set engine idle speed with the low-speed mixture needle. Incorrect setting of the low-speed mixture needle can cause engine damage. Refer to Synchronize Carburetors in this chapter to adjust the engine idle speed.

1. Remove the seat and engine cover. Allow the engine compartment to air out.

2. Locate the craft in quiet water about 3 ft. (0.9 m) deep.

3. Secure the craft, with a strong rope attached to the rear of the craft, to a dock, a tree or other immovable object.

4. Turn each of the 3 low-speed mixture needles (**Figure 59**) in until seated lightly then back each out the number of turns specified in **Table 8**.

CAUTION
Never force a mixture needle into its seat. You will damage the adjustment needle and its seat in the carburetor.

5. Start and warm the engine. Check that the engine idles smoothly.

WARNING
The exhaust gases are poisonous. Do not run the engine in a closed area. Make sure there is plenty of ventilation.

CAUTION
Prolonged running without coolant will cause serious engine damage. Do not run the engine for more than 10 seconds without water or the rubber parts of the exhaust system will be damaged. Even with freshwater supplied to the engine by the flushing attachment, never operate the engine at maximum speed out of the water.

6. Push the throttle lever 2 or 3 times in short, quick bursts, checking to see if the engine accel-

erates without stalling or hesitation and returns to a smooth low idle. If it hesitates, readjust the low-speed mixture needles until the engine accelerates from idle smoothly.

> *CAUTION*
> *Do not attempt to set engine idle speed with the low-speed mixture needle. Incorrect low-speed mixture adjustment can cause engine damage.*

High-speed Mixture

> *CAUTION*
> *The rider may not notice if 1 of the 3 carburetors is operating lean, except for a slight loss of power. This condition is especially critical at high engine speed, because the cylinder that is affected by the lean mixture may be seriously damaged by overheating before power is low enough to cause the rider to complain.*

The high-speed mixture needles permit external adjustment of the fuel circuit that controls the fuel mixture while the engine is operating at high-speed. The high-speed mixture needles should have limiter caps installed that allow adjustment of only 1/4 turn. Turning a high-speed mixture needle counterclockwise (OUT) enrichens the mixture for that carburetor/cylinder.

> *CAUTION*
> *Be very cautious and do not attempt to remove the limiter cap to turn the main jet screw more than 1/4 turn, unless the*

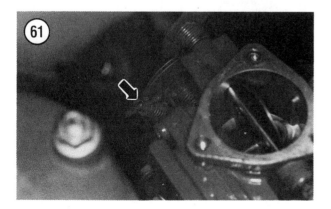

carburetor is being serviced. If it is necessary to change the needle settings a great deal from the setting listed in Table 8, check the carburetor and other engine systems for problems. Only very minor differences from the standard needle setting should be necessary.

Refer to **Figure 60** for the location of the high-speed mixture needles. Initial setting after servicing the carburetor is listed in **Table 8**. Turn the high-speed mixture needle for each carburetor in until it seats lightly then back it out the turns specified. If it is necessary to set any of the high-speed mixture needles much different than listed in **Table 8**, the carburetor or the cylinder should be inspected for damage.

> *CAUTION*
> *Never force a mixture needle into its seat. You will damage the adjustment needle and its seat in the carburetor.*

Start and warm the engine. Check that the engine idles and accelerates smoothly.

> *WARNING*
> *The exhaust gases are poisonous. Do not run the engine in a closed area. Make sure there is plenty of ventilation.*

> *CAUTION*
> *Prolonged running without coolant will cause serious engine damage. Do not run the engine for more than 10 seconds without water or the rubber parts of the exhaust system will be damaged. Even with freshwater supplied to the engine by the flushing attachment, never operate the engine at maximum speed out of the water.*

Idle Speed Adjustment

The idle speed stop screw controls engine idle by holding the carburetor throttle open slightly. The idle speed screw (**Figure 61**) located on the front carburetor controls the idle speed setting for all 3 carburetors. A second stop screw is located on the rear carburetor (**Figure 62**). The throttle control shafts on all 3 carburetors should be synchronized as described in this chapter. Throttle valve synchronization is not affected by idle speed adjustment.

1. Remove the seat and engine cover.

2. Connect an induction tachometer to the spark plug wire for the front cylinder, following its manufacturer's directions.

NOTE
It is difficult or impossible to adjust the idle speed correctly with the craft out of the water. More accurate adjustment is possible with the craft in quiet water about 3 ft. (0.9 m) deep. Secure the craft, with a strong rope attached to the rear of the craft, to a dock, a tree or other immovable object. Be sure to use an object that is strong enough to withstand the full thrust of the craft.

3. Start and warm the engine.

WARNING
The exhaust gases are poisonous. Do not run the engine in a closed area. Make sure there is plenty of ventilation.

4. Push the throttle lever 2 or 3 times in short, quick bursts, checking to see if the engine accelerates without stalling or hesitation and returns to a smooth idle. If it hesitates, readjust the low-speed mixture screw as described in this chapter.

CAUTION
Do not attempt to set engine idle speed with the low-speed mixture screw. Incorrect low-speed mixture screw adjustment can cause engine damage.

5. Turn the idle speed screw (**Figure 61**) so the engine idles at the idle speed listed in **Table 8**. If necessary, turn the stop screw (**Figure 62**) for the rear carburetor out to allow adjustment of the front screw.

6. Check to make sure the engine accelerates smoothly without stalling or hesitation and returns to the correct idle speed.

a. Push the throttle lever and accelerate the engine 2 or 3 times in short, quick bursts.

b. Let the throttle return to the idle position.

c. The engine should accelerate smoothly and should return to a smooth idle speed within the speed range listed in **Table 8**.

d. If the engine does not accelerate smoothly or if engine speed does not return to the correct idle speed quickly, the carburetors are probably not adjusted correctly. It is also possible that the carburetors are dirty or damaged.

NOTE
If the engine stumbles when trying to accelerate, the idle mixture is probably incorrect (too lean).

e. When carburetor adjustment is correct, proceed to Step 8.

7. Turn the idle speed adjustment screw (**Figure 62**) for the rear carburetor in until it just contacts the lever, but does not change the engine speed. The stop screw for the rear carburetor should stop movement at exactly the same time as the stop screw on the front carburetor.

8. Turn the engine OFF.

9. Remove the service tachometer from the engine.

BATTERY

Refer to Chapter Seven for complete battery service procedure.

Table 1 PERIODIC MAINTENANCE SCHEDULES

Each time the watercraft is filled with gasoline	Check the oil tank for proper level. Check the water trap for the presence of water.
Pre-ride (or daily)	Check the hull for damage. Check the fuel/water separator for the presence of water. Check the throttle and choke cables for proper operation and lubrication. Check the steering and jet nozzle for proper operation. Check that the muffler, battery and oil reservoir are properly fastened. Check battery condition It may be necessary to add water more frequently in hot weather. Check that the bilge system and watertrap drains are clean and do not leak. Check location and condition of the fire extinguisher.
Post-ride	Turn fuel off at shutoff valve. Inspect the bilge Lubricate the driveshaft couplers and bearing housing if water has been above the level of the coupler. Check the hull for damage. If operated in saltwater, flush cooling system with fresh water at the end of each day.

Pre-season	Check the fuel tank. Drain old gasoline from the tank and fill with fresh gasoline.
	Check the water trap for the presence of water.
	Remove the seat and engine cover.
	Remove, clean and check spark plug gap. Install new spark plugs if necessary.
	Inspect and lubricate the throttle and choke cables.
	Check adjustment of the carburetor mixture and operating cables.
	Lubricate and coat all metal parts to protect against corrosion.
	Check the fuel and oil filters Install new filters at the beginning of each season.
	Retorque the cylinder head retaining nuts.
	Check to be sure the handlebar clamp and nuts hold the handlebars tightly.
	Check the steering column and bearings for wear.
	Check the steering and jet nozzle for proper movement.
	Check the steering cable adjustment. Make sure that cable is mounted tightly.
	Check all components in the engine compartment for looseness or damage. Repair or replace components as required.
	   a. Carburetor mounting screws.
	   b. Engine mount screws.
	   c. Muffler and exhaust.
	   d. Battery mounting and cables.
	   e. Reservoir mounting.
	Check all fuel and oil hoses and connections for leakage or other damage.
	Inspect the oil injection system for proper operation.

(continued)

Table 1 PERIODIC MAINTENANCE SCHEDULES (continued)

Pre-season (continued)	Clean and inspect water trap drains. The bilge should be dry.
	Check the condition of the battery and starter cables. Clean cables and connections.
	Check connections for the engine overheating signal.
	Check the tone for the low oil level signal.
	Check the condition of the impeller and clearance to the wear ring.
	Check the condition of the driveshaft shroud.
	Lubricate the driveshaft couplers and bearing housing.
	Inspect the condition of the water intake grate. Make sure that grate is properly attached.
	Flush the cooling system.
	Inspect the rubber parts of the cooling system Install new parts if necessary.
	Remove and inspect the cooling system thermostat Install new thermostat if necessary.
	Remove and inspect the cooling system filters including the exhaust cooling hose screen. Clean or install new filters.
	Check the engine mounts for damage Install new mounts if damaged.
	Check to be sure that the engine stop switch and the tether switch both stop the engine instantly.
	Check the fire extinguisher.
	Clean the hull and inspect for cracks or other damage.
Monthly (or after every 25 hours of operation)	Check the water trap for the presence of water.
	Lubricate and coat all metal parts to protect against corrosion. Coat all metal parts with corrosion protection at least once each month if operated in saltwater.
	Check the condition of the fuel filter.
	Check the condition of the oil filter.
	Check the steering column and bearings for wear.
	Check the steering cable adjustment. Make sure that cable is mounted tightly.
	Check to be sure the handlebar clamp and nuts hold the handlebars tightly.
	If operated in saltwater, clean and inspect water trap drains at least once each month.
	Check the condition of the driveshaft shroud.
	If operated in salt water, lubricate the driveshaft couplers and bearing housing. Grease the driveshaft couplers and bearing housing immediately if water has been above the level of the coupler.
	Clean and inspect the hull for cracks.
Every 3 months (or after 50 hours of operation)	Check the water trap for the presence of water.
	Remove, clean and check spark plug gap Install new spark plugs if necessary.
	Inspect and lubricate the throttle and choke cables.
	Check adjustment of the carburetor mixture and operating cables.

(continued)

Table 1 PERIODIC MAINTENANCE SCHEDULES (continued)

Every 3 months (or after 50 hours of operation) (continued)	Check clearance between the impeller and wear ring, after the first 3 months of operation. Check clearance at least every 6 months or after 100 hours of operation.
	Check the condition of the driveshaft shroud, after the first 3 months of operation. Check condition at least every 6 months or after 100 hours of operation.
	Lubricate the driveshaft couplers and bearing housing. Grease the driveshaft couplers and bearing housing immediately if water has been above the level of the coupler.
	Inspect the water intake grate for damage or missing fasteners, after the first 3 months of operation. Check condition at least every 6 months or after 100 hours of operation.
	Flush the cooling system.
	Inspect the rubber parts of the cooling system Install new parts if necessary.
	Remove and inspect the cooling system thermostat. Install new thermostat if necessary
	Remove and inspect the cooling system filters including the exhaust cooling hose screen. Clean or install new filters.
Every 6 months (or after 100 hours of operation)	Check the water trap for the presence of water.
	Check the fuel and oil filters Install new filters if necessary.
	Check the steering and jet nozzle for proper operation.
	Check all components in the engine compartment for looseness or damage. Repair or replace components as required.
	a. Carburetor mounting screws.
	b. Engine mount screws.
	c. Muffler and exhaust.
	d. Battery mounting and cables.
	e. Reservoir mounting.
	Check all hoses and hose connections for leakage or other damage.
	Clean and inspect water trap drains. The bilge should be dry.
	Check the condition of the battery and starter cables. Clean cables and connections.
	Check connections for the engine overheating signal.
	Check the tone for the low oil level signal.
	Check the condition of the impeller and clearance to the wear ring.
	Check the condition of the driveshaft shroud.
	Inspect the condition of the water intake grate. Make sure that grate is properly attached.
	Lubricate the driveshaft couplers and bearing housing. Grease the driveshaft couplers immediately if water in the compartment has been above the level of the couplers.
	Inspect the condition of the water intake grate. Make sure that grate is properly attached.
	Check the engine mounts for cracks or other damage and attaching screws for tightness.
	Clean the hull and check for cracks or other damage.

3

Table 2 INITIAL 10 HOUR MAINTENANCE SCHEDULE

Check all nuts, bolts and other fasteners for tightness.
Check all hose clamps for tightness.
Clean spark plugs and check gap. Replace plug if necessary.
Check adjustment of carburetors.
Check fuel filter for contamination or damage. Replace filter if necessary.
Check all components in the engine compartment for looseness or damage. Repair or replace components
    as required.
Check battery electrolyte level It may be necessary to check more frequently in hot weather.
Check all electrical connections and wires for corrosion, contamination or damage. Make sure all
    connectors are tight.
Check the starter switch for proper operation.
Check the engine stop switch and tether switch for proper operation.
Check the front hatch lock for proper operation.
Check the hatch seal for proper sealing.
Check the seat latch for proper operation.
Check the hull for damage. Repair if damaged in any way.
Check the steering column for proper operation.

Table 3 APPROXIMATE REFILL CAPACITY

Oil injection reservoir		
SL650 & SL750	3.3 L	3.5 qt.
SLT750	4.7 L	5 qt.
Fuel tank		
SL650 & SL750	37.1 L	9.8 gal.
SLT750	41.6 L	11 gal.

Table 4 MAINTENANCE TIGHTENING TORQUES

	N·m	ft.-lb.
Carburetor mounting	21.7	16
Cylinder head	24.4	18
Cylinder base	38	28
Crankcase		
8 mm	21.7	16
10 mm	35.2	26
Drive coupler	216.9	160
Engine to mount plate	61	45
Exhaust manifold	21.7	16
Flywheel screw	74.6	55
Flywheel housing	8.81	78 in.-lb.
Impeller	135.6	100
Intake manifold	8.81	78 in.-lb.
Plastic air intake	2.26	20 in.-lb.
Steering cable adjusting nuts		
1992-1994 (rear)	40.7	30
1995-on (front)	40.7	30

(continued)

Table 4 MAINTENANCE TIGHTENING TORQUES (continued)

	N·m	ft.-lb.
Water outlet manifold	8.81	78 in.-lb.
Other fasteners		
5 mm	5.1-5.9	45-52 in.-lb.
6 mm	7.5-8.8	66-78 in.-lb.
8 mm	17.6-21.7	13-16
10 mm	35.2-40.7	26-30
12 mm	54.2-59.7	40-44

Table 5 COMPRESSION TEST RECORD

Date (MM/DD/YY)	Front cylinder	Center cylinder	Rear cylinder
Notes:			
Notes:			
Notes:			
Notes:			

Table 6 SPARK PLUGS

	NGK type	Champion type	Gap mm (in.)
1992-1993 models	BR8ES	RN-3C	0.7 (0.028)
1994-on	BPR7ES	–	0.7 (0.028)

Table 7 IGNITION TIMING

Year and model	CDI box identification	Ignition timing @ 3,000 rpm (BTDC) degrees	mm	in.
1992				
SL 650 B924058				
Early *	F8T16271	22.5-25.5	3.54	0.139
Late **	F8T16272	22.5-25.5	3.54	0.139
1993				
SL 650 B934058	F8T16273	16.5-19.5	2.01	0.079
SL 750 B934070	F8T16273	14.5-17.5	1.59	0.063
(continued)				

Table 7 IGNITION TIMING (continued)

Year and model	CDI box identification	Ignition timing @ 3,000 rpm (BTDC) degrees	mm	in.
1994				
SL 650 B944058	F8T16274 (65W95)	16-20	2.01	0.079
SL 750 B944070	F8T32071 (75W95)	22-26	3.54	0.139
SLT 750 B944170	F8T32071 (75W95)	22-26	3.54	0.139
1995				
SL 650 B954058	F8T16274 (65W95)	16-20	2.01	0.079
SL650 Std. B954358	F8T16274 (65W95)	16-20	2.01	0.079
SL 750 B954070	F8T32071 (75W95)	22-26	3.54	0.139
SLT 750 B954170	F8T32071 (75W95)	22-26	3.54	0.139

* Early models with large harmonic balancer.
** Serial No.PLE04039F292 and later models.

Table 8 CARBURETOR TUNE-UP SPECIFICATIONS

Year and model	Idle rpm (in water)	Idle needle (turns out)	High-speed needle (turns out)
1992			
SL 650 (early)*	1450-1650	1 3/8	front (mag) 3/8 center 1/8 rear (pto) 1/4
SL 650 (late)*	1450-1650	1 3/8	front (mag) 3/8 center 3/8 rear (pto) 1/4
1993			
SL 650	1200-1400	1/4	front (mag) 7/8 center 3/8 rear (pto) 5/8
SL 750	1200-1300	1/2	front (mag) 7/8 center 1/2 rear (pto) 5/8
1994			
SL 650 (early)**	1250-1350	1 1/4	front (mag) 3/4 center 1/4 rear (pto) 1/2
SL 650 (late)**	1250-1350	1	front (mag) 7/8 center 1/2 rear (pto) 3/4
SL 750 & SLT 750	1200-1300	1/2	front (mag) 1 1/4 center 3/8 rear (pto) 7/8
1995 SL 650 & SL650 Std.			
	1200-1300	1 1/8	front (mag) 1 1/8 center 1/4 rear (pto) 7/8
SL 750 & SLT 750	1200-1300	1/2	front (mag) 1 center 1/2 rear (pto) 3/4

* Early models manufactured before June; late models manufactured in 1992 from June on.
** Early models are serial No. 94-0001–94-02010; late models are serial No. 94-02011-on.

Chapter Four

Engine

All Polaris personal watercraft covered in this manual are equipped with a 3 cylinder, water cooled, 2-stroke engine (**Figure 1**). All models use a reed valve type intake system and 3 carburetors. The crankshaft, connecting rods, crankpins and connecting rod bearings are a pressed-together unit. Alignment of the various parts and clearances between the parts are critical. Assembly of the crankshaft should not be attempted by anyone except the most competent trained technicians who are equipped with the required special tools. Even removing the crankshaft can damage the alignment and should be accomplished with great care. It is recommended that all crankshaft work except replacing the outer seals be performed by a Polaris dealer or other specialist.

This chapter covers information necessary for routine service and disassembly of the engine including the procedure for removal of the engine crankshaft.

Work on the engine requires considerable mechanical skill. You should carefully consider your own capabilities before attempting any operation involving major disassembly of the engine.

Much of the labor charge for dealer repairs involves the removal and disassembly of other parts to reach the defective component. Even if you decide not to perform the entire engine overhaul after studying the text and illustrations in this chapter, it may be less expensive to perform the preliminary operations yourself, then take the engine to a dealer. Since dealers have lengthy waiting lists for service (especially during the spring and summer riding seasons), this practice can reduce the time your unit is in the shop. If you have done much of the preliminary work, your repairs can be scheduled and performed much quicker.

General engine specifications are listed in **Table 1**. Engine service specifications are listed in

Table 2. Recommended tightening torques are listed in **Table 3**. **Tables 1-3** are found at the end of this chapter.

ENGINE LUBRICATION

The engine is lubricated by oil stored in a separate oil tank, which is delivered and metered by the oil injection pump. It is important to keep the oil tank (**Figure 2**) filled at all times. Refer to Chapter Eight for *Oil Pump Service*.

SERVICE PRECAUTIONS

Observe the following precautions when disassembling, inspecting and reassembling the watercraft's engine.

1. The text frequently mentions left and right sides of the engine. This refers to the engine as it sits in the hull, not as it sits on your workbench. See **Figure 3**.

2. Always replace a worn or damaged fastener with one of the same size, type and torque requirements. Make sure to identify each screw or nut before replacing it with another.

3. Lubricate fastener threads with engine oil, unless otherwise specified, before torque is applied.

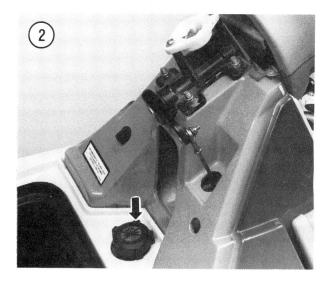

4. Use special tools where noted. In some cases, it may be possible to perform the procedure with makeshift tools, but this is not recommended. The use of makeshift tools can damage the components and may cause serious personal injury. Where factory tools are required, they may be purchased through a Polaris dealership. Other tools can be purchased through a parts dealer, motorcycle or automotive accessory store. Remember that all threaded parts that screw into the engine must have metric threads.

5. Before removing the first bolt, get several boxes, plastic bags and containers to store the parts as they are removed (**Figure 4**). These storage items will prevent frustration during assembly. Also have on hand a roll of masking tape

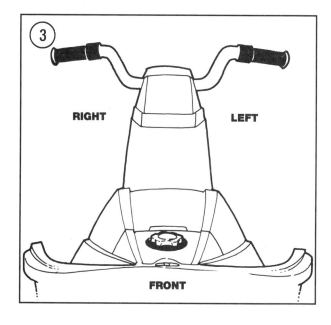

and a permanent, waterproof marking pen to label parts or assemblies as required.

6. Make notes or label each electrical connection before disconnecting it. Marking is particularly important if it appears that some of the wiring may have been changed or replaced and is not standard.

7. To prevent damage, use a vise with protective jaws to hold parts. If protective jaws are not available, insert soft plastic, aluminum, or wooden blocks on each side of the part(s) before clamping them in the vise.

8. Remove and install parts that are pressed together using appropriate mandrels, supports

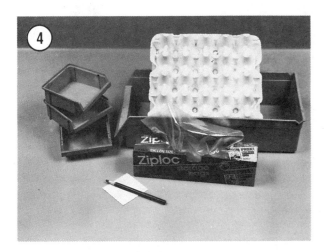

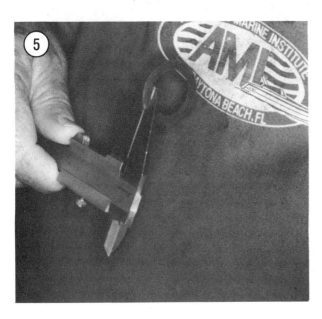

and a hydraulic press. Do not try to pry, hammer or otherwise force parts apart or together.

9. Refer to **Table 3** at the end of this chapter for torque specifications. Proper torque is essential to ensure long life and satisfactory service from the engine. If the tightening torque for a specific fastener is not listed in **Table 3** (end of this chapter), refer to the standard torque information listed in Chapter One.

10. Discard all O-rings and oil seals during disassembly. During reassembly apply a small amount of grease to the inner lips of each oil seal to prevent damage when the engine is first started.

11. When disassembling, keep a detailed record of all shims and where they came from. As soon as shims are removed, inspect them for damage and write down their thickness and location. Measure shim thickness with a micrometer or vernier caliper (**Figure 5**).

12. Work in an area where there is sufficient lighting and room for component storage.

13. Before tipping the watercraft on its side, turn the fuel valve OFF and remove the battery. Tip the craft by raising the right side, with the left side down. This precaution is important, because if the left side is higher than the right, water can run out of the cooling system, through the exhaust ports and into the cylinders. Refer to Chapter Seven for *Battery Installation* and Chapter Eight for *Oil Pump Bleeding*.

SERVICING THE ENGINE IN THE HULL

The following components can be serviced while the engine is mounted in the hull:

    a. Exhaust pipe and manifold.

    b. Cylinder heads.

    c. Cylinders.

    d. Pistons and rings.

    e. Carburetors and reed valves.

    f. Oil pump.

    g. Starter motor.

Even though some components of the engine can be serviced without removing the engine, it may be more practical to first remove the engine, remove, repair and reinstall the component, then reinstall the engine. Some of the components are very difficult to service with the engine in the hull.

SPECIAL TOOLS

Where special tools are required or recommended for engine overhaul, the tool part numbers are provided. The special tools can be ordered from Polaris dealerships.

PRECAUTIONS

Because of the explosive and flammable conditions that exist around gasoline, always observe the following precautions:

1. Immediately after removing the engine cover, check for the presence of raw gasoline fumes. If strong fumes can be smelled, determine their source and correct the problem.

2. Allow the engine compartment to air out before beginning work.

3. Detach the straps (**Figure 6**) retaining the electrical box and the battery, then disconnect the negative battery cable.

> *WARNING*
> *Gasoline dripping onto a hot engine component may cause a fire.*

4. Always allow the engine to cool completely before working on any part of the fuel system.

5. Spilled gasoline should be wiped up with dry rags immediately. Store the rags in a suitable metal container until they are removed for cleaning or disposal. Do not store gas or solvent-soaked rags in the hull.

6. Do not service any fuel system component while in the vicinity of open flames, sparks or while anyone is smoking.

7. Always have a Coast Guard approved fire extinguisher close at hand when working on the engine.

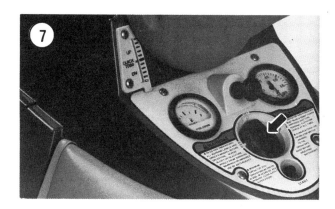

ENGINE REMOVAL

Engine removal and crankcase separation are required for repair of the crankshaft, connecting rods and bearings.

The following procedure describes a step-by-step sequence for removing the engine from the hull. If you plan to remove the engine intact, a minimum of 2 helpers or a hoist is required.

NOTE
Many of the clamps used to secure oil, fuel and cooling system hoses are not reusable. Make a note of the clamps removed so that new ones can be ordered.

1. Secure the watercraft so that it will not move when removing the engine.
2. Turn the fuel valve (**Figure 7**, typical) OFF.
3. Remove the seat and engine cover. Cover the edge of the hull with tape to protect the hull from damage.

CAUTION
Do not damage the oil lines attached to the air intake on 1995 models.

4. Remove the air intake silencer cover (**Figure 8**) and flame arrestor screen (**Figure 9**). Cover the carburetor openings so nothing can fall into them.
5. Remove the exhaust water box. Loosen the hose clamps, detach hoses (**Figure 10** and **Figure 11**), remove the hold down strap, then lift out the exhaust water box.
6. Remove the battery hold down straps.
7. Lift the electrical box from the battery carrier.
8. Remove the top of the battery box.
9. Detach the battery ground cable from the negative (–) terminal of the battery.

NOTE
Some service can be accomplished with the engine resting on boards placed across the hull. If the engine is not completely removed, the battery box can remain attached. Be extremely careful to support the engine securely.

10. If necessary, remove the electrical box as follows:
   a. Remove the 6 screws attaching the halves of the electrical box.
   b. Remove wire clamp (**Figure 12**) that seals the electrical wires to the engine. These wires run below the engine and into the alternator/ignition stator.

c. Separate the wiring harness connectors (**Figure 13**).

d. Remove the harness grommet bracket.

e. Pull the wiring harness out of the electrical box.

f. Move the electrical box out of the way and secure it. The cover can be temporarily reinstalled to protect components in the electrical box.

11. Detach the wire from the engine coolant temperature sensor (**Figure 14**).

12. Lift the front hatch and remove the storage basket (**Figure 15**).

NOTE
Be prepared to plug all of the openings for both the fuel and oil lines before detaching the hoses. Plug the lines and the attachment fittings to prevent the unnecessary loss of oil and to prevent the entrance of dirt.

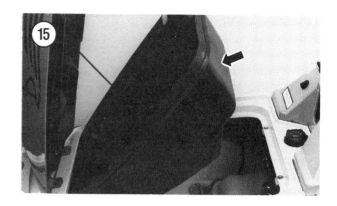

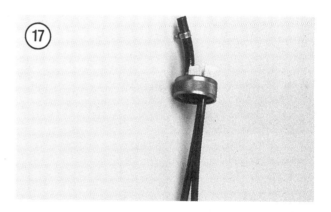

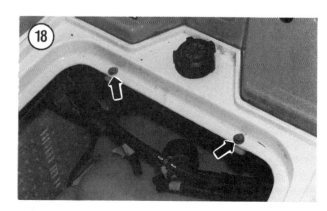

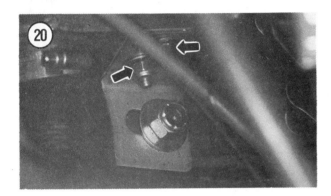

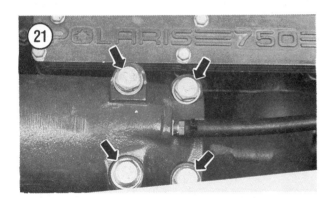

13. Mark the fuel lines (**Figure 16**) and the connectors of the fuel tank adapter, then detach the lines from the adapter.

14. Remove the retainer nut, then withdraw the adapter from the fuel tank. Refer to **Figure 17**.

15. Detach the supply and vent lines from the oil tank and plug all openings.

16. Remove the 2 bolts (**Figure 18**) attaching the front of the oil tank, then remove the oil tank.

17. Remove the screws and nuts attaching the exhaust system front mounting bracket to the front of the engine. Refer to **Figure 19**.

18. Remove the nuts (**Figure 20**) attaching the exhaust system to the rear mounting bracket. The bracket is attached to the hull with the left rear mounting nut.

19. Remove the 4 screws (**Figure 21**) attaching the exhaust pipe to the manifold.

NOTE
The manifold mounting screws on some models may be installed using a high-strength threadlocking compound. These screws may break if you attempt to remove them with an impact wrench. Apply slow even pressure to loosen these screws.

20. Remove the 9 screws attaching the exhaust manifold, then remove the manifold (**Figure 22**) and the exhaust pipe (**Figure 23**). It is necessary to move the exhaust pipe to reach the manifold screws, but the exhaust pipe cannot be removed before the manifold.

21. Detach the large cable (**Figure 24**) from the starter motor.

22. Unbolt the lower part of the intake silencer (**Figure 25**) from the carburetors, detach the necessary hoses from the fuel pump, then remove the silencer base with the fuel pump attached (**Figure 26**).

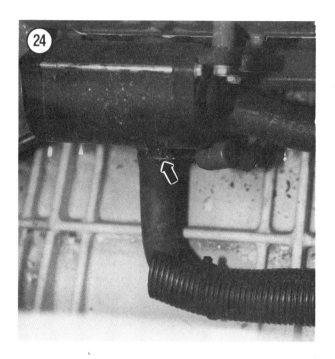

> *NOTE*
> *Even though the fuel lines were already detached from the fuel tank in Step 13, some fuel will drain when the hoses are detached from the fuel pump.*

> *NOTE*
> *The oil tank was removed in Steps 15-16, but oil will still drain from the hose detached from the oil pump. Be prepared to plug the supply hose as soon as it is detached.*

23. Detach the oil supply line from the oil pump.

24. Detach the throttle and choke cables from the front carburetor levers and the bracket (**Figure 27**).

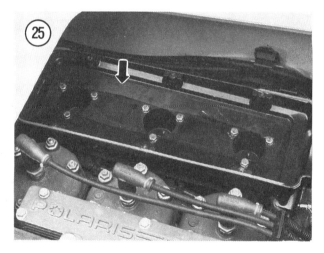

25. Detach the cooling (water) lines from the engine.

26. Refer to Chapter Five and remove the jet pump and the driveshaft as an assembly.

27. Remove the drive coupling from the rear of the crankshaft as outlined in this chapter.

28. Remove the 4 engine mounting nuts.

> *NOTE*
> *A hoist can be used by using lifting eyes screwed into 2 of the spark plug holes. The lifting eyes can be fabricated by welding a large washer to the steel shell of a spark plug from which the insulator and center electrode has been removed.*

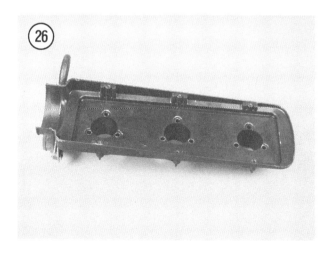

> *CAUTION*
> *Be careful not to damage the oil check valves in the intake manifolds or other parts while lifting the engine from the hull.*

NOTE
*If the engine is lifted by hand, 2 helpers are required. Padded wooden boards that are strong enough to hold the engine can be positioned across the hull opening to temporarily support the engine before lifting it away from the craft. Refer to **Figure 28**.*

29. Lift the engine, then move it toward the rear. Lift the engine from the craft.

NOTE
*Do not mix any shims (1, **Figure 29** or 1, **Figure 30**) from the 4 different engine mounts. The shims are selected to align the engine crankshaft with the jet pump drive. Special alignment tool (part No. 2871343) must be used and the jet pump must be disassembled to check the alignment. Refer to Engine/Jet Pump Align-*

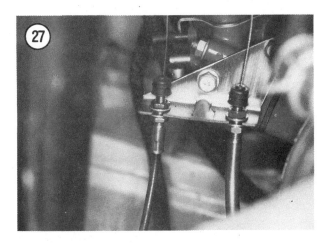

ment in this chapter for the alignment procedure.

30. Check the hull carefully for damage before installing the engine.
31. Inspect the wiring, hoses and other components that are difficult to repair or replace when the engine is in place.
32. Repair or replace damaged parts as necessary.

4

ENGINE SUPPORT PLATE AND RUBBER MOUNTS

The engine support plate and the 4 rubber mounts are critical parts of the water vehicle's drive train. See 2 and 3 **Figure 29** or 2 and 3 **Figure 30**. Damaged or loose engine mounts will allow the engine to shift or pull out of alignment during operation. Engine misalignment will result in excessive engine vibration and reduced performance. The engine support plate (2, **Figure 29** or 2, **Figure 30**) and rubber mount assemblies (3, **Figure 29** or 3, **Figure 30**) should be inspected carefully whenever the engine is removed from the hull or when engine misalignment becomes a problem. Refer to *Engine/Jet Pump Alignment* in this chapter.

NOTE
*Shims (1, **Figure 29** or 1, **Figure 30**) located on the engine mounts are used to align the engine with the jet pump drive. Identify each shim and its original location as the rubber mounts are removed in the following steps so each shim can be reinstalled in its original mounting position.*

Removal

Refer to **Figure 29** or **Figure 30** when performing this procedure.

1. Remove the engine and mount plate as described in this chapter.

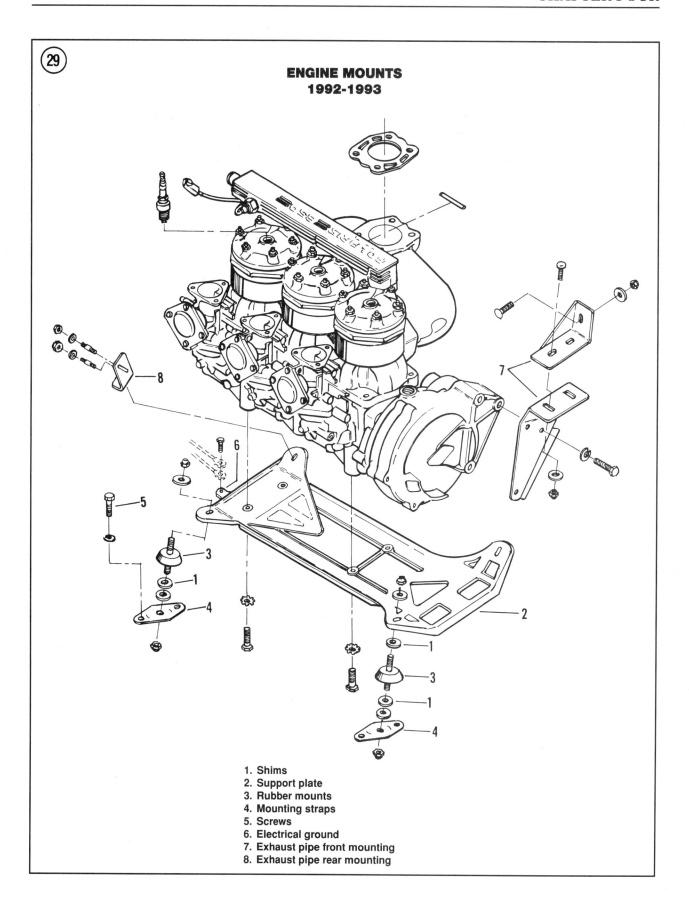

(29)

**ENGINE MOUNTS
1992-1993**

1. Shims
2. Support plate
3. Rubber mounts
4. Mounting straps
5. Screws
6. Electrical ground
7. Exhaust pipe front mounting
8. Exhaust pipe rear mounting

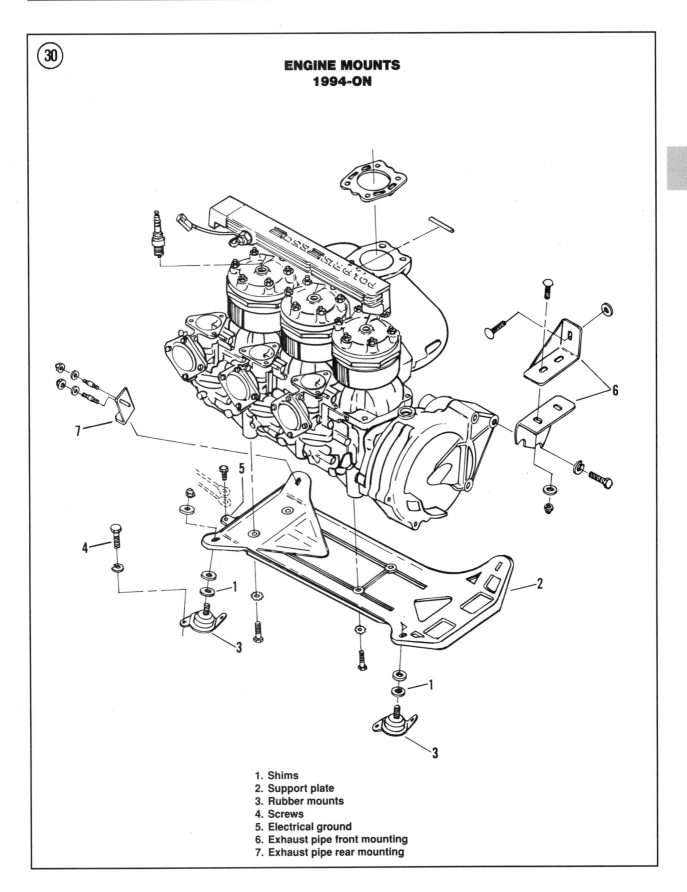

30

**ENGINE MOUNTS
1994-ON**

4

1. Shims
2. Support plate
3. Rubber mounts
4. Screws
5. Electrical ground
6. Exhaust pipe front mounting
7. Exhaust pipe rear mounting

2. Turn the engine and mounting plate over and remove the screws and washers securing the engine support to the engine. Refer to **Figure 31**. Remove the engine support.

3. Visually inspect the rubber mounts (**Figure 32**) for cracks or damage, then try to twist the rubber mount by hand to see if it is loose. If it is necessary to remove a rubber mount, proceed as follows.

4. Remove the 2 bolts and washers securing each rubber mount to the hull. The mounts on 1992-1993 models are attached to a plate (4,

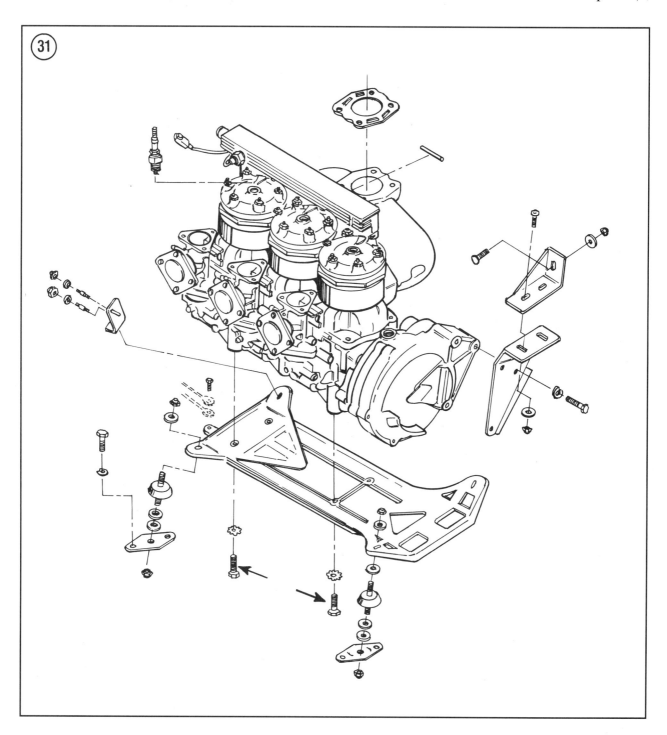

(31)

Figure 29) and spacers may be located between the rubber mount and the lower plate. The mounts on 1994-on models have 2 mounting tabs as shown in **Figure 30**.

5. Remove the rubber mount and its shim (if used). Measure the shim thickness with a vernier caliper or micrometer, then record the thickness and its mounting position on a piece of paper.

6. Repeat for the remaining rubber mounts and shims. Store each rubber mount and shim set in a separate plastic bag so that it can be reinstalled in its original location.

Inspection

Refer to **Figure 29** or **Figure 30** when performing this procedure.

1. Check the engine mount plate (2, **Figure 29** or 2, **Figure 30**) for cracks or damage. A bent or damaged engine mount will cause engine misalignment.

2. Check the rubber mounts (3, **Figure 29** or 3, **Figure 30**) for cracks or damage.

3. Clean nuts and bolts to remove all Loctite residue.

4. Check all of the nuts and bolts for thread damage. Replace damaged fasteners with the same grade material. Weaker materials will loosen and allow the engine to slip when under power.

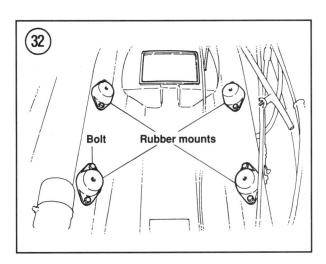

Bolt   **Rubber mounts**

5. Inspect the washers for splitting or other damage. Replace washers if necessary.

6. Visually check the shims (1, **Figure 29** or 1, **Figure 30**) for cracks or damage. Replace shims with the same type and thickness. Verify thickness with a vernier caliper or micrometer.

7. Check the threads in the lower crankcase for stripped threads or other damage.

8. The screws (5, **Figure 29** or 4, **Figure 30**) that attach the rubber mounts to the hull thread into inserts installed in the hull. Check these inserts for looseness or thread damage. Clean and flush insert threads with contact cleaner and compressed air. Loose or damaged inserts should be repaired at a dealership or mechanic who is qualified to do extensive hull repair.

9. Replace worn or damaged parts as required.

Installation

Refer to **Figure 29** or **Figure 30** when performing this procedure.

1. To attach the rubber mounts to the hull:
   a. Lay out the rubber mounts with its shims positioned in its original location.
   b. Assemble each rubber mount with its shims. On 1992-1993 models, assemble the mount (3, **Figure 29**) to its mounting strap (4, **Figure 29**).
   c. Attach the engine mount to the hull with the 2 screws and lockwashers. Tighten the screws (5, **Figure 29** or 4, **Figure 30**) securely, but do not cross thread, strip or otherwise damage the threaded inserts in the hull.

2. To attach the support plate to the engine:
   a. Turn the engine over so that the lower crankcase half faces up.
   b. Align the support plate with the ground tab (6, **Figure 29** or 5, **Figure 30**) for the engine toward the rear of the engine.
   c. Install a lockwasher onto each of the 4 screws.

d. Align the holes in the mount plate with the threaded holes in the engine lower case and install all 4 screws finger tight.

e. Tighten the 4 screws attaching the engine support plate to the engine in a crisscross sequence to the torque specification listed in **Table 3**.

CAUTION
A torque wrench must be used when tightening the screws in substep e. Over-tightening can damage the engine crankcase.

f. Turn the engine upright.

3. Refer to *Engine/Jet Pump Alignment* in this chapter to select the shims necessary to align the engine with the jet pump.

ENGINE INSTALLATION

1. Secure the watercraft so that it will not move when installing the engine.

2. Before installing the engine, be sure to observe the following:

a. Clean the threads of all fasteners, especially those originally coated with the Loctite threadlocker.

b. Coat 10 mm and larger threaded fasteners (not secured with Loctite) with antiseize compound.

c. Have new gaskets to seal the electrical box and the exhaust system.

d. Have RTV sealer available to seal the air intake cover.

e. Clean the inside of the hull and make sure that hoses and wires are pulled up, out of the way.

f. Leave the exhaust manifold and exhaust pipe off until the engine is installed. The engine cannot be installed with the exhaust manifold and exhaust pipe attached.

g. Make sure any shims previously located on the engine mounts are reinstalled in their original locations. Do not mix any shims (1,

Figure 29 or 1, **Figure 30**) from the 4 different engine mounts. The shims are selected to align the engine crankshaft with the jet pump drive. Special alignment tool (part No. 2871343) must be used and the jet pump must be disassembled to check the alignment. Refer to *Engine/Jet Pump Alignment* in this chapter.

h. Position the cable for the electric starter and the wires from the alternator/ignition stator before lowering the engine into position.

NOTE
If the engine is lifted by hand, 2 helpers are required. Padded wooden boards that are strong enough to hold the engine can be positioned across the hull opening to temporarily support the engine before lowering it into the craft. Refer to **Figure 33**.

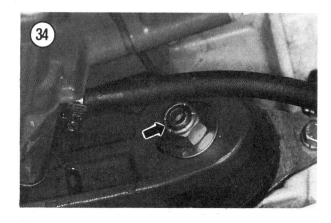

3. Lower the engine into the hull, then move the engine toward the front onto the mounting studs.

4. Install the engine mounting nuts located at the right front, left front and right rear (**Figure 34**). The mounting nut for the left rear and the exhaust pipe bracket should be installed after the exhaust pipe is installed. Refer to Step 8.

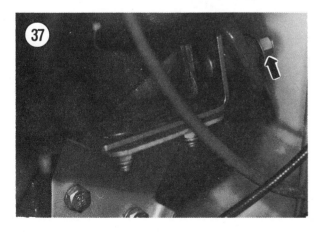

5. Attach the large cable (**Figure 35**) to the starter motor.

NOTE
*It is necessary to move the exhaust pipe to reach some of the manifold screws, but the exhaust pipe (**Figure 23**) must be in position while installing the manifold (**Figure 22**).*

6. Position a new exhaust gasket, the exhaust manifold and the exhaust pipe on the left side of the engine, then install the 9 screws attaching the exhaust manifold to the cylinders.

NOTE
It may be helpful to use guide studs in 2 of the manifold-to-engine attaching holes, to temporarily hold the manifold in position while installing the remaining screws. The studs can be made from screws of the same type that are sufficiently long to permit removal after the manifold is installed. Be sure to remove the guide studs and install the correct screws before continuing the installation.

7. Install the 4 screws attaching the exhaust pipe to the manifold.

8. Install the exhaust pipe bracket (**Figure 36**) on the left rear engine mount, then install the 2 nuts attaching the bracket to the exhaust pipe.

9. Attach the fuel line to the fuel pump

10. Attach the oil line to the oil pump.

NOTE
It may be necessary to adjust the choke and throttle cables as described in Chapter Three.

11. Attach the throttle and choke cables to the front carburetor.

12. Install the mounting bracket for the front of the exhaust pipe to the front of the engine. Install the cross bolt (**Figure 37**) clamping the engine front bracket to the bracket on the exhaust pipe.

13. Connect the oil delivery line, low oil warning wires and the vent line to the oil tank, then

install the tank. Attach the tank to the hull with the 2 bolts (**Figure 38**).

14. Position the fuel tank adapter and pickup hoses (**Figure 39**) in the fuel tank.

15. Check the condition of the fuel tank sealing ring and install a new seal if damaged. Install the adapter retaining nut (**Figure 40**).

16. Attach the fuel lines to the fuel tank adapter using the identifying marks attached before removing. The longer pickup line is for reserve fuel, the shorter line is the regular pickup. The fuel return line is connected to the fitting on an adapter that extends into the tank and the vent line connects to the remaining fitting. Clamp all of the lines to the adapter.

17. Attach wires to the electrical box as follows:

   a. If the cover for the electrical box was temporarily installed, remove it.

   b. Pull the wiring harness that runs below the engine and into the alternator/ignition stator into the electrical box.

   c. Attach the wiring harness connectors inside the electrical box. Refer to **Figure 41**. Wires are color coded the same. The ground is attached to the base mount for the CDI module.

   d. Install the wire clamp that seals the wires where they enter the electrical box.

   e. Install the gasket and electrical box cover. Attach the cover with the 6 screws.

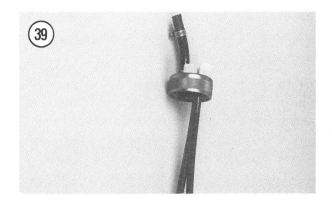

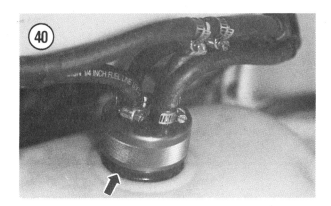

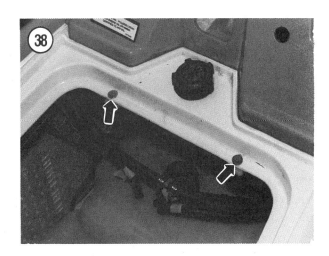

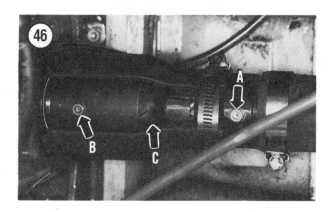

18. Attach the wire from the engine coolant temperature sensor (**Figure 42**) to the wiring harness.

19. Remove any covers from the carburetors and install the screen for the air intake.

20. Position the exhaust water box in the hull and install the hold down strap. Attach the hoses and tighten the hose clamps. Refer to **Figure 43** and **Figure 44**.

21. Install the air intake silencer. Seal the air intake cover with RTV silicone sealer.

22. If removed, install the rear coupler to the engine crankshaft as outlined in this chapter.

23. Install the driveshaft seal and bearing assembly, leaving the clamps loose.

24. Check the driveshaft to be sure that the bumpers (**Figure 45**) are in place in the ends of the shaft.

25. Lubricate the driveshaft, then insert the driveshaft through the seals and bearing and into the splines of the engine coupling.

26. Refer to Chapter Five and install the jet pump.

27. Turn the bearing and seal housing until the grease fitting (A, **Figure 46**) is toward the top, then tighten clamps.

28. Turn the engine coupling until the grease fitting (B, **Figure 46**) is toward the top.

29. Install the driveshaft cover (C, **Figure 46**) with the slot toward the top.

30. Grease the engine coupling and the bearing and seal housing through fittings (A and B, **Figure 46**).

31. Turn the driveshaft cover (C, **Figure 46**) until the slot is down, then tighten the clamp.

32. Attach the cooling (water) lines to the engine.

33. If removed, attach the battery ground cable to the engine mounting plate. Refer to **Figure 47**.

34. Install the battery in the lower part of the carrier, then install the battery and lower carrier in the hull.

35. Attach the positive cable from the electrical box to the positive (+) terminal of the battery.

4

36. Attach the negative (ground) cable to the negative (–) terminal of the battery.

37. Install the battery upper cover (carrier), then position the electrical box on top of the battery.

38. Install both retainer straps over the battery and electrical box and attach to the hull.

39. Launch the craft, start the engine and check for proper operation and leaks before putting the craft into operation.

40. Install the storage basket (**Figure 48**) and close the front hatch.

41. Install the seat and engine cover.

ENGINE/JET PUMP ALIGNMENT

Shims located under the engine mounts are used to align the engine with the jet pump drive. Refer to **Figure 49** for a view typical of 1992-1993 models or **Figure 50** typical of 1994-on models.

Identify each shim and its original location as it is removed so that each can be reinstalled in its original position. Shims from the 4 different mounts should not be mixed. Engine misalignment will result in excessive vibration and reduced performance. Inspect the engine support and rubber mount assembly carefully whenever the engine is removed from the hull or if engine misalignment becomes a problem.

Special alignment tool (part No. 2871343) must be used and the jet pump must be disassembled to check the alignment. The engine must be removed to install or remove the shims, but must be securely attached to the mounts when checking the alignment.

1. Detach the ground (negative) cable from the battery.

2. Remove the jet pump as described in Chapter Five.

3. Withdraw the driveshaft if not removed with the pump.

4. Remove the bearing and seal housing (**Figure 46**).

5. Remove the extension housing, impeller and stub shaft from the pump as described in Chapter Five.

6. Insert the special alignment tool (part No. 2871343) into the engine coupling.

7. Install the partially disassembled pump housing. The special alignment tool will protrude through the bearings in the pump housing.

8. Tighten the nuts attaching the pump housing to the hull lightly, then withdraw the special alignment tool from the engine coupling.

9. Torque the 4 pump attaching nuts in a crossing pattern to 28 ft.-lb. The top 2 nuts are shown in **Figure 51**.

10. Withdraw the special alignment tool and coat the end of the tool with grease.

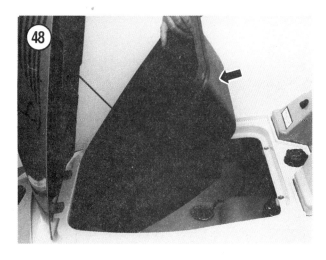

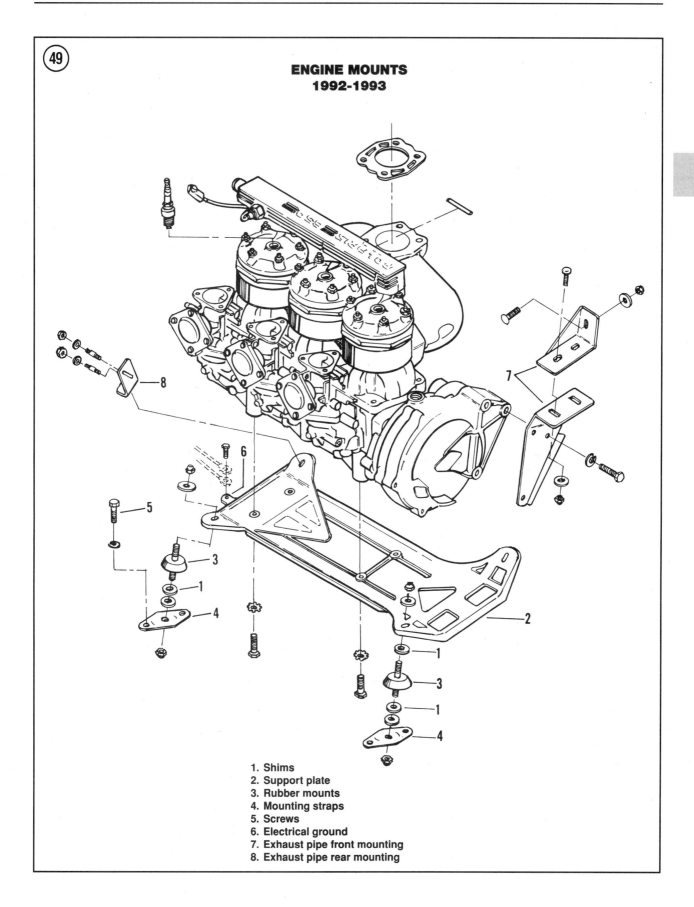

**ENGINE MOUNTS
1992-1993**

1. Shims
2. Support plate
3. Rubber mounts
4. Mounting straps
5. Screws
6. Electrical ground
7. Exhaust pipe front mounting
8. Exhaust pipe rear mounting

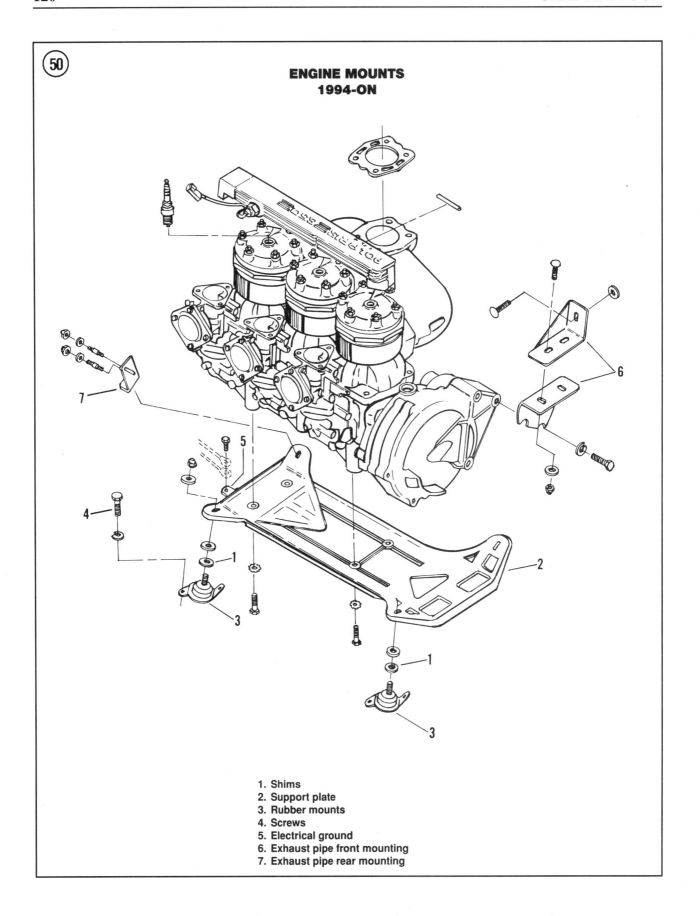

50

**ENGINE MOUNTS
1994-ON**

1. Shims
2. Support plate
3. Rubber mounts
4. Screws
5. Electrical ground
6. Exhaust pipe front mounting
7. Exhaust pipe rear mounting

11. Slide the alignment tool straight into the engine coupling, then withdraw it straight out of the coupling.

12. Inspect the marks in the grease.

   a. If the alignment is correct, the splines will leave marks in the grease evenly all around the shaft.

   b. If the spline marks are much heavier in the grease on the bottom of the alignment tool, add shims to both front engine mounts. This will tip the engine rear coupling down. Return to Step 11 and recheck alignment.

13. When the marks on the alignment tool are even all the way around the tool, remove the pump.

14. Remove the special alignment tool and reassemble the pump as described in Chapter Five.

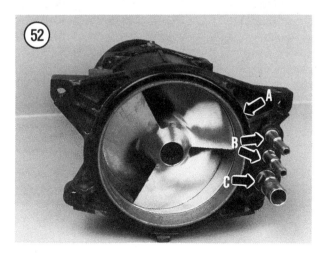

15. Reinstall the driveshaft bearing and seal housing.

16. Lubricate the driveshaft and make sure the bumpers (**Figure 45**) in the ends are in place and in good condition.

17. Insert the driveshaft through the bearing and seals. Make sure the front splines correctly engage the splined coupling at the rear of the engine.

18. Apply antiseize compound to the threads of the pump mounting studs and nuts.

19. Before installing the pump, coat all of the O-rings located at the front of the pump with marine grease. Refer to **Figure 52**.

20. Install the jet pump and tighten the 4 mounting nuts to the torque listed in **Table 3** in a crossing pattern. Make sure the pump fits flush against the hull.

NOTE
The studs are provided with hexagon flats that must fit into the spaces provided in the pump housing. If the pump does not fit against the hull properly, check to see if studs have turned. Loosen the nuts located in the engine compartment and relocate the studs if necessary. Be sure to retighten the inner nuts to the torque listed in **Table 3** *before tightening the rear nuts.*

21. Grease the driveshaft bushing and engine rear coupling through the fittings as described in Chapter Three.

22. Install the driveshaft cover, make sure the slot is down and tighten the clamps.

23. Complete reassembly by reversing the disassembly procedure.

EXHAUST PIPE AND MANIFOLD

1. Remove the seat and engine cover. Cover the edge of the hull with tape to protect the hull from damage.

2. Loosen the clamps attaching hoses (**Figure 43** and **Figure 44**) to the exhaust water box.

Detach the hoses, remove the hold down strap, then lift out the exhaust water box.

3. Remove the battery hold down straps.

4. Lift the electrical box from the battery carrier.

5. Remove the top of the battery box.

6. Detach the battery ground cable from the negative (–) terminal of the battery.

7. Lift the front hatch and remove the storage basket (**Figure 48**).

> *NOTE*
> *Be prepared to plug all of the openings for both the fuel and oil lines before detaching the hoses. Plug the lines and the attachment fittings to prevent the unnecessary loss of oil and to prevent the entrance of dirt.*

8. Mark the fuel lines (**Figure 40**) and the connectors on the fuel tank adapter, then detach the lines from the adapter.

9. Remove the retainer nut, then withdraw the adapter (**Figure 39**) from the fuel tank.

10. Detach the supply and vent lines from the oil tank and plug all openings.

11. Remove the 2 bolts (**Figure 38**) attaching the front of the oil tank, then remove the oil tank.

12. Remove the screws and nuts attaching the exhaust system front mounting bracket (**Figure 53**) to the front of the engine.

13. Remove the nuts attaching the exhaust system at the rear mounting bracket (**Figure 54**).

14. Disconnect cooling hose from the exhaust pipe and remove the 4 screws (**Figure 55**) attaching the exhaust pipe to the manifold.

> *NOTE*
> *The manifold mounting screws on some models may be installed using a high-strength threadlocking compound. These screws may break if you attempt to remove them with an impact wrench. Apply slow even pressure to loosen these screws.*

15. Remove the 9 screws attaching the exhaust manifold, then remove the manifold and the exhaust pipe. It is necessary to move the exhaust

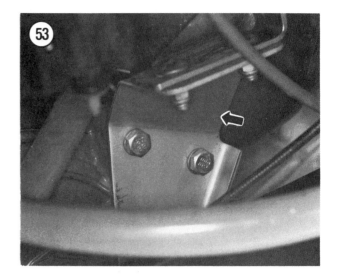

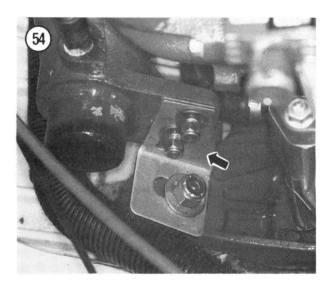

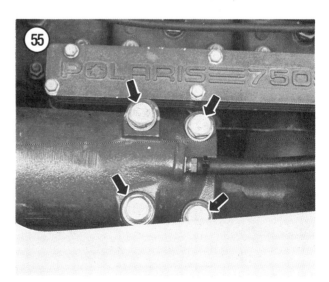

pipe to reach the manifold screws, but the exhaust pipe cannot be removed before the manifold.

16. Clean all of the old gasket material from the exhaust pipe, manifold and cylinder surfaces.

NOTE
It is necessary to move the exhaust pipe (Figure 56) to reach some of the manifold screws, but the exhaust pipe must be in position while installing the manifold (Figure 57).

17. Position a new exhaust gasket, the exhaust manifold and the exhaust pipe on the left side of the engine, then install the 9 screws attaching the exhaust manifold (**Figure 57**) to the cylinders.

NOTE
It may be helpful to use guide studs in 2 of the manifold to engine attaching

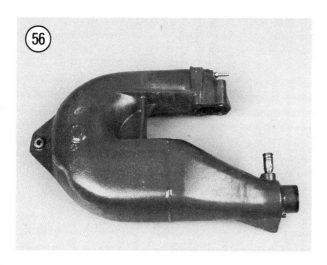

holes, to temporarily hold the manifold in position while installing the remaining screws. The studs can be made from screws of the same type that are sufficiently long to permit removal after the manifold is installed. Be sure to remove the guide studs and install the correct screws before continuing the installation.

18. Install the 4 screws (**Figure 55**) attaching the exhaust pipe to the manifold.
19. Install the exhaust pipe bracket (**Figure 54**) to the left rear engine mount, then install the 2 nuts attaching the bracket to the exhaust pipe.
20. Install the front bracket (**Figure 53**) and tighten all of the fasteners securely.
21. Complete the remaining reassembly by reversing the disassembly procedure.

ENGINE TOP END

The engine top end consists of the cylinder heads, cylinders, pistons, piston rings, piston pins and the connecting rod small-end bearings.

The engine top end can be serviced with the engine installed in the hull; however, most mechanics prefer to remove the engine. The following service procedures are shown with the engine removed for clarity.

Refer to **Figure 58** when servicing the engine top end.

Cylinder Head Removal

CAUTION
To prevent warpage and damage to any component, remove the cylinder head(s) only when the engine is at room temperature.

NOTE
If the engine is being disassembled for inspection, check the compression as described in Chapter Three before disassembly.

1. If the engine is mounted in the hull, perform the following:

    a. Loosen the hose clamp and detach the coolant hose (**Figure 59**) from the outlet manifold.

    b. Disconnect the wire from the water temperature sender (**Figure 60**).

    c. Unbolt and remove the water outlet manifold from the cylinder head.

    d. Detach the spark plug caps from the spark plugs.

2. Loosen the spark plugs if they are to be removed later.

3. Loosen the cylinder head mounting nuts and washers in a crossing pattern. After all of the nuts are loosened, remove the nuts. Refer to **Figure 61**.

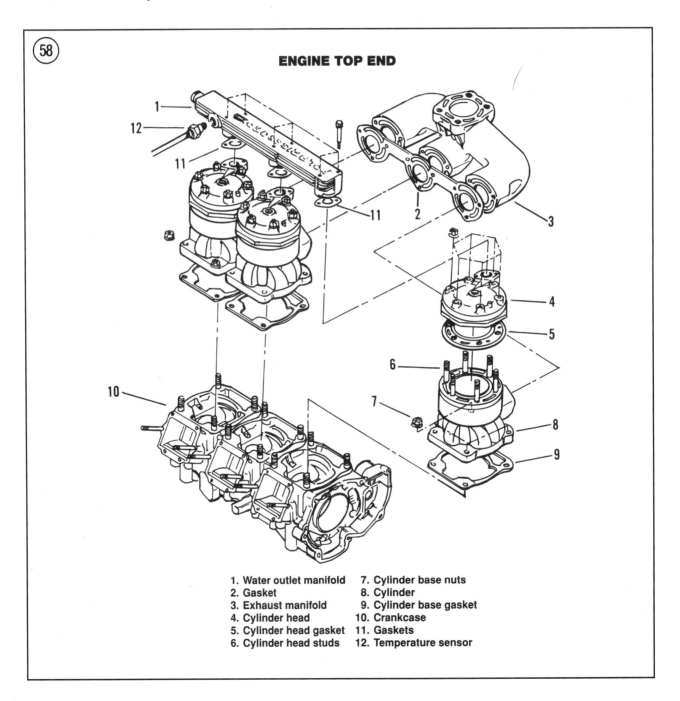

58

ENGINE TOP END

1. Water outlet manifold
2. Gasket
3. Exhaust manifold
4. Cylinder head
5. Cylinder head gasket
6. Cylinder head studs
7. Cylinder base nuts
8. Cylinder
9. Cylinder base gasket
10. Crankcase
11. Gaskets
12. Temperature sensor

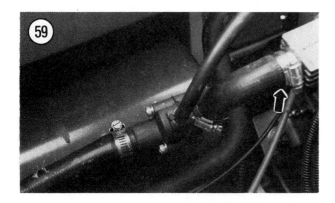

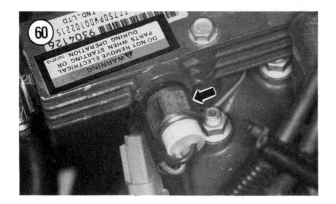

4. Lift the cylinder head from the retaining studs. If the head is tight, tap it lightly with a rubber or plastic mallet.

5. Remove the gasket from the cylinder block studs.

Inspection

1. Clean sand and salt deposits from the water passages in the cylinder head.

2. Wipe away any soft deposits in the combustion chambers (**Figure 62**). Remove hard deposits using a soft metal scraper. Be careful not to gouge the aluminum surfaces. Burrs created from improper cleaning can cause preignition and result in heat erosion.

NOTE
Always use an aluminum thread fluid or Kerosene on the thread chaser and cylinder head threads when performing Step 3.

3. With the spark plugs removed, check the spark plug threads in the cylinder head for carbon buildup or cracks. The carbon can be removed with a 14 mm spark plug chaser. After cleaning the threads, check by installing the spark plug into the cylinder head threads. The plug should thread easily by hand.

4. Clean the gasket surfaces of the cylinder head.

NOTE
Make sure the cylinder head mating surface is clean before performing Step 5.

5. Use a straightedge or flat plate and feeler gauge and measure cylinder head flatness. Refer to **Figure 63**. If the cylinder head shows minor warpage, resurface the cylinder head as follows:

    a. Tape a piece of 400-600 grit wet emery sandpaper onto a piece of thick plate glass or surface plate.

    b. Slowly resurface the head by moving it in a figure-eight pattern on the sandpaper.

c. Rotate the head several times to avoid removing too much material from one side. Check progress often with the straightedge and feeler gauge.

> *NOTE*
> *Removing material from the cylinder head mating surface will change the compression ratio. Removing material will also lower the mating surface for the water outlet manifold. Consult with a Polairs dealer or machinist about the results of removing material from the cylinder head.*

d. If the cylinder head warpage still exceeds the wear limit, it is necessary to have the head resurfaced by a machine shop familiar with water vehicle and motorcycle machining.

6. Wash the cylinder head in hot soapy water and rinse thoroughly before installation.

7. Check the cylinder head for cracks, gouges or damage.

8. Make sure the gasket surfaces, water passages and combustion chamber of the cylinder head are clean and smooth.

Installation

1. Prior to installation, inspect parts carefully to make sure all defective parts have been repaired or replaced. The cylinder head should be thoroughly cleaned before installation.

2. Clean all old sealer residue from the cylinder block.

> *NOTE*
> *Make sure the correct gasket is used. Installing the incorrect gasket or installing the gasket incorrectly can damage the engine.*

3. Install a new cylinder head gasket over the studs with the side marked EX UP toward the top. The tab (A, **Figure 64**) must be under the hole for the water outlet housing as shown. The

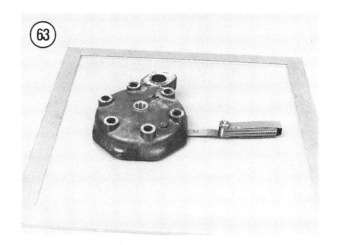

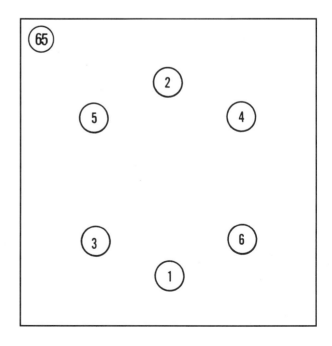

large hole (B, **Figure 64**) in the head gasket must be located in front of the stud on the intake (right) side as shown.

4. Install the cylinder head over the retaining studs. The mounting for the water outlet manifold must be toward the left side.

5. Apply Loctite 242 (blue) to the cylinder studs, then install all of the cylinder head nuts finger tight.

6. Tighten the cylinder head nuts in a crossing pattern as shown in **Figure 65** to the torque listed in **Table 3**.

7. If the spark plugs were removed, gap and install them as described in Chapter Three.

8. Position new gaskets for the water outlet manifold on the cylinder heads.

9. Position the water outlet manifold on the cylinder heads.

10. Apply Loctite 242 (blue) to the threads retaining the water outlet manifold, then install all of the screws finger-tight.

11. Tighten the water manifold retaining screws to the torque listed in **Table 3**.

12. Attach the coolant hose to the water outlet manifold. See **Figure 59**.

13. Attach the spark plug caps to the spark plugs (**Figure 66**).

14. Attach the wire from the temperature sensor (**Figure 60**) to the wiring harness.

CYLINDERS

Individual aluminum cylinder blocks, each with a cast iron liner, are used. If excessive wear is experienced, the cylinder liner can be honed or bored oversize and new pistons and rings installed.

Refer to **Figure 58** when performing the following service procedures.

Removal

1. Remove the cylinder head as described in this chapter.

2. Remove the exhaust manifold as described in this chapter.

3. Gradually loosen the cylinder retaining nuts (**Figure 67**) in a crisscross pattern, then remove the nuts. Each cylinder is retained by 4 base nuts.

NOTE
Mark the cylinders before removal so they can be reinstalled in their original location. Each cylinder must be reinstalled in its original position.

4. Pull the cylinder block straight up, away from the crankcase studs. Secure the piston so that it cannot fall against the crankcase. Refer to **Figure 68**.

5. Repeat the procedure to remove the other cylinders.

6. Remove and discard the cylinder base gaskets.

7. Stuff clean rags around the connecting rods to keep dirt and loose parts from falling into the crankcase.

Inspection

A precision inside micrometer or bore gauge is required to measure accurately the cylinder bore. If you don't have the right tools, have your dealer or a machine shop measure these parts.

1. Clean all gasket residue from the cylinder head gasket surfaces.

2. Clean all gasket residue from the cylinder base gasket surfaces.

3. Clean all gasket residue from the exhaust manifold gasket surfaces.

4. Use a soft scraper or other cleaning tool to remove all carbon deposits from the exhaust port.

> *CAUTION*
> *When cleaning the exhaust port in Step 4, do not allow the scraper or other tool to slip into the cylinder and damage the cylinder bore. Be careful and do not gouge, nick or otherwise damage any metal surface of the cylinder. This caution is especially important if power tools are used to clean the cylinder port.*

5. Check the cylinder area around the ports (**Figure 69**) for excessive wear, sharp edges, cracks or other damage that could snag or damage the piston rings.

6. Wash the cylinder in solvent to remove any oil and carbon particles. The cylinder bore must

be cleaned thoroughly before attempting any measurement to prevent incorrect readings.

7. Measure the cylinder bore diameter as described under *Piston/Cylinder Clearance Check* in this chapter.

> *NOTE*
> *It may be possible to reduce piston-to-cylinder clearance by installing new pistons without reboring the cylinders. New pistons will often reduce excessive pis-*

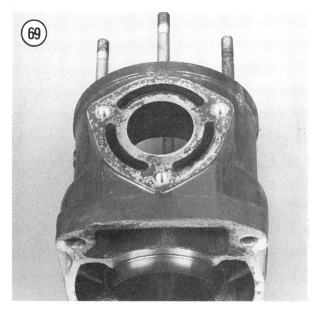

ton-to-cylinder clearance; however, do not install new pistons in a cylinder that is damaged or worn past the wear limit.

8. If the piston-to-cylinder bore clearance is not excessive, check the bore carefully for scratches or gouges. The bore may still require reconditioning.

NOTE
If the engine experienced a slight seizure, there may be bits of aluminum stuck to the cylinder wall. A machine shop may be able to remove the aluminum without having to rebore the cylinder. However, if the surface of the cylinder wall has been scarred by the seizure, the cylinder will require honing or boring.

9. Check the threaded holes in the cylinder block for thread damage. Minor damage can be cleaned up with the correct size metric tap. Refer to Chapter One for information on threads, fasteners and repair tools. If damage is severe, a thread insert should be installed.

10. Check the cylinder block studs for stripping or other damage. Replace damaged studs, nuts and washers.

11. After the cylinder is serviced, wash the bore in hot soapy water. This is the only way to clean

the fine grit left on the cylinder wall after boring or honing. After washing, wipe the cylinder wall with a clean white cloth. If the cylinder wall is clean, the white cloth will remain clean. If the cloth shows any sign of grit or debris, the cylinder wall is not clean and must be rewashed. After the cylinder is thoroughly cleaned, lubricate the cylinder walls immediately with clean engine oil to prevent the cylinder liners from rusting.

CAUTION
A combination of soap and hot water is the only solution that should be used to clean the cylinder wall. Kerosene and other solvents will wash fine grit into very small imperfections in the cylinder surface. Any grit left in the cylinder will act as a grinding compound and cause severe wear to the rings, piston and cylinder bore.

Installation

1. Clean the cylinder bore as described under *Inspection* in this chapter.
2. Be sure the top surface of the crankcase and the bottom surface of the cylinder are clean prior to installation.
3. Install new base gaskets over the cylinder base studs.

NOTE
Check the pistons to make sure each piston is correctly installed with the mark on the top pointing toward the magneto end (front) of the engine. Check that piston pin clips are installed, correctly positioned in their grooves and that the gap is toward the top or bottom of the piston.

4. Align the end gap of each piston ring with the locating pins in the piston ring grooves. Both of the pins are toward the right (reed valve) side of the engine. Refer to A, **Figure 70**.
5. Lightly oil the piston rings and the inside of the cylinder bores with engine oil.

6. Place a piston holding tool under 1 piston and turn the crankshaft until the piston is down firmly against the tool. This will make cylinder installation easier. You can make this tool out of wood as shown in **Figure 71**.

NOTE
When installing the cylinders, make sure to install each cylinder in its original location. The cylinders should have been marked to indicate their original location before removal. If the cylinders were rebored, make sure to match each cylinder with the piston for which it was fitted.

7. Align the cylinder with the piston so that the exhaust port faces to the left side of the engine.

8. Lower the cylinder block over the piston while compressing each piston ring with your fingers as the cylinder starts to slide over the ring. After both rings have entered the cylinder, slide the cylinder all the way down.

NOTE
If the rings are hard to compress, make sure that the ends of the ring are on each side of the ring locating pins in the piston grooves. Ring compressors are available from most tools suppliers that can be used to compress the rings into the piston grooves, but the rings should not be difficult to compress using your fingers.

9. Remove the piston holding tool (**Figure 71**) and lower the cylinder against the crankcase and gasket.

10. Install the cylinder retaining nuts hand tight.

11. Repeat the installation procedure (Steps 1-10) for the other cylinders.

12. Turn the engine with the driveshaft (engine installed) or crankshaft (engine removed). Check that the rings do not snag in a port. If the engine is hard to turn and it seems there is excessive pressure being exerted from one or more cylinders, a piston ring may be incorrectly installed. Remove the cylinder(s) and check ring alignment.

13. Tighten the cylinder retaining nuts in a crossing pattern to the torque listed in **Table 3**.

14. Install the cylinder head using new gaskets as described in this chapter.

CAUTION
If the exhaust manifold or water outlet manifold does not seem to fit squarely against all 3 cylinders, it may be necessary to loosen the cylinder base retaining nuts to move the cylinders. If it is difficult to align the cylinders, the exhaust manifold can be temporarily installed without gaskets to hold the cylinders in alignment while tightening the base nuts. Be sure the base nuts are

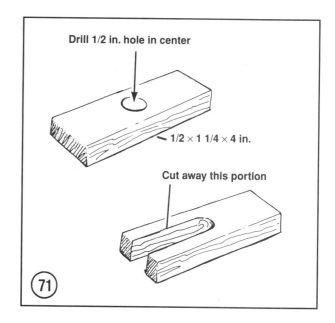

Drill 1/2 in. hole in center

1/2 × 1 1/4 × 4 in.

Cut away this portion

71

72

tightened evenly to the torque listed in **Table 3**. *Remove the manifold and install a new gasket when completing assembly.*

15. Install the water outlet housing using new gaskets and tighten the screws to the torque listed in **Table 3**.

16. Install the engine as described in this chapter.

17. Install the exhaust manifold using new gaskets as described in this chapter. The engine must be installed in the hull and the exhaust pipe must be located in the hull before installing the manifold retaining screws.

18. If new components were installed or if the cylinders were bored or honed, the engine must be broken-in as if it were new. Refer to *Break-In Procedure* in Chapter Three.

PISTON, PISTON PIN AND PISTON RINGS

The pistons are made of an aluminum alloy. The piston pin is a precision fit in the piston and is held in place by a clip at each end. A caged needle bearing is located in the small end of the connecting rod.

Piston and Piston Ring Removal

1. Remove the cylinder head and cylinder as described in this chapter.

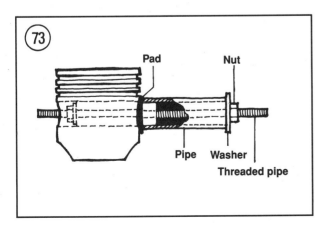

(73)

Pad   Nut

Pipe   Washer

Threaded pipe

2. Identify the original location of each piston by marking the top of each piston with its position. Some suggested marks are F, C & R or 1, 2 & 3. In addition, keep each piston together with its own pin, bearing assembly and piston rings to avoid confusion during reassembly.

3. Before removing the piston, hold the rod tightly and rock the piston. Refer to **Figure 72**. Any rocking motion (do not confuse this movement with the normal sliding motion) indicates wear on the piston pin, needle bearing, piston pin bore, or more likely a combination of all 3.

4. Stuff clean shops rags under all of the pistons to keep the clips or other items from falling into the crankcase.

WARNING
Wear safety glasses when performing Step 5.

5. Remove the piston pin clip from the one side of the piston (B, **Figure 70**) using needlenose pliers. Hold your thumb over one edge of the clip when removing it to prevent it from springing out. Remove the second clip retaining the piston pin from the other side of the piston.

6A. To remove the piston pin without using a special piston pin removal tool, use a proper size wooden dowel or socket extension and push the piston pin from the piston.

CAUTION
If the engine ran hot or seized, the piston pin may be difficult to remove. If so, do not drive the piston pin out of the piston. This may damage the piston, needle bearing and connecting rod. If the piston pin will not push out by hand, remove it as described in Step 6B.

6B. If it is difficult to remove the piston pin, a removal tool can be fabricated as shown in **Figure 73**. Assemble the tool onto the piston and pull the piston pin from the piston. Make sure to install a pad between the piston and the removal tool to avoid scoring the side of the piston.

7. Lift the piston from the connecting rod.

4

8. Remove the caged needle bearing from the upper end of the connecting rod.

CAUTION
Be careful to keep any loose rollers or other pieces of damaged bearings from falling into the crankcase. If the needle bearing is damaged, the bearing surfaces in the upper end of the connecting rod and other parts are probably damaged too.

9. Repeat the removal procedure (Steps 1-8) for the other pistons.

CAUTION
Do not mix the piston pins and needle bearing assemblies from the 3 cylinders. Each set of parts including the cylinder head, cylinder, piston, rings, piston pin clips, piston pin and piston pin needle bearing must be kept together. Install the parts in their original location.

10. Place a piece of foam insulation tube, or shop cloth, over the end of each rod to protect it.

NOTE
Always remove the top piston ring first.

11. Remove the upper ring by spreading the ends with your thumbs just enough to slide it up over the piston (**Figure 74**). Repeat the procedure and remove the lower ring.

Piston Pin and Needle Bearing Cleaning and Inspection

1. Clean the piston pin in solvent and dry thoroughly.
2. Inspect the piston pin for excessive wear or scoring. Also check the piston pin for cracks. Install a new piston pin if any damage is noticed.
3. Clean one needle bearing assembly at a time to prevent mixing parts from different cylinders. Perform the following:
   a. Place one caged bearing in a suitable container filled with solvent.

b. Rock the container to loosen all grease, sludge and other contamination from the needles and from the cage.
c. Remove the bearing assembly from the container and place it on a clean lint-free cloth and allow it to air dry.
d. Check each bearing needle for flat spots or other damage. If any bearing needle is defective, replace the bearing assembly.
4. Check the piston pin and needle bearing play as follows:
   a. Wipe the inside of the piston pin bore in the upper end of the connecting rod with a clean rag.
   b. Insert the caged needle bearing into the bearing bore at the upper end of the connecting rod.

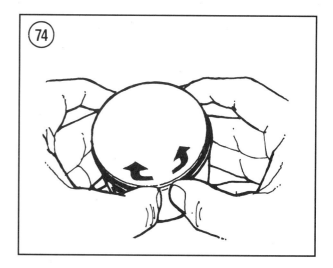

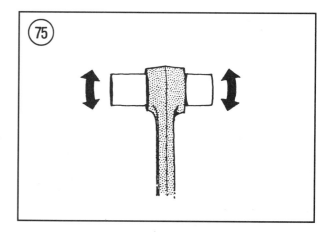

c. Align the piston pin with the caged bearing in the connecting rod and push the pin through the connecting rod.

d. Push against the piston pin as shown in **Figure 75**. There should be no radial (up-and-down) play. If any play exists, replace the pin and bearing assembly.

e. Remove the piston pin and needle bearing assembly.

5. Repeat the procedure described in Step 4 to check the other piston pin assemblies.

CAUTION
If there are signs of piston seizure or overheating, replace the piston pins and caged needle bearings. These parts are weakened by excessive heat and may fail later if not replaced.

Connecting Rod Inspection

1. Wipe the piston pin bore in the upper end of the connecting rod with a clean rag and inspect it for galling, scratches or any other signs of wear or damage. If any of these conditions exist, replace the connecting rods and crankshaft assembly.

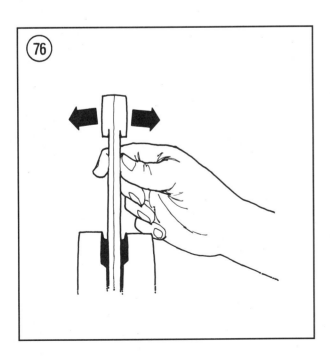

2. Check the connecting rod big end axial play. You can make a quick check by simply rocking the connecting rod back and forth (**Figure 76**). If there is more than a very slight rocking motion (some side-to-side sliding is normal), you should have the crankshaft inspected at a Polaris dealership or competent machine shop.

Piston and Ring Inspection

1. Carefully check the piston for cracks, especially at the top, rounded edge of the transfer cutaways. Install a new piston if any cracks are found. Check the piston skirt for brown varnish buildup. Even a slight amount is an indication of worn or sticking rings.

2. Check the piston skirt for galling or deep scratches which may have resulted from piston seizure. If light galling is present, smooth the affected area with No. 400 emery paper and oil or a fine oilstone. However, if galling is severe or if the piston is deeply scored, replace it.

3. If the piston is damaged, it is important to pinpoint the cause so that the failure will not repeat after engine assembly. Note the following when checking damaged pistons:

a. If the piston damage is contained to the area above the piston pin bore, the engine probably overheated. Seizure or galling conditions contained to the area below the piston pin bore is usually caused by a lack of lubrication, rather than overheating. Severe damage in either location may continue past the piston pin bore making identification of the original problem more difficult.

b. If the piston has seized and appears very dry (apparent lack of oil or lubrication on the piston), a lean fuel mixture probably caused overheating. Overheating can result from incorrect jetting, air leaks, over advanced ignition timing or a faulty or incorrectly adjusted oil pump.

c. Preignition will cause a sand-blasted appearance on the piston crown. This condition is discussed in Chapter Two.

d. If the piston damage is confined to the exhaust port area of the piston, look for incorrect jetting (too lean) or over advanced ignition timing.

e. If the piston has a melted pocket in the crown or if there is a hole in the piston crown, the engine is running too lean. This can be due to incorrect jetting, an air leak or ignition timing that is too far advanced. A spark plug that is too hot can also cause this type of piston damage.

f. If the piston is seized around the skirt but the dome color indicates proper lubrication (no signs of dryness or excessive heat), the damage may indicate a condition referred to as cold seizure. This condition typically results from running the engine too hard without first properly warming it up. A lean fuel mixture can also cause skirt seizure.

4. Check the piston ring locating pins in the piston grooves. The pins must be tight. If a locating pin is loose, replace the piston. A loose pin will fall out and cause severe engine damage.

5. Inspect the grooves (B, **Figure 70**) in the piston for the piston pin clips. If a clip comes out when the engine is running, it will cause severe engine damage. Install a new piston if either groove shows any signs of wear or damage.

NOTE
Maintaining proper piston ring end gap helps to ensure peak engine performance. Excessive ring end gap reduces engine performance and can cause overheating. If there is too little ring end gap, the ring ends will butt together and cause the ring to break. Either condition can result in severe engine damage.

6. Measure piston ring end gap. Push a ring in the top of the cylinder until it is 13 mm (1/2 in.) below the top of the cylinder. The piston can be used to push the ring squarely into position.

Measure the gap with a flat feeler gauge (**Figure 77**) and compare the gap to the specification listed in **Table 2**. Always replace the rings.

NOTE
When installing new rings, measure the end gap in the same manner as for old ones. If the gap is less than specified, make sure you have the correct piston rings. If the replacement rings are correct but the end gap is too small, carefully file the ends with a fine cut file until the gap is correct. Insufficient ring end

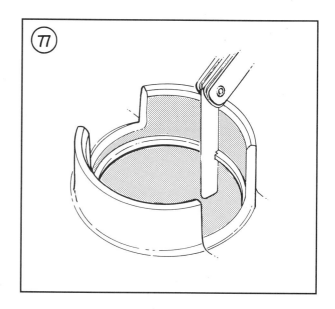

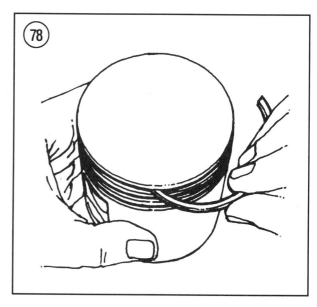

gap can result in ring breakage and severe damage to the cylinder and piston.

7. Carefully remove all carbon buildup from the ring grooves with a broken ring (**Figure 78**), making sure you do not gouge or widen the groove. Inspect the pistons carefully for burrs or nicks in the grooves and for cracked or broken lands. Install a new piston if it is damaged.

CAUTION
Be careful not to damage the piston when cleaning. The soft aluminum of the piston can easily gouge or scratch while attempting to remove the hard, baked on carbon deposits. Do not remove the ar-

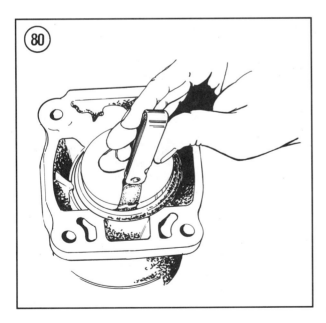

row or other manufacturer's marks from the piston while cleaning. If temporary identification marks are removed by cleaning, attach new marks for reference during assembly.

8. Inspect the top of the piston. Normal carbon buildup can be removed with a scraper (**Figure 79**). If the piston shows signs of overheating, pitting or other abnormal conditions, the engine may be experiencing preignition or detonation; both conditions are discussed in Chapter Two.

CAUTION
Do not use a wire brush to clean the piston skirts or ring lands. A wire brush will remove aluminum which will increase piston clearance and round the corners of the ring lands, decreasing support for the piston and the rings.

9. Check *Piston/Cylinder Clearance* as described in this chapter.

10. If new piston rings will be installed, the cylinders should be honed before assembling the engine. Refer to *Cylinder Honing* in this chapter.

Piston/Cylinder Clearance

Measure piston clearance in the cylinder with the bottom of the piston skirt positioned at the bottom of the cylinder.

1. Inspect the piston and cylinder to make sure neither is scored or dirty. Clean the parts, if dirty, before measuring the piston-to-cylinder clearance.

2. Insert the piston into the cylinder. The piston must be oriented in the cylinder the same as when it is installed. The arrow on the piston crown must point toward the front of the cylinder.

3. Move the piston down in the cylinder until the skirt is at the bottom of the cylinder.

4. Insert a flat feeler gauge between the piston skirt and the cylinder as shown in **Figure 80**. The clearance is the thickest gauge that can be inserted.

5. Refer to **Table 2** for the recommended clearance and wear limit.

6. If clearance between the piston and cylinder bore exceeds the recommended limit, it may be possible to restore the correct clearance by installing a new piston.

NOTE
Obtain the new pistons first before the cylinders are bored so that the pistons can be measured. The cylinders must be bored to match the pistons. Piston-to-cylinder clearance is listed in **Table 2**.

7. If the clearance exceeds the limit listed in **Table 2** after installing a new piston, bore the cylinder to the next oversize and install new piston and rings. The cylinder must also be rebored if it is scored.

Glaze Breaking

New piston rings will not seat properly in a cylinder that is shiny and glazed from normal operation. The smooth glassy surface must be removed using cylinder hone. The operation of removing the glaze is sometimes called deglazing, glaze breaking or honing.

When installing new piston rings, hone the cylinder bore only enough to roughen up the glazed surface slightly to provide a lightly textured or crosshatched surface. This surface finish controls wear of the new rings and helps them to seat and seal properly. Honing can be performed by a Polaris dealer or machine shop equipped to repair small displacement high-performance engines. The cost of having the cylinder honed by a dealer is usually minimal compared to the cost of purchasing a hone and doing the job yourself. If you choose to hone the cylinder yourself, follow the hone manufacturer's directions closely.

CAUTION
After a cylinder has been reconditioned by honing, clean the bore with hot soapy

water to remove all material left from the machining operation. Refer to **Inspection** *under* **Cylinder** *in this chapter. Improper cleaning will not remove all of the machining residue and will result in rapid wear.*

Cylinder Reboring or Honing Oversize

The cylinder can be bored or honed oversize using specialized machine tools. Reboring or honing oversize should be accomplished by properly equipped and trained personnel. Consult with your local Polaris dealer concerning reboring services.

Obtain new, oversize pistons before resizing the cylinders so the pistons can be measured. The cylinders must be bored to match the pistons.

Remove the sharp edges from the top and bottom of the cylinder ports after reboring to keep the rings from catching. Do not chamfer the sides of the ports. Be extremely careful, because this operation is extremely important, but can destroy an otherwise good cylinder.

After a cylinder has been reconditioned by boring or honing, wash the bore in hot soapy water. This is the only way to clean the cylinder wall of the fine grit material left from the bore or honing job. After washing the cylinder wall, run

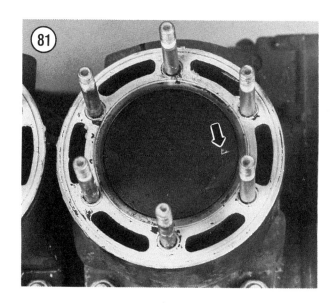

a clean white cloth through it. The cylinder wall should show no traces of grit or other debris. If the cloth shows any sign of debris, the cylinder wall is not clean and must be rewashed. After the cylinder is thoroughly cleaned, lubricate the cylinder walls immediately with clean engine oil to prevent the cylinder liners from rusting.

CAUTION
A combination of soap and hot water is the only solution that should be used to clean the cylinder wall. Kerosene and other solvents will wash fine grit into very small imperfections in the cylinder surface. Grit left in the cylinder will act as a grinding compound and cause severe wear to the rings, piston and cylinder bore.

Piston Assembly

Used pistons must be installed in their original positions. Mark each piston to indicate its original location, before removing it. Install the pistons on their respective connecting rods by following the marks made prior to removal. The top of the piston is marked with an arrow that must point toward the front (magneto end) of the engine. If new pistons are being installed and the cylinders were bored or honed oversize, the cylinder and piston matched by the machinist or dealer must be installed as a set. Remember, cylinders are bored to fit individual pistons.

NOTE
Before installing, wash the piston and the cylinder bore in hot soapy water. After washing, coat the piston and cylinder bore with the same oil as used in the injection oil system. Use a premium marine waterproof grease (part No. 2871066 or equivalent) where grease is called for.

1. Check the piston for its identification mark made during disassembly and match each piston with its correct connecting rod and needle bearing assembly.

2. Stuff shop cloths into the crankcase openings to prevent anything from falling into the crankcase during assembly.

3. Coat the connecting rod small end bore with grease.

4. Insert the caged bearing into the connecting rod.

5. Coat the piston pin and piston pin bore with oil.

6. Insert the piston pin part way into the piston.

7. Align the piston with the connecting rod so that the arrow on the piston crown (**Figure 81**) points forward, then place the piston carefully over the connecting rod.

8. Align the piston pin bore with the connecting rod bore, then push the piston pin through the connecting rod.

NOTE
If you cannot push the piston pin through the piston, remove the piston from the connecting rod and the piston pin from the piston. Warm the piston to approximately 50-60° C (122-140° F). Wear heavy gloves when handling the hot piston and install as described in Steps 6-8.

WARNING
Safety glasses should be worn when performing Step 9.

9. Install new piston pin clips with needlenose pliers. Position the clips so their openings are either up or down.

CAUTION
Do not install used piston pin clips. Make sure that the opening in the clip is either up or down, never toward the side of the piston. A used clip or a clip that is improperly installed could dislodge during operation and cause severe engine damage.

10. Check piston installation by rocking it back and forth around the pin axis and from side to side along the axis. It should rotate freely back and forth but not from side to side.

4

11. Repeat the procedure and install the other pistons.

Piston Ring Installation

Check new rings carefully before installation.
1. Install the piston rings by carefully spreading the ends of the ring with your thumbs and slipping the ring over the top of the piston. Observe the following:
   a. First install the lower ring, then install the top piston ring.
   b. Make sure the manufacturer's marks on the piston rings are toward the top of the piston. Align the ends of the rings with the pins as shown in **Figure 82**.
   c. It is recommended that new piston rings be installed if the rings are removed from the piston. If used rings are reinstalled, it is important to install them on the pistons from which they were removed. It is usually better if they are not removed from the piston.
2. Make sure the ring(s) are seated completely in the grooves, all the way around the circumference, and that the ends are aligned with the locating pins (**Figure 82**). If the rings will not seat completely in the groove, check for dirt or nicks that would prevent proper assembly.
3. If new components were installed, the engine must be broken-in as if it were new. Refer to *Break-In Procedure* in Chapter Three.

CRANKCASE AND CRANKSHAFT

Disassembly of the crankcase is sometimes referred to as splitting the cases or separating the crankcase halves. To remove the crankshaft assembly, the engine must be removed from the hull, the pistons must be removed from the connecting rods and the crankcase must be disassembled.

The crankcase is made of 2 halves of precision diecast aluminum alloy. To avoid damaging

them, do not hammer or pry on any of the interior or exterior projected walls. These areas are easily damaged if stressed.

The crankcase halves are assembled without a gasket; only a thin coat of sealer is used between the halves. The crankcase halves are available only as a matched set. If one crankcase half is damaged, both must be replaced.

The crankshaft, connecting rods, connecting rod bearings, crankpins and center main bearings are a pressed-together assembly. See **Figure 83**. Alignment of the various crankshaft components is critical. Crankshaft disassembly/reassembly should not be attempted by anyone except competent, trained technicians who are equipped with the necessary special equipment and tools. The only individual components readily available for the crankshaft are the outer seals and bearings. All other crankshaft components may not be available as individual parts.

The following procedure is presented as a complete, lower end overhaul.

Crankshaft Misalignment

The crankshaft is pressed together and the pieces may become misaligned. Any misalignment will affect the overall performance and will damage engine parts. Misalignment occurs where the main and connecting rod journals are pressed together.

(83) **ENGINE CRANKSHAFT, CONNECTING ROD AND PISTON ASSEMBLY**

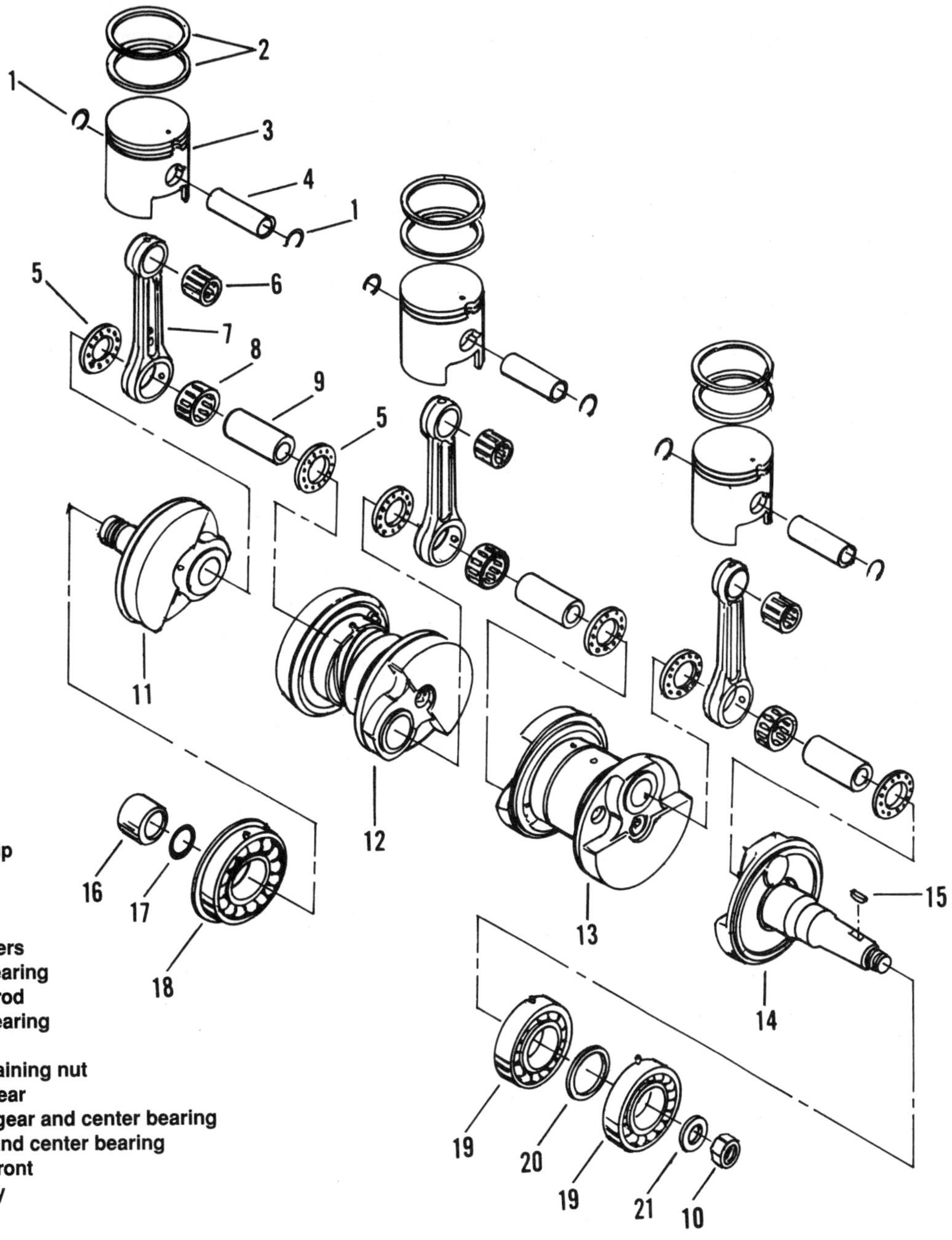

4

1. Piston pin clip
2. Rings
3. Piston
4. Piston pin
5. Thrust washers
6. Small end bearing
7. Connecting rod
8. Large end bearing
9. Crankpin
10. Flywheel retaining nut
11. Crankshaft rear
12. Crankshaft, gear and center bearing
13. Crankshaft and center bearing
14. Crankshaft front
15. Woodruff key
16. Wear ring
17. O-ring
18. Rear main bearing
19. Front main bearing
20. Spacer
21. Washer

The connecting rod crankpins must be evenly spaced exactly 120° apart. It is possible to twist the crankshaft so that crankpin spacing is not equal. This type of misalignment will change the engine's timing and affect the overall performance of the watercraft.

A crankshaft can slip and become misaligned under severe use; however, misalignment is frequently a result of careless handling when disassembling or assembling the engine. If you suspect a misaligned or twisted crankshaft, perform the following procedure.

Crankshaft Main Journal Alignment Check

The following procedure describes how to check for a twisted crankshaft. The only special tools required are a dial indicator (part No. 2870459 or equivalent) and a degree wheel that can be attached to the engine crankshaft at the rear coupling.

1. Remove the jet pump and driveshaft as described in Chapter Five.
2. Remove the spark plugs.
3. Install a dial indicator in the spark plug hole for the *front* cylinder.
4. Use the dial indicator to determine top dead center (TDC) of the *front* piston. Do not move the crankshaft after finding TDC.
5. Attach a degree wheel to the rear drive coupling. Make sure the degree wheel is centered on the coupling.
6. Attach a pointer to the engine and align the pointer with the degree wheel marks.
7. Move the degree wheel to align the 0-360° mark with the pointer, without turning the engine crankshaft.
8. Attach the degree wheel to the rear coupling so that the degree wheel will not move on the coupling.

NOTE
The dial indicator can be removed from the front cylinder for this check, or another may be installed in the center cyl-

inder. Do not use the degree wheel to find top dead center for the center piston.

9. Install a dial indicator in the spark plug hole for the *center* cylinder.
10. Use the dial indicator to determine top dead center (TDC) of the *center* piston.
11. Observe the degree wheel and pointer. The pointer should be pointing to exactly 120°.

NOTE
The dial indicator can be removed from another cylinder for this check, or another may be installed in the rear cylinder. Do not use the degree wheel to find top dead center for the rear piston.

12. Install a dial indicator in the spark plug hole for the *rear* cylinder.
13. Use the dial indicator to determine top dead center (TDC) of the *rear* piston.
14. Observe the degree wheel and pointer. The pointer should be pointing to exactly 240°.
15. If the crankshaft appears to be twisted, check the position of the pistons again. The accuracy of this check depends upon the care to locate each piston at exactly top dead center.
16. The crankshaft must be removed before it can be realigned. Crankshaft alignment should only be attempted by competent trained technicians who are equipped with the special tools.

Crankcase Disassembly

This procedure describes disassembly of the crankcase halves and removal of the crankshaft.

Refer to **Figure 84**.

1. Remove the engine as described in this chapter.
2. Unbolt and remove the carburetors and reed valve assemblies from the right side of the engine as described in Chapter Six.
3. Remove the drive coupling from the rear of the crankshaft as described in this chapter.
4. Unbolt and remove the engine front cover.

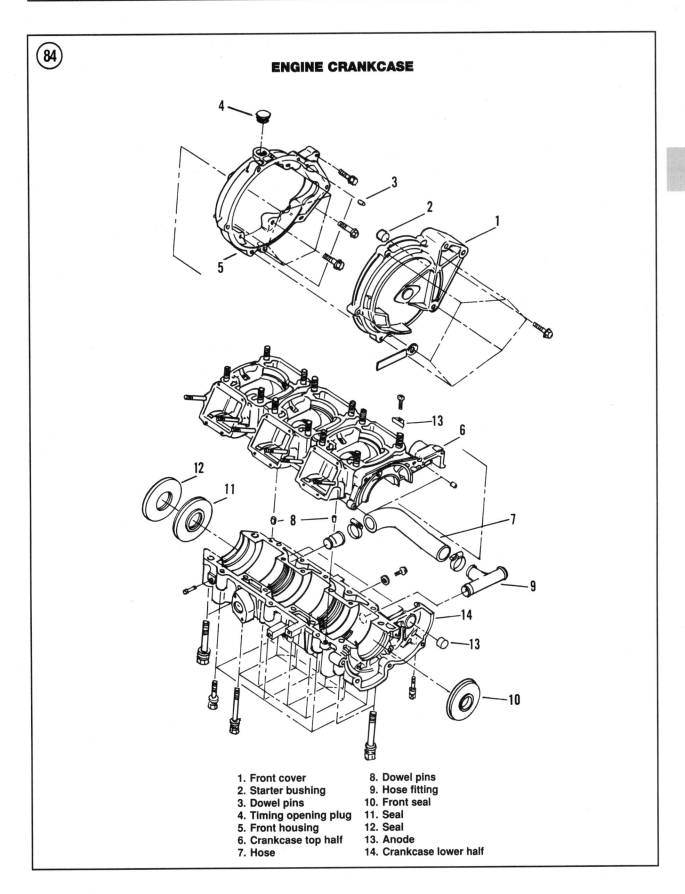

ENGINE CRANKCASE

1. Front cover
2. Starter bushing
3. Dowel pins
4. Timing opening plug
5. Front housing
6. Crankcase top half
7. Hose
8. Dowel pins
9. Hose fitting
10. Front seal
11. Seal
12. Seal
13. Anode
14. Crankcase lower half

4

5. Remove the flywheel and stator plate as described in Chapter Seven.

6. Unbolt and remove the electric starter.

7. Remove the oil pump from the crankcase.

8. Remove the cylinders and pistons as described in this chapter.

CAUTION
Do not damage the cylinder block studs in the crankcase or the connecting rods when performing the following procedures.

9. Turn the crankcase assembly so that it rests upside down. Make sure the engine is stable and will not slide or fall when removing screws.

10. Remove the engine mount plate from the bottom of the crankcase as described in this chapter.

11. Loosen the 21 screws attaching the crankcase halves together in reverse of the numerical order shown in **Figure 85**. Remove all of the screws.

CAUTION
Make sure that you have removed all the fasteners. If the cases are hard to separate, check for any fasteners you may have missed.

12. Lift the lower half of the crankcase from the upper half.

CAUTION
It is very difficult to clean the crankshaft if it is allowed to get dirty. Make sure that no dust or other small particles·enter the connecting rod bearings or main bearings. Cover the crankshaft with a clean plastic bag to keep it clean while it is removed.

13. Lift the crankshaft from the upper crankcase half. Support the crankshaft on the workbench so that it cannot roll off.

Cleaning

Refer to **Figure 84** for this procedure.

1. Clean both halves of the crankcase with cleaning solvent. Thoroughly dry with compressed air and wipe the crankcase with a clean shop cloth. Be sure to remove all traces of old sealer from all mating surfaces.

2. Clean the passages in the case halves. Use compressed air to ensure that they are clean.

3. Clean the crankshaft assembly and check the condition of all connecting rod and main bear-

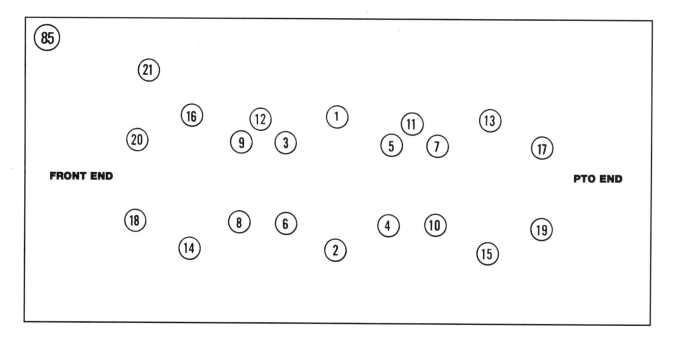

ings. Oil the bearings with engine oil to prevent rusting.

4. Cover the crankshaft assembly with a plastic bag.

Crankcase Inspection

Refer to **Figure 84** for this procedure.

1. Inspect the case halves for cracks and fractures. Especially check the areas around the stiffening ribs, bearing bosses and threaded holes. If any cracks are found, have them repaired by a shop specializing in the repair of precision aluminum castings or replace the crankcase assembly.

2. Check the bearing surface areas in the upper and lower halves.

3. Check the threaded holes in both crankcase halves for thread damage and for dirt or oil buildup. If necessary, clean or repair the threads with a suitable size metric tap. Lubricate the tap threads with kerosene or an aluminum tap fluid before use.

4. Check the oil seal grooves in the upper and lower crankcase halves for cracks or damage.

Crankshaft Inspection

Refer to **Figure 83** for this procedure.

1. Check the oil seals located at each end of the crankshaft. Replace the seals when reassembling the engine and inspect the crankshaft surfaces, especially if the seals are damaged.

2. Check each connecting rod around both ends for discoloration or other evidence of excessive heat damage.

NOTE
A set of V-blocks can be made out of hardwood to perform the check described in Step 3. However, only machined V-blocks should be used to check crankshaft runout described in Step 8B.

3. Place the crankshaft on V-blocks and spin each bearing and connecting rod by hand. Check for excessive noise or roughness.

WARNING
When drying a bearing with compressed air, do not allow the air jet to spin the bearing. The air jet could cause the bearing to spin too fast and fly apart.

4. Carefully examine the condition of the crankshaft main bearings. Clean the bearings in solvent and dry thoroughly with compressed air. Oil each bearing before checking it. Roll each bearing around by hand, checking that it turns quietly and smoothly and there are no rough spots. There should be no apparent radial play. Defective bearings must be replaced.

5. Check the oil pump drive gear, located near the center of the crankshaft, for deep scoring, excessive wear, nicks or other damage. If the gear is damaged, check the oil pump driven gear for damage.

6. Check the crankshaft threads for stripping or other damage.

7. Check the key seat in the crankshaft for cracks or other damage. If the key seat is damaged, refer service to a dealership or machine shop.

8A. To check the crankshaft runout with the crankshaft supported in the upper crankcase half:

   a. Support the upper case half (6, **Figure 84**) on wooden blocks. Then place the crankshaft in the upper case half. Make sure the wooden blocks are tall enough the connecting rods can hang down without contacting the workbench.

   b. Check runout with dial indicator located near one end of the crankshaft.

   c. Turn the crankshaft slowly and note the gauge reading.

   d. The maximum difference recorded is crankshaft runout.

4

e. Move the dial indicator to the other end of the crankshaft and check the runout at the opposite end.

f. If the runout exceeds the limit in **Table 2**, take the crankshaft assembly to a Polaris dealership or machine shop that specializes in the repair and alignment of crankshafts.

8B. To check crankshaft runout on precision V-blocks:

a. Remove the end bearings (18 and 19, **Figure 83**) from the crankshaft.

b. Place the crankshaft on a set of machined V-blocks located where the end bearings were removed from the crankshaft.

NOTE
Do not check crankshaft runout with the crankshaft placed between centers or in a lathe. V-blocks must be used as described in sub-step b.

c. Position the dial indicator near one end of the crankshaft to check runout.

d. Turn the crankshaft slowly and note the gauge reading.

e. Move the dial indicator to each of the main bearings nearest the center cylinder crankpin and check the runout at these bearings.

f. Move the dial indicator to near the remaining end of the crankshaft and check the runout at this location.

g. The maximum difference recorded at any of these locations (checked in substeps c through f) is crankshaft runout. If the runout at any position exceeds the limit in **Table 2**, the crankshaft should be checked and aligned by a technician who is trained and equipped to service this type of crankshaft.

9. Replace the crankshaft if it exceeds any of the limits listed in **Table 2** or if any of the bearings are damaged.

10. Replace all O-rings and seals that are removed.

11. Check the seal collar located at the rear of the crankshaft for wear or other damage, before installing the crankshaft.

Crankshaft Installation

Refer to **Figure 83** and **Figure 84** for this procedure.

1. Install the O-ring (17, **Figure 83**) on the rear of the crankshaft, then install the wear ring (16, **Figure 83**).

2. Fill the lip cavities of the oil seals at each end of the crankshaft with low-temperature grease, then install the seals (10-12, **Figure 84**) on the crankshaft. Install the narrow outermost rear seal with its rubber coated side out (toward the rear). The metal side of the 2 rear seals should be together.

3. Fill the 2 labyrinth seal areas located between the cylinders with low-temperature grease.

4. Support the upper crankcase (6, **Figure 84**) on wooden blocks so the connecting rods can hang free through the crankcase.

NOTE
Step 5 describes crankshaft installation. Because of the number of separate procedures required during installation, read Step 5 through first before actually installing the crankshaft.

5. Align the crankshaft with the upper crankcase half and lower the crankshaft into position. Note the following:

    a. Make sure the connecting rods hang freely through the openings for the cylinders.

    b. Align the retaining rings on the main bearings with grooves in the crankcase.

    c. Make sure the crankshaft oil seals and bearings fit into the crankcase reliefs.

    d. Turn the main bearings so the locating pins in each outer race engages the relief in the upper crankcase half.

    e. Recheck substeps a through d to be sure everything is still aligned.

Crankcase Assembly

1. Install the crankshaft in the upper crankcase half as described in this chapter.

2. Lubricate the crankshaft gear and the bottom end bearings with the same oil used in the injection system.

3. Make sure the crankcase mating surfaces are clean, then apply Loctite Gasket Eliminator 515 to the sealing surface of one crankcase half.

4. Position the lower case half (14, **Figure 84**) on the upper half and check the mating surfaces to make sure they are together evenly.

5. Apply Loctite 242 (blue) to the threads of the 21 bolts that attach the crankcase halves together, then install the bolts finger tight.

6. Tighten the crankcase bolts in the order shown in **Figure 85** to the torque listed in **Table 3**.

> *CAUTION*
> *While tightening the crankcase bolts, Check frequently to be sure the crankshaft turns easily and the case halves come together evenly.*

7. After the crankcase halves are tightened, check to be sure the crankshaft still turns freely. If it is binding, separate the crankcase halves and determine the cause, then correct the problem. If the cases are separated, be sure to clean the sealer from the mating surfaces. Reassemble the crankcase as previously described.

8. Turn the engine right side up.

9. Coat the connecting rods, crank pins and bearings liberally with the same oil as used in the oil injection system.

10. Install the engine as described in *Engine Top End* this chapter.

11. Install the *Reed Valves* and *Carburetors* as described in Chapter Six.

12. Install the stator plate and engine flywheel as described in Chapter Seven.

13. Install the coupler to the rear end of the crankshaft.

14. Install the engine mounting plate. Tighten the retaining screws to the torque listed in **Table 3**.

15. Install the engine in the hull as described in this chapter.

16. If new components were installed, the engine must be broken-in as if it were new. Refer to *Break-In Procedure* in Chapter Three.

REAR COUPLING

The driveshaft coupling (**Figure 86**), attached to the rear of the engine crankshaft, can be removed with the engine mounted in the hull. A special tool (part No. 2871037) is available for removing the rear coupling. The special tool engages the splines in the coupling. Large flats are located on the rear coupling that can be used if the special tool is not available.

Removal/Installation

1. If the engine is mounted in the hull:

    a. Remove the seat and engine cover.

    b. Detach the cooling (water) lines from the engine.

    c. Refer to Chapter Five and remove the jet pump and the driveshaft as an assembly.

2. Remove the spark plug from the rear cylinder.

3. Turn the rear coupling until the rear piston is at approximately top dead center, then turn the coupling clockwise until the piston moves down approximately 25.4 mm (1 in.).

NOTE
Leave some of the rope outside the spark plug hole to allow the rope to be removed.

4. Insert approximately 30 cm (1 ft.) of 5/16 in. diameter nylon rope into the cylinder through the spark plug hole. The rope will stop the piston from reaching the top of the cylinder when trying to turn the rear coupling.

5. Insert the special coupling tool (part No. 2871037) into the splines of the rear coupling.

NOTE
The coupling has large flats that can be used if the special coupling tool is not available.

6. Turn the rear coupling counterclockwise until the rope is trapped between the cylinder head and piston.

CAUTION
Do not use an impact wrench or pipe wrench to remove the coupler. The rear coupling may be damaged by improper removal procedures or using the wrong type of wrench.

7. Continue to turn the coupling counterclockwise to unscrew the coupler from the engine crankshaft.

8. Installation is the reverse of these steps. Observe the following.

   a. Clean the rear coupling and crankshaft threads.

   b. Grease the crankshaft threads, then install the rear coupling onto the crankshaft.

   c. Use the rope in the cylinder to hold the crankshaft and tighten the rear coupling to the torque listed in **Table 3**.

Table 1 ENGINE SPECIFICATIONS

Year and model	Engine model	Bore mm (in.)	Stroke mm (in.)	Disp. cc (cid.)	HP @ rpm
1992					
SL 650	EC65PW	65 (2.56)	65 (2.56)	647 (39.5)	68@6500
1993					
SL 650	EC65PW	65 (2.56)	65 (2.56)	647 (39.5)	68@6500
SL 750	EC75PW	69.72 (2.74)	65 (2.56)	744 (45.4)	78@6500
1994					
SL 650	EC65PW	65 (2.56)	65 (2.56)	647 (39.5)	68@6350
SL 750	EC75PW	69.72 (2.74)	65 (2.56)	744 (45.4)	80@6150
SLT 750	EC75PW	69.72 (2.74)	65 (2.56)	744 (45.4)	80@6250
1995					
SL 650	EC65PW	65 (2.56)	65 (2.56)	647 (39.5)	68@6500
SL650 Std.	EC65PW	65 (2.56)	65 (2.56)	647 (39.5)	68@6500
SL 750	EC75PW	69.72 (2.74)	65 (2.56)	744 (45.4)	80@6000
SLT 750	EC75PW	69.72 (2.74)	65 (2.56)	744 (45.4)	80@6000

4

Table 2 SERVICE SPECIFICATIONS

	mm	in.
Maximum crankshaft		
Runout	0.10	0.004
Oil injection pump		
End play	0.3-0.6 mm	0.012-0.024
Piston ring end gap*	0.20-0.47	0.008-0.018
Piston skirt clearance		
1992-1993 SL650 & SL750		
New	0.1-0.15	0.004-0.006
Wear limit	0.2	0.008
1994 & 1995 SL650		
New	0.13-0.18	0.0051-0.0071
Wear limit	0.2	0.008
1994 & 1995 SL750		
New	0.1-0.16	0.0042-0.0062
Wear limit	0.2	0.008
Reed petal air gap		
Maximum	0.38	0.015
* Measure piston ring end gap with ring 1.3 cm 1/2 in. from top of the cylinder bore.		

Table 3 TIGHTENING TORQUES

	N·m	ft.-lb.
Carburetor mounting	21.7	16
Cylinder head	24.4	18
Cylinder base	38	28
Crankcase		
8 mm	21.7	16
10 mm	35.2	26
Carburetor adapters/reed valves		
Screws	8.3	6 (72 in.-lb.)
Nuts	8.6	6 (72 in.-lb.)
Carburetor mounting	21.7	16
Cylinder head	24.4	18
Cylinder base	38	28
Crankcase		
8 mm	21.7	16
10 mm	35.2	26
Drive coupler	216.9	160
Engine to support plate	61	45
Exhaust manifold	21.7	16
Flywheel housing	8.81	6.5 (78 in.-lb.)
Flywheel nut	74.6	55
Impeller	135.6	100
Intake manifold	8.81	6.5 (78 in.-lb.)
Plastic air intake	2.26	1.67 (20 in.-lb.)
Starter mounting screws	7.5-8.1	5.5-6.0
Water manifold	8.81	6.5 (78 in.-lb.)
Other fasteners		
5 mm	5.1-5.9	3.8-4.3 (45-52 in.-lb.)
6 mm	7.5-8.8	5.5-6.5 (66-78 in.-lb.)
8 mm	17.6-21.7	13-16
10 mm	35.2-40.7	26-30
12 mm	54.2-59.7	40-44

Chapter Five

Drive System

The drive train consists of the coupling at the rear of the engine, the driveshaft and the jet pump assembly. This chapter describes procedures for servicing the driveshaft and jet pump assemblies. Service and torque specifications are listed in **Tables 1-2** at the end of this chapter.

SERVICE PRECAUTIONS

When working on the drive system, there are several precautions that should be followed to help safely disassemble, inspect and reassemble the components.

1. When working on the drive system, it is necessary to work on the bottom of the craft. The bottom of the craft is sufficiently open on some trailers to remove the jet pump. If it is not, you can either mount the craft on a suitable stand (where you can work underneath it) or you can rotate the craft so the left side is down. Whatever method you use, make sure the vehicle is secured

properly. Do not rotate the craft on its side unless all of the water has been drained from the engine and exhaust systems. Before turning the water vehicle on its side, remove the battery. Refer to Chapter Seven for *Battery Removal*. In addition, make sure the fuel valve is turned OFF. After turning the craft upright, reinstall the battery (Chapter Seven) and bleed the oil pump (Chapter Eight).

> *CAUTION*
> *Do not rotate the craft so the right side is lower than the left. Even when most of the water drained, if the right side is lower than the left, any water remaining can drain from the exhaust through the exhaust ports and into the cylinders.*

2. Always replace a worn or damaged fastener with one of the same size, type and torque requirements. Make sure to identify each bolt before replacing it with another. Lubricate bolt threads with antiseize compound, unless other-

wise specified, before torque is applied. If a tightening torque is not listed in **Table 2** (end of this chapter), refer to the torque and fastener information in Chapter One.

3. Where special tools are recommended or mandatory, they are called out in the text. Factory tools can be purchased through a Polaris dealership. Some aftermarket companies offer a few of the more general types of special tools required to service the drive system.

4. Use a vise with protective jaws to hold parts. If protective jaws are not available, insert wooden blocks on each side of the part(s) before clamping them in the vise.

5. Remove and install pressed-on parts with an appropriate mandrel, support and hydraulic press. Do not try to pry, hammer or otherwise force them on or off.

6. Refer to **Table 2** at the end of this chapter for torque specifications. Proper torque is essential to ensure long life and satisfactory service from water vehicle components.

7. Keep a record of all shims and where they came from. As soon as the shims are removed,

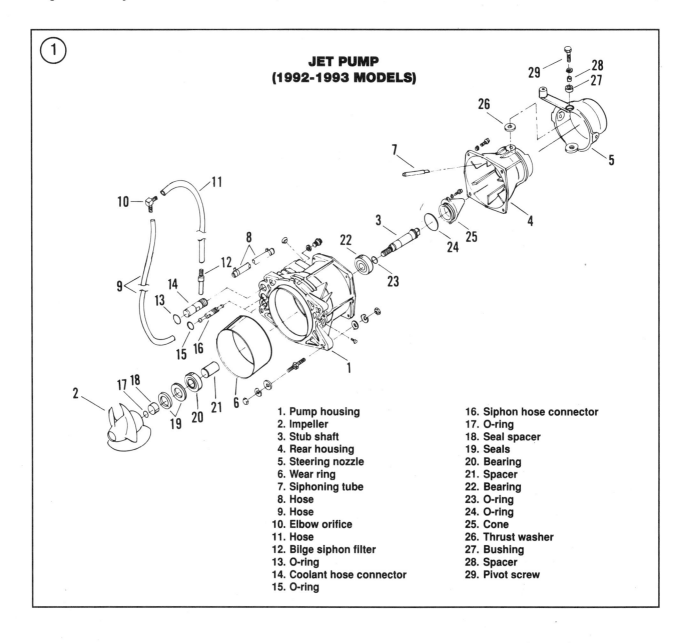

**JET PUMP
(1992-1993 MODELS)**

1. Pump housing
2. Impeller
3. Stub shaft
4. Rear housing
5. Steering nozzle
6. Wear ring
7. Siphoning tube
8. Hose
9. Hose
10. Elbow orifice
11. Hose
12. Bilge siphon filter
13. O-ring
14. Coolant hose connector
15. O-ring
16. Siphon hose connector
17. O-ring
18. Seal spacer
19. Seals
20. Bearing
21. Spacer
22. Bearing
23. O-ring
24. O-ring
25. Cone
26. Thrust washer
27. Bushing
28. Spacer
29. Pivot screw

inspect them for damage and write down their thickness and location. Measure shim thickness with a micrometer or vernier caliper.

JET PUMP

An axial flow, single stage jet pump is used on all models. The pump used on 1992-1993 models is different from the pump used on later

(1994-on) models. Servicing differences are noted, where applicable.

The pump used on 1992-1993 models consists of a pump housing (1, **Figure 1**), impeller (2, **Figure 1**), impeller (stub) shaft (3, **Figure 1**), rear housing (4, **Figure 1**), and steering nozzle (5, **Figure 1**).

The jet pump assembly on 1994-on models is of modular design. It consists of the front (wear ring) housing (1, **Figure 2**), impeller (2, **Figure 2**), bearing housing (3, **Figure 2**), impeller (stub)

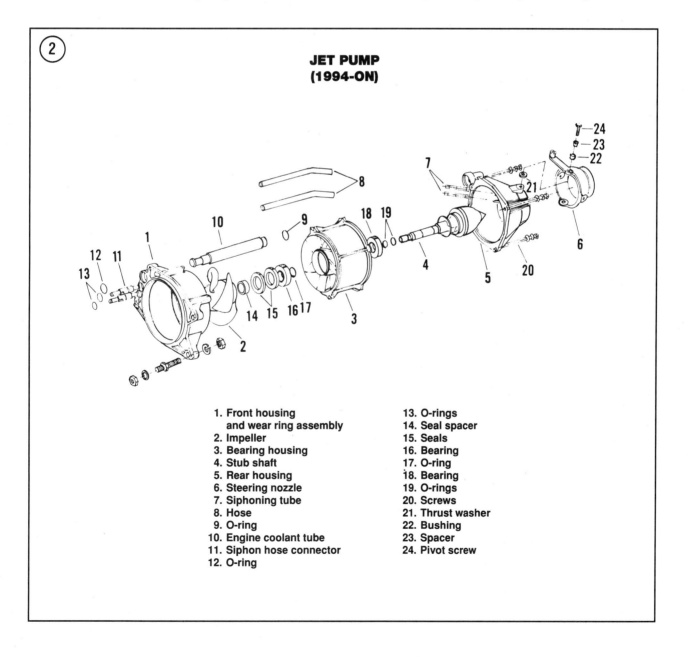

JET PUMP (1994-ON)

1. Front housing
   and wear ring assembly
2. Impeller
3. Bearing housing
4. Stub shaft
5. Rear housing
6. Steering nozzle
7. Siphoning tube
8. Hose
9. O-ring
10. Engine coolant tube
11. Siphon hose connector
12. O-ring
13. O-rings
14. Seal spacer
15. Seals
16. Bearing
17. O-ring
18. Bearing
19. O-rings
20. Screws
21. Thrust washer
22. Bushing
23. Spacer
24. Pivot screw

5

shaft (4, **Figure 2**) and steering nozzle (6 **Figure 2**). The impeller (stub) shaft is supported by 2 bearings (16 and 18, **Figure 2**) pressed into the bearing housing.

The coupling (1, **Figure 3**) at the rear of the engine turns the impeller (2, **Figure 3**) of the jet pump via the splined driveshaft (3, **Figure 3**).

NOTE
*The impeller is also shown at 2, **Figure 1** and 2, **Figure 2**. The spline at the forward end of the driveshaft (3, **Figure 3**) is different from the spline at the rear.*

As the impeller rotates, water is drawn through the intake grate (**Figure 4**) on the bottom of the craft and into the pump intake. Water is forced through the impeller housing, then it exits through the rear housing and steering nozzle (5, **Figure 1** or 6, **Figure 2**). As engine speed increases, a higher volume of water is forced through the jet pump, increasing the craft's speed. Stationary vanes in the pump housing control water flow for improved thrust and effi-

ciency. A cable, attached to the steering column at the front (**Figure 5**) and the steering nozzle (**Figure 6**) at the rear, controls steering movement. Models equipped with the variable trim system have a rod attached to a trim ring attached to the steering nozzle. The trim system is discussed later in this chapter.

When performing the following service procedures, refer to the jet pump and driveshaft figure for your model:

a. **Figure 1** shows the jet pump for 1991-1992 models.

b. **Figure 2** shows the jet pump typical of 1994-on models.

Impeller and Wear Ring Inspection

There should be very little clearance between the tips of the impeller blades and the wear ring surrounding the impeller. Both the ring and the impeller blades will wear and as the clearance increases, pump thrust (force) will decrease.

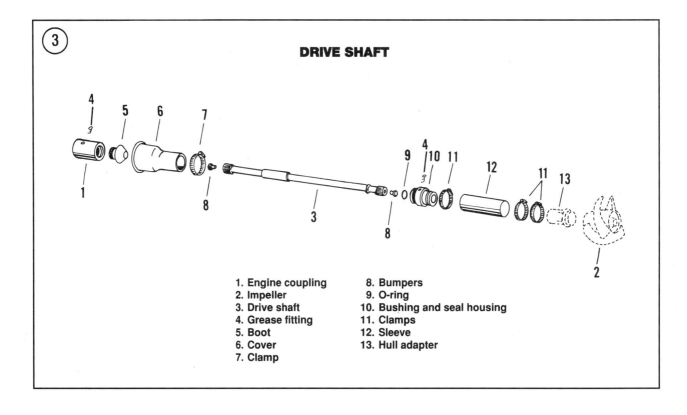

(3)

DRIVE SHAFT

1. Engine coupling
2. Impeller
3. Drive shaft
4. Grease fitting
5. Boot
6. Cover
7. Clamp
8. Bumpers
9. O-ring
10. Bushing and seal housing
11. Clamps
12. Sleeve
13. Hull adapter

The impeller and wear ring can be inspected for wear without removing the jet pump from the hull. If wear or damage is noted, the jet pump must be removed to service these parts.

1. Refer to Step 1 under *Service Precautions* in this chapter to secure the craft for impeller and wear ring inspection.

2. Unbolt and remove the ride plate (**Figure 7**).

3. Remove the screw (**Figure 4**) securing the intake grate to the hull and remove the intake grate.

4. Look through the water inlet opening and check the physical condition of the impeller (2, **Figure 1** or 2, **Figure 2**) and the wear ring (6, **Figure 1** or 1, **Figure 2**). Check for chipped, broken or blunted impeller blades. These conditions will cause the impeller to be out of balance. When out of balance, an impeller will cause wear ring damage. An unbalanced impeller will also damage the impeller shaft (3, **Figure 3**), shaft bearing and seal assembly (4, **Figure 3**) and impeller housing bearings (20 and 22, **Figure 1** or 16 and 18, **Figure 2**).

5. Working from the water inlet opening, check the clearance between the impeller and the wear ring (**Figure 8**) with a feeler gauge. Measure impeller-to-wear ring clearance in at least 3 locations and compare with the specification listed in **Table 1**.

6. If the clearance in Step 5 exceeds the wear limit in **Table 1**, or if the wear ring or impeller

appears damaged, remove the jet pump as described in this chapter.

Intake Grate and Ride Plate Removal/Installation

Remove the ride plate before removing the jet pump.

1. The intake grate is accessible without removing the craft from some trailers. If it is necessary to tip the craft on its side to inspect or clean the intake, observe the following:

    a. Turn the fuel valve OFF.

    b. Remove the seat and engine cover.

    c. Remove the battery.

CAUTION
It is important to raise the right side, not the left, because if the left side is higher than the right, water can run out of the cooling system, through the exhaust ports and into the cylinders.

    d. Tip the craft by lifting the right side, with the left side down.

2. Remove the screws attaching the ride plate (**Figure 9**) to the hull.

NOTE
The ride plate is installed with RTV sealer across the front. The sealer will stick the ride plate to the hull, making removal difficult. However, be sure all retaining screws are removed if the ride plate is difficult to separate from the hull.

3. Pull the ride plate away from the hull.

4A. On 1992-1993 models, hold the lock nut inside the hull (under the driveshaft) and remove the screw (**Figure 10**).

4B. On 1994-on models, screw (**Figure 10**) is threaded into a threaded insert in the hull.

5. Pull the intake grate down and away from the recess in the hull.

6. Reassemble by reversing the disassembly procedure, observing the following:

    a. On 1992-1993 models, seal the screw (**Figure 10**) to the hull with RTV sealer.

    b. On 1994-on models, coat the threads of screw (**Figure 10**) with Loctite 242 (blue) when installing.

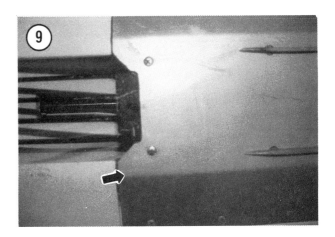

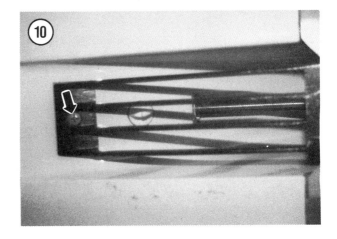

c. Clean and dry the front edge of the ride plate and the mating surface of the hull so that RTV sealer will stick to both surfaces.

NOTE
Any leak in the seal at the front of the ride plate can cause cavitation. Be sure there are no pin holes or gaps in the continuous bead of sealer. Apply sealer to

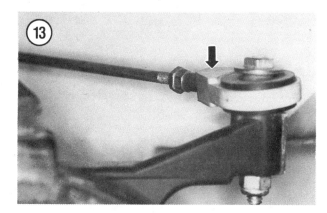

cleaned surfaces just before installing the ride plate.

d. Coat the entire front edge of the ride plate with a continuous bead of RTV sealer.

e. Coat threads of the screws attaching the ride plate with Loctite 242 (blue) before installing.

f. Tighten the ride plate retaining screws securely and wipe any remaining sealer from the hull.

Jet Pump Removal

1. Remove the engine cover. Allow the engine compartment to air out before disconnecting the negative battery lead.

2. Remove the straps retaining the electrical box and remove the electrical box from the top of the battery.

3. Remove the top of the battery carrier and disconnect the negative battery lead. See Chapter Seven.

4. Loosen the clamp (A, **Figure 11**) and remove the cover (B, **Figure 11**).

5. Loosen the hose clamps and detach the coolant hose (A, **Figure 12**) and the bilge siphon hoses (B, **Figure 12**).

6. Refer to Step 1 under *Service Precautions* in this chapter to secure the craft for jet pump removal.

7. Disconnect the steering cable from the steering nozzle. See **Figure 13**.

8. On models with trim adjustment, detach the trim rod (**Figure 14**) from the trim ring.

9. Remove the ride plate as described in this chapter.

NOTE
Sealer is used between the jet pump housing and hull, which may make separation of the housing from the hull difficult.

10. Support the jet pump, so it will not fall when it is detached from the hull.

11. Remove the 4 nuts attaching the jet pump to the hull. The left 2 are shown in **Figure 15**.

12. Pull the jet pump assembly to the rear away from the hull. Refer to **Figure 16**.

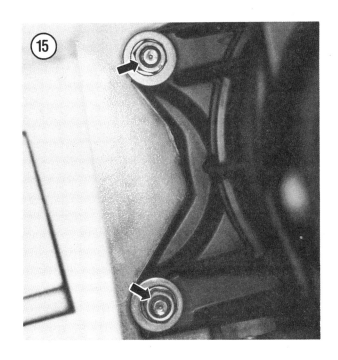

NOTE
The driveshaft may either stay attached to the splines of the engine coupling or it may stay attached to the jet pump impeller. If the driveshaft is stuck in the pump, apply penetrating oil along the driveshaft and into the impeller. Then, hold the driveshaft in one hand and tap around the impeller housing with a soft-faced hammer to separate the driveshaft and impeller. If the driveshaft is stuck in the engine coupling, pull the shaft straight to the rear.

13. If the driveshaft remained in the hull, pull the shaft from the engine coupling and from the bearing and seal assembly.

NOTE
*Do not lose or damage the rubber bumpers located in the ends of the driveshaft or O-ring located ahead of the rear splines of the driveshaft (**Figure 17**). Also, do not lose or damage the seal located in the engine coupler.*

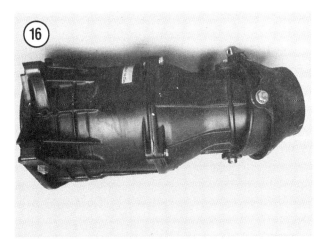

Jet Pump Disassembly

The jet pump for 1992-1993 models (**Figure 1**) is different from the pump used on 1994-on models (**Figure 2**); however, many of the service procedures are the same.

1. Remove the large O-ring located around the pump intake.

2. Remove the 3 O-rings that seal where the water fittings pass through the hull.

3. Loosen the hose clamps and remove the bilge siphon hoses (**Figure 18**).

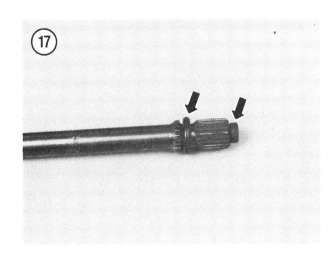

NOTE
*The 4 screws removed in Step 4 attach the rear housing to the pump housing on 1992-1993 models (**Figure 1**). The 4 re-*

moved screws attach the 3 housings together on 1994-on models (**Figure 2**).

4. Remove the 4 screws attaching the rear housing, then separate the housings (**Figure 19**).

5. Remove the screws attaching the cone (**Figure 20**). The cone is retained by 2 screws on
1992-1993 models and 3 screws on 1994-on
models.

NOTE
*The O-ring may secure the cone to the
housing enough to make removal of the
cone difficult.*

6. The impeller is threaded onto the impeller
stub shaft. To remove the impeller, perform the
following:

   a. The Polaris impeller remover (part No.
   2871036) or equivalent is required to remove the impeller. A suitable tool can be
   made from a discarded driveshaft.

CAUTION
*Improper removal will damage parts.
The splines of the tool must fit those in
the impeller properly. Do not use an
impact wrench to loosen the impeller.*

   b. Align the 2 flats on the impeller stub shaft
   in a vise equipped with soft jaws. Tighten
   the vise to lock the stub shaft in place.

   c. Insert the special tool into the impeller splines (**Figure 21**).

   d. Turn the impeller (**Figure 21**) counterclockwise and unscrew the impeller from
   the impeller stub shaft.

   e. Lift the impeller from the housing.

7. Remove the impeller stub shaft from the vise,
then remove the shaft from the bearings and
housing.

8. Further disassembly is not required unless it
is necessary to replace worn or damaged parts.
Refer to *Inspection* this chapter.

Parts Cleaning

1. All RTV residue must be removed from the hull, jet pump, ride plate and intake grate surfaces. To remove silicone:

    a. Before removing silicone from the pump housing (1, **Figure 1**) or bearing housing (3, **Figure 2**), cover both bearings with tape or clean shop rags.

    b. Use a hand scraper to remove as much silicone from the surfaces as possible.

    c. If a commercial silicone remover is used, follow its manufacturer's directions, apply it only to the affected area, then scrape it off. Be careful to keep the stripper from contacting any painted surfaces, because it will damage the paint.

    d. Remove the tape or shop rags from the impeller housing bearings.

2. Clean all silicone, sand or other residue from the threads of screws, studs and threads in housings.

3. Clean parts in solvent and allow to dry thoroughly.

4. Clean all threaded fasteners (bolts and washers) in solvent.

5. Clean water passages thoroughly, then blow low-pressure compressed air through the passages to make sure they are clean.

> *NOTE*
> *The inlet for the engine cooling water is fitted with a screen (**Figure 22**) on 1995-on models. The screen can be installed on 1994 models using kit part No. 5431523. Installing the screen will reduce the possibility of overheating damage to the engine caused by the pump becoming plugged with debris.*

Inspection

Worn or damaged jet pump parts will reduce jet pump thrust and top speed, even if the engine is running correctly. Problems can also be caused by obstructions in the pump. Carefully inspect the jet pump assembly and replace all worn or damaged parts.

Driveshaft

Engine power and thrust is transmitted through the driveshaft (**Figure 23**) to the jet pump. The driveshaft is supported by bearings located in the seal and bearing housing (**Figure 24**). The driveshaft is splined on both ends to mate with the engine coupling at the front and the pump impeller at the rear.

Drive train vibration may indicate a bent driveshaft. A bent driveshaft can also cause dam-

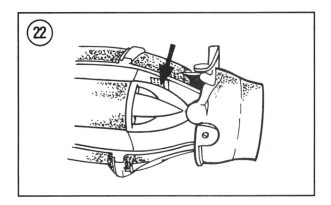

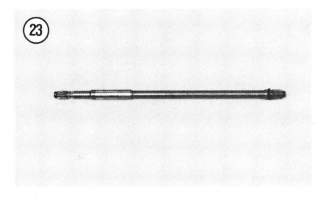

age to the impeller, drive coupling and to the seals and bearings in the housing (**Figure 24**). To check for a bent driveshaft, proceed as follows.

1. Mount the removed driveshaft on V-blocks at points near the splines at the ends.

2. Mount a dial indicator so that it contacts the driveshaft near the center, just behind the bushing and seal surface.

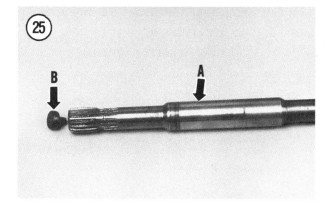

3. Turn the driveshaft slowly and observe the runout indicated by the dial indicator. Runout is the difference between the highest and lowest dial indicator reading.

4. Replace the driveshaft if runout exceeds the maximum allowable runout listed in **Table 1**.

5. Check the bearing and seal surfaces (A, **Figure 25**) for damage. Inspect the splines at the ends of the driveshaft for excessive wear or other damage. Install a new driveshaft if necessary.

6. Replace the bumpers (B, **Figure 25**) if hard or damaged. Driveshaft end play should be within the limits listed in **Table 1** with new bumpers installed.

Impeller stub shaft, bearings and seals

The impeller stub shaft (3, **Figure 1** or 4, **Figure 2**) is supported by 2 bearings in the pump housing (1, **Figure 1**) or bearing housing (3, **Figure 2**). Install 2 seals ahead of the front bearing. A damaged impeller stub shaft and/or bearings will cause excessive vibration. Worn or damaged parts must be replaced.

1. Check the impeller shaft seals (A, **Figure 26**) for wear or other damage. If the surface of the spacer (B, **Figure 26**) is damaged, replace the spacer.

2. Check the bearings (20 and 22, **Figure 1** or 16 and 18, **Figure 2**) for damage by rolling the inner race by hand. Replace damaged bearings as described later in this chapter.

3. Inspect the impeller stub shaft for any damage. Always install a new seal ring (**Figure 27**) during reassembly.

Impeller Stub Shaft Bearings and Seal Replacement

This procedure describes replacement of both bearings and seals at the same time. To replace only the seals, refer to *Impeller Stub Shaft Seal Replacement* this chapter.

5

1. To remove the seals and both bearings from the impeller housing:

   a. First remove the seal spacer (B, **Figure 26**).

   b. Use a long punch and push the spacer (located between the bearings) to the side as shown in **Figure 28** so that the punch can press against the inner race of the rear bearing.

   c. Use a suitable driver inserted through the front against the inner race of the rear bearing (**Figure 28**).

   d. Bump the rear bearing from the housing. The spacer will also be removed.

   e. Insert a proper sized driver through the housing from the rear to push the front bearing and both seals from the housing.

2. Check the bores in the housing for cracks, burrs, gouges or other damage. If necessary, smooth the bore with crocus cloth. Install a new housing if it is cracked or damaged.

3. Clean the bearing bores in the housing thoroughly with solvent, then blow dry.

NOTE
Facing out means that the identification mark on the bearing should be visible when the bearing is installed in the housing.

4. Use a press and a driver that fits against the outer race to install new bearings. Identification marks on bearings must face out (away from housing).

   a. Press the rear bearing into the bore until the outer race is seated in housing bore.

   b. Turn the impeller housing over and install the spacer between the 2 bearings.

   c. Press the front bearing into the bore until it is seated in housing bore.

   d. Pack the cavity of both seals with grease.

   e. Stack the 2 seals (19, **Figure 1** or 15, **Figure 2**) with the spring loaded lips facing up, then insert the seal spacer (B, **Figure 26**) through both seals.

   f. Position the 2 seals (with spacer) over the housing bore, then use a driver that presses against the outer edge of the seals to press both seals into the front of housing bore. Refer to **Figure 28** for the installed view.

Impeller Stub Shaft Seal Replacement

Seals (19, **Figure 1** or 15, **Figure 2**) can be removed and installed from the housing without removing the shaft bearings.

1. Use a seal puller to remove the seals from the housing.

CAUTION
Do not attempt to remove the seal by knocking it out with a punch. This method could damage the bearing and/or the housing.

2. Wipe the housing and the seal with a clean cloth.

3. Pack the cavity of both seals with grease.

4. Stack the 2 seals (19, **Figure 1** or 15, **Figure 2**) with the spring loaded lips facing up, then insert the seal spacer (B, **Figure 26**) through both seals.

5. Position the 2 seals (with spacer) over the housing bore, then use a driver that presses against the outer edge of the seals to press both seals into the front of housing bore. Refer to **Figure 28** for the installed view.

Impeller Inspection

The impeller is the final link between the drive system and the water. A perfectly maintained engine and hull are useless if the impeller is the wrong type or damaged. A severely worn or nicked impeller will cause vibration. The vibration can also damage the wear ring, impeller shaft bearings, impeller shaft and seals.

> *NOTE*
> *The impeller is a 1-piece unit, but it is composed of several different parts. Damage to only 1 blade may not look severe, but can affect the impeller's balance. Keep this in mind when inspecting the impeller.*

1. Visually inspect the impeller (**Figure 29**) for the following conditions:

  a. Blades that are nicked or gouged.

  b. Chipped, cracked or broken impeller blades.

  c. Blunted impeller blade tips.

2. If the impeller is severely worn or damaged, replace it. If damage is minor, smooth damaged areas with an abrasive paper or file.

3. Clean the threads in the impeller with solvent, then use compressed air to remove solvent and all sand and grit. Check the threads for damage.

Impeller Identification

Impellers with 3 blades are used on 1992-1993 models. Impellers with 4 blades are installed on models from 1994-on. All 3 blade impellers are not alike and all 4 blade impellers are not alike. Be sure to check the appropriate parts catalog for specific application.

Wear Ring Inspection and Replacement

A replaceable impeller wear ring (6, **Figure 1**) is installed in the impeller housing on 1992-1993 models. The inside of the replacement wear ring must be machined after installation to provide the correct clearance between the tips of the impeller blades and the wear ring.

Refer to **Table 1** for the recommended operating clearance between the impeller and the wear ring. Because the clearance between the tips of the impeller blades and the wear ring are so close, a loose or damaged impeller will damage the wear ring. Likewise, debris that flows through the jet pump will cause damage in this area. If the clearance becomes too wide, performance will suffer.

> *NOTE*
> *The wear ring shown in **Figure 30** is typical of 1992-1993 models, but the wear ring on later models (1, **Figure 2**) should be similarly inspected for wear or damage.*

1. Inspect the wear ring for deep scratches, excessive wear or damage.

2. If the wear ring is worn or damaged, replace the wear ring as described in the following steps.

3A. On 1994-on models, install a new housing.

3B. On 1992-1993 models, the wear ring can be removed and replaced as follows:

> *CAUTION*
> *It is easy to damage the pump housing, during the following operation. When cutting the wear ring in substep a, work slowly and do not cut into the impeller housing.*

5

a. Very carefully cut the wear ring with a die grinder or hack saw at 2 locations 180° apart.

b. The wear ring can then be removed from the housing.

c. Clean and inspect the housing for damage. Check the surface for cracks or other damage.

d. Spray the outer surface of the wear ring with a penetrating lubricant.

NOTE
Use a flat steel plate over the wear ring and a hydraulic press to push the wear ring into the housing. The thin metal ring can be easily damaged while attempting to install it.

e. Align the wear ring with the impeller housing bore and press the new wear ring into the housing until it is fully seated. Check to make sure the wear ring is evenly seated all the way around.

f. Machine the inside of the wear ring to provide the proper clearance for the impeller. Refer to **Table 1**.

Main Component Inspection

1. Inspect the ride plate (**Figure 31**) and intake grate (**Figure 32**) for severe wear or cracks.

2. To check the rear housing:

a. Check the housing for dents.

b. Inspect the machined surfaces for burrs, cracks or other damage. Repair minor damage with a fine-cut file or oilstone.

c. Check threaded holes for stripping, cross-threading or contamination. Remove all sand and other residue with compressed air.

3. Inspect the intake scoop located in the hull ahead of the pump. If damaged, refer to *Intake Scoop Replacement* in this chapter.

4. Check for cracked or damaged vanes in the pump housing (1, **Figure 1**) or bearing housing (3, **Figure 2**).

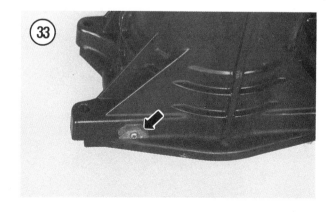

5. Check the condition of the sacrificial anode (**Figure 33**). If the anode is badly eroded or broken off, it must be replaced.

6. To check the steering nozzle (**Figure 34**):

   a. Check the bushings (A, **Figure 35**) for excessive wear.

   b. Check the pivot bolts (B, **Figure 35**) for excessive wear or thread damage.

   c. Check the thrust washers (C, **Figure 35**) for wear or damage.

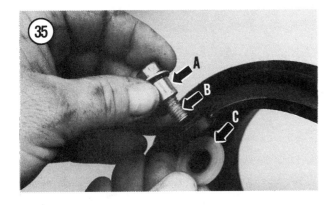

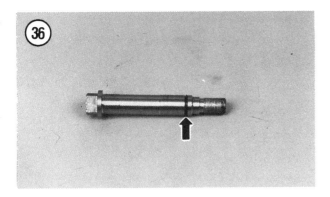

   d. Check the steering nozzle mounting tabs for damage.

   e. Check the steering cable (A, **Figure 34**) and trim rod (B, **Figure 34**, if used) for wear or damage. Make sure that connections are not loose.

7. Replace all worn or damaged parts.

Jet Pump Assembly

Refer to **Figure 1** or **Figure 2** for your model when performing the following.

1. Prior to assembly, perform the inspection procedures in this chapter to make sure all worn or defective parts have been repaired or replaced. Thoroughly clean all parts before assembly or installation.

2. Install a new O-ring (**Figure 36**) in the groove of the impeller stub shaft.

> *NOTE*
> *Make sure the seal spacer (B, **Figure 26**) is in place before inserting the stub shaft. The spacer should be in place when pressing the 2 new seals into the housing and should not be removed unless new seals are being installed. Removal may cause leakage.*

3. Apply marine grease to the impeller stub shaft and O-ring, then carefully insert the shaft from the rear, through the seals and bearings.

4. Install the outer O-ring (**Figure 37**). Be careful when passing the O-ring over the shaft threads.

5. Clamp the 2 flats of the impeller stub shaft in a vise. Tighten the vise to hold the shaft and the housing in place.

6. Coat the threads of the impeller stub shaft with antiseize compound.

> *NOTE*
> *A special tool (part No. 2871036), shown in **Figure 38**, is available to engage the splines of the impeller so the proper torque can be applied.*

7. Install the impeller and tighten to the torque listed in **Table 2**.

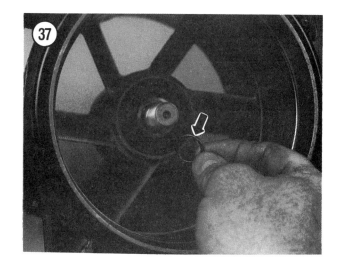

CAUTION
Do not use an impact wrench to tighten the impeller in Step 7.

8. Remove the stub shaft from the vise after the impeller is tightened.

9. Install a new O-ring (**Figure 39**) in the groove of the cone.

10. Coat the O-ring and housing bore with marine grease.

11. Insert the cone into the housing and install the retaining screws. Two retaining screws are used on 1992-1993 models; 3 screws are used to retain the cone on 1994-on models.

12A. On 1992-1993 models, attach the rear housing (4, **Figure 1**) to the main housing (1, **Figure 1**).

12B. On 1994-on models, attach the front housing (1, **Figure 2**), the bearing housing (3, **Figure 2**) and the rear housing (5, **Figure 2**). Install the screws (20, **Figure 2**), clamping the sections together, finger tight. Make sure that alignment is correct before tightening the clamping screws.

13. Turn the impeller by hand. It should rotate freely and there should be no noticeable wobble or noise.

Jet Pump Installation

The pump must be sealed to the hull. Make sure that all old sealer is removed before installing new sealer. Make sure that the proper type of sealer is used. Remove all of the old O-rings and carefully install new O-rings (A, B and C, **Figure 40**). The old O-rings may be stuck to the hull.

NOTE
Coat the threads of the pump mounting studs with antiseize compound before installing the self locking nuts.

DRIVE SYSTEM   **165**

1. Make sure that the pump mounting studs are tightened against the hull. Self locking nuts are located inside the hull.

NOTE
The pump mounting studs have hexagon lugs that can be used to hold the stud while tightening the retaining nuts.

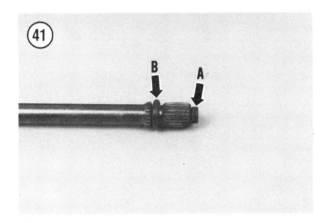

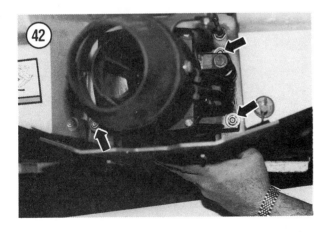

These hexagon lugs on the studs fit inside reliefs in the pump housing. If the studs are not turned to the proper position, the hexagon lugs can prevent the pump from fitting against the hull. Be sure the studs are properly positioned when installing the pump.

2. Coat the threads of the mounting studs with antiseize compound.

3. Lubricate the O-rings (**Figure 40**) with marine grease.

4. Make sure to install the driveshaft as described in Chapter Four, if removed.

    a. Check the driveshaft to be sure the bumper (A, **Figure 41**) in each end is in place and in good condition.

    b. Make sure the O-ring (B, **Figure 41**) is in place and in good condition.

NOTE
*The splines at each end of the driveshaft is different. The groove for the O-ring (B, **Figure 41**) is located at the rear (pump) end.*

    c. Lubricate the splines at both ends of the driveshaft and the bushing and seal journal.

    d. Insert the driveshaft through the seals and bearing and into the splines of the engine rear coupling.

    e. Make sure the driveshaft is completely seated in the engine coupling and the bumper (A, **Figure 41**) is in place at the rear of the installed driveshaft.

5. Position the jet pump against the hull over the mounting studs and the driveshaft. Make sure the pump fits snugly against the hull. Refer to the NOTE following Step 1.

6. Install and tighten the 4 retaining nuts to the torque listed in **Table 2**. Three of the 4 retaining nuts are shown in **Figure 42**.

7. Turn the engine coupling until the grease fitting (A, **Figure 43**) is toward the top.

8. Turn the driveshaft bearing and seal housing until the grease fitting (B, **Figure 43**) is toward the top, then tighten the rear clamps.

9. Install the driveshaft cover with the slot toward the top.

10. Inject marine grease into fittings (A and B, **Figure 43**) until grease comes from the coupling and the seal housing.

11. Turn the driveshaft cover until the slot is down, then tighten the clamp (C, **Figure 43**).

12. Attach the bilge siphon hoses to the lower fittings (B, **Figure 40**) and tighten the hose clamps.

13. Attach the engine cooling hose (**Figure 44**) to the fitting and tighten the hose clamp.

14. Attach the steering control cable (A, **Figure 34**) and the trim rod (B, **Figure 34**) if so equipped. Refer to Chapter Three for adjustment of the steering controls.

NOTE
The ride plate must be sealed to the hull, using Loctite Superflex or similar silicone sealer.

15. Install and seal the ride plate as described in *Ride Plate and Intake Grate Installation* in this chapter.

Driveshaft Alignment

The engine support and the 4 rubber engine mounts are critical parts of the water vehicle's drive train. Damaged or loose engine mounts will allow the engine to shift or pull out of alignment during operation. Engine misalignment will result in excessive engine vibration and reduced performance. Shims located under the engine mounts are used to align the engine with the jet pump drive. If shims are identified as they are removed and each is reinstalled in its original location, alignment will not be changed. If alignment is wrong, the engine must be removed to change the position of alignment shims. Refer to *Engine/Jet Pump Alignment* in Chapter Four.

Driveshaft Removal and Installation

1. Remove the jet pump as described in this paragraph.

2. If the driveshaft remains with the engine and hull, pull the driveshaft straight to the rear to remove it. If the driveshaft remains with the jet pump, pull the driveshaft straight out of the impeller splines.

3. Loosen the clamps and remove the driveshaft center bearing and seal assembly.

4. Remove the drive coupling from the rear of the crankshaft as outlined in Chapter Four, if removal is required.

5. Check the driveshaft splines for damage.

6. Inspect the rubber bumpers (A, **Figure 41**) at the ends of the driveshaft for damage.

7. Inspect the O-ring (B, **Figure 41**) located at the impeller end of the driveshaft for damage.

8. Check the bearing surface of the driveshaft for wear or scoring.

9. Check the driveshaft for straightness as follows.

   a. Position the driveshaft on precision V blocks near the splined ends of the driveshaft.

   b. Locate the indicator pin of a dial indicator just behind the bushing journal.

   c. Rotate the driveshaft and check for runout indicated by the dial indicator. Runout should not exceed the limit listed in **Table 1**.

10. Install new rubber bumpers and O-ring (A and B, **Figure 41**).

11. If removed, install the drive coupler to the rear of the engine crankshaft as outlined in Chapter Four.

12. Install the driveshaft seal and bearing assembly, leaving the clamps loose.

13. Check the driveshaft to be sure that the bumpers are in place in the ends of the shaft.

14. Lubricate the driveshaft, then insert the driveshaft through the seals and bearing and into the splines of the engine coupling.

15. Install the jet pump as described in this chapter.

16. Turn the bearing and seal housing until the grease fitting (B, **Figure 43**) is toward the top, then tighten clamps.

17. Turn the engine coupling until the grease fitting (A, **Figure 43**) is toward the top.

18. Install the driveshaft cover with the slot toward the top.

19. Grease the engine coupling and the bearing and seal housing.

20. Turn the driveshaft cover until the slot is down, then tighten the clamp (C, **Figure 43**).

Intake Scoop Replacement

The water intake scoop for the jet pump must be completely sealed to the hull with Loctite Ultra Blue silicone sealer or equivalent. Apply a 13 mm (1/2 in.) or wider continuous bead of sealer to the contact areas of the hull, then press the intake scoop into position. Wipe off any excess sealer, then complete the assembly. Allow the sealant to cure 12 hours before operating the craft.

DRIVESHAFT BEARING, SEALS AND HOUSING

The seal and bearing housing (**Figure 45**) is clamped to the driveshaft tunnel in the hull. The assembly seals and supports the driveshaft between the engine and the jet pump. The bearing and seal assembly consists of the carrier housing, a bearing and 2 seals. Install a new assembly if any part is damaged.

Removal

1. Remove the jet pump and driveshaft as described in this chapter.

2. Loosen the clamp retaining the housing in the attaching hose.

3. Pull the bearing housing assembly from the hose.

4. Loosen the clamp retaining the hose to the hull attaching coupling, then pull the hose from coupling.

Inspection

1. Clean all sealer residue from the housing, seal carrier and hull mating surfaces.
2. Visually check both carrier seals for excessive wear or damage.
3. Visually check the bearing for damage. Also check the bearing journal of the driveshaft.
4. If damaged, install a new bushing, seal and housing assembly.
5. The coupling attached to the hull should be securely attached to the hull. If loose, attach the coupling using a 2 part structural adhesive such as 3M part No. 08101.

Installation

1. Apply Loctite 587 Superflex Ultra Blue around the inside of the connecting hose.
2. Slide the hose onto the hull coupling. Make sure the hose is fully on and is aligned with the engine rear coupling.
3. Install and tighten the clamps to hold the hose to the hull coupling. Allow the sealer to cure before proceeding to Step 4.
4. Insert the bearing housing assembly into the front of the hose.
5. Make sure the grease fitting (B, **Figure 43**) is up and align the bearing with the engine coupling. Then install and tighten the hose clamp to secure the bearing housing in the hose.
6. To complete installation, follow the procedures described under *Jet Pump Installation* in this chapter.

ELECTRIC QUICK TRIM SYSTEM

Some models are equipped with an electric trim system actuated by a thumb operated switch (**Figure 46**) located on the left handle bar. The switch controls a trim motor (**Figure 47**) located at the rear of the craft to raise or lower the trim ring (**Figure 48**) attached to the jet pump steering nozzle for optimum performance. The trim angle

of the jet nozzle can be changed to compensate for the different weight of riders or loads.

Major components include the control switch (**Figure 46**), electric trim motor (**Figure 47**) and the trim adjusting ring (**Figure 48**). Electrical wires connect the switch to the trim motor and a connecting rod (**Figure 49**) relays the movement of the trim motor to the trim ring. A cable con-

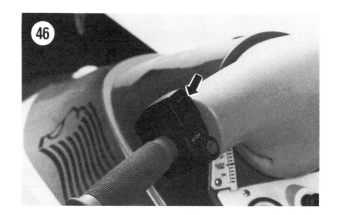

nects the trim indicator (**Figure 50**) to a lever on the trim motor to show the operator the relative position of the trim nozzle.

Pushing the lower part of the switch (**Figure 46**), lowers the trim nozzle, forcing the bow of the vehicle down. Pushing the top of the switch, raises the nozzle, raising the bow of the vehicle.

Troubleshooting

If the trim motor does not operate or operates in only 1 direction, proceed as follows.

1. Remove the seat and engine cover.

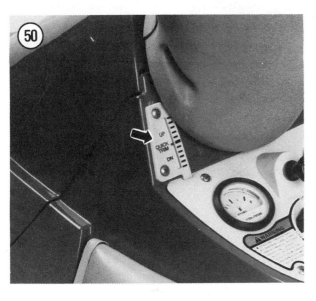

2. Unbolt the cover from the trim motor (**Figure 47**).

3. Detach the 2 wires from the trim motor.

4. Temporarily connect a jumper wire from 1 of the trim motor wires to 1 of the battery terminals.

5. Temporarily connect a jumper wire from the second wire attached to the trim motor to the other battery terminal.

6. Observe if the motor runs or does not run.

7. Switch the connection of the temporarily attached jumper wires on the battery. The trim motor should operate in the reverse direction.

8. If the motor only operates in 1 direction (Step 5 or Step 7) or if the motor does not operate in either direction, remove the motor as described in this chapter.

9. If the motor operates satisfactorily in both directions, proceed to Step 10.

10. Check the electrical wires to the handle bar mounted switch and the wires from the switch.

   a. Make sure the black wire to the trim switch is grounded (negative).

   b. Make sure the orange wire to the trim switch is provided with positive voltage.

   c. Determine the cause if voltage is not properly supplied to the switch through the black and orange wires.

11. If the wires are satisfactory, check the condition of the blue/white and green/white wires from the switch.

12. If the condition of the blue/white and green/white wires from the switch are satisfactory, replace the trim switch.

Trim Motor Removal and Installation

The trim motor is located in the rear of the craft as shown in (**Figure 47**).

1. Remove the seat and engine cover.

2. Unbolt the cover from the trim motor (**Figure 47**).

3. Remove bolt (A, **Figure 51**) that attaches the trim rod to the operating lever of the trim motor.

The trim rod is also attached to the trim ring on the jet pump nozzle.

4. Remove the 3 screws (B, **Figure 51**) that attach the trim motor to the hull.

5. Lift the trim motor up from the hull. The cable to the trim indicator and the electrical wires to the control switch will still be attached.

6. Detach the 2 wires from the trim motor.

7. Push the operating lever up (in) and remove the pin (C, **Figure 51**), then remove the operating lever from the motor shaft.

8. Loosen the screw attaching the indicator cable to the operating lever, then detach the cable and housing.

NOTE
Attach the electrical wires to the trim motor and test operation before attaching the trim motor to the hull.

9. Install the trim motor by reversing the removal procedure.

Trim Ring Removal/Installation

The trim ring (**Figure 48**) is attached to the steering nozzle.

1. Remove cotter pin, then detach the trim rod (A, **Figure 51**) from the trim ring.

2. Remove the 2 pivot screws (A, **Figure 52**) securing the trim ring to the steering nozzle, then, remove the trim ring.

3. Clean all sealer residue from the pivot and mounting screws.

4. Inspect the arms of the trim ring for cracks or other damage.

5. Check the trim ring for cracks or other damage.

6. Install the trim ring on the steering nozzle so the pivot for the control rod is positioned at the top of the nozzle.

7. Apply Loctite 242 (blue) to both trim ring screws, then install and tighten the screws.

8. Attach the trim control rod (B, **Figure 52**) and install the retaining cotter pin.

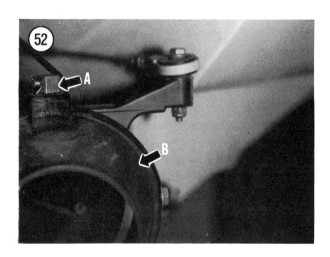

Table 1 SERVICE CLEARANCES

	Desired mm (in.)	Wear limit mm (in.)
Pump impeller to wear ring	0.05-0.20 (0.002-0.008)	0.51 (0.020)
Driveshaft		
Runout *	–	0.13 (0.005)
Driveshaft end play **	–	2.5-5.1 (0.1-0.2)

* Support driveshaft near ends and measure runout near the center behind the bushing and seal journal.
** With new bumpers installed in both ends of the driveshaft.

Table 2 TIGHTENING TORQUES

	N·m	ft.-lb.
Impeller	135.6	100
Pump to hull	38	28
Other fasteners		
5 mm	5.1-5.9	3.8-4.3 (45-52 in.-lb.)
6 mm	7.5-8.8	5.5-6.5 (66-78 in.-lb.)
8 mm	17.6-21.7	13-16
10 mm	35.2-40.7	26-30
12 mm	54.2-59.7	40-44

5

Chapter Six

Fuel System

This chapter includes removal and repair procedures for the carburetors, fuel pump and fuel tank. Refer to Chapter Three for carburetor adjustment. **Tables 1-2** are at the end of this chapter.

> *WARNING*
> *Because of the explosive and flammable conditions that exist around gasoline, always observe the following precautions:*

1. Immediately after removing the engine cover, check for the odor of raw gasoline fumes. If strong fumes can be smelled, determine the source and correct the problem.

2. Allow the engine compartment to air out before beginning work.

3. Disconnect the battery cable from the negative (ground) terminal of the battery before working on the fuel system.

4. Gasoline dripping onto a hot engine component may cause a fire. Always allow the engine to cool completely before working on any fuel system component.

5. Wipe up spilled gasoline immediately using dry rags. Store the gasoline soaked rags in a suitable metal container until they can be cleaned or disposed of. Never store gasoline or solvent-soaked rags in the hull.

6. Do not service any fuel system component while in the vicinity of open flames, sparks or while anyone is smoking near the work area.

7. Do not use any type of electric powered tool in the hull or on the watercraft until the fuel

system has been checked for leaks, and if found, repaired and the system retested.

8. Always have a Coast Guard approved fire extinguisher close at hand while working on the engine.

FUEL SYSTEM IDENTIFICATION

You must disconnect a number of fuel lines and hoses when removing many of the fuel system components for service. The first step when servicing the fuel system is to label all of the hoses. As you disconnect a hose, identify it and record its location on the label and attach the label to the hose. Identifying each hose as it is disconnected helps during reassembly. You can make labels with strips of masking tape and a permanent marking pen. A permanent marking pen should be used because many ink marks, as well as lead pencil marks, fade on the tape. Check to make sure that ink from the marking pen does not smear when coated with gasoline or oil.

When servicing the fuel system, refer to the fuel system diagram for your model as listed below. Compare the fuel system drawing to the fuel system hose routing in your water vehicle. There may be differences, especially if you purchased the vehicle second hand, but differences may also be due to normal production changes. Note and record any discrepancies on the appropriate drawing for reassembly reference.

   a. **Figure 1**: 1992-1993 models.
   b. **Figure 2**: 1994 SL 650 and SL 750 models.
   c. **Figure 3**: 1994 SLT 750 models and all 1995 models.

AIR INTAKE SILENCER AND FLAME ARRESTOR

The air intake silencer and flame arrestor assembly consists of the flame arrestor screen, cover, silencer housing, gasket, air inlet and fasteners. Routine service requires removal of the

flame arrestor only. If carburetor removal is required, the housing must also be removed. Before removing the housing, make sure to have a new gasket on hand for reassembly. The air silencer (**Figure 4**) and flame arrestor must be installed whenever the engine is running.

Removal

1. Read the WARNING at the beginning of this chapter.

2. Remove the seat and engine cover.

3. Disconnect the negative battery cable.

4. Loosen the clamp (**Figure 5**) and remove the air intake from the air silencer.

5. Remove the 6 screws attaching the cover, then lift the cover from the air intake silencer housing.

6. Lift the flame arrestor (**Figure 6**) from the housing.

7. If necessary, remove the silencer housing as follows:

   a. Pull the choke knob out to close the chokes and prevent objects from falling into the carburetors.

> *NOTE*
> *Be prepared to plug the lines and fittings as hoses are detached in the following substeps b through f. Plugging the openings will prevent fuel or oil from leaking into the hull. It will also prevent dirt from entering the openings.*

   b. On 1995 and later models, loosen the spring clamps on the hoses to the 3 oil injector check valves located in the silencer housing, then detach the hoses from the check valves. Refer to **Figure 7**.

   c. Detach the vacuum line from the automatic shutoff valve (A, **Figure 8**). This vacuum line is attached to the reed valve housing (A, **Figure 9**).

6

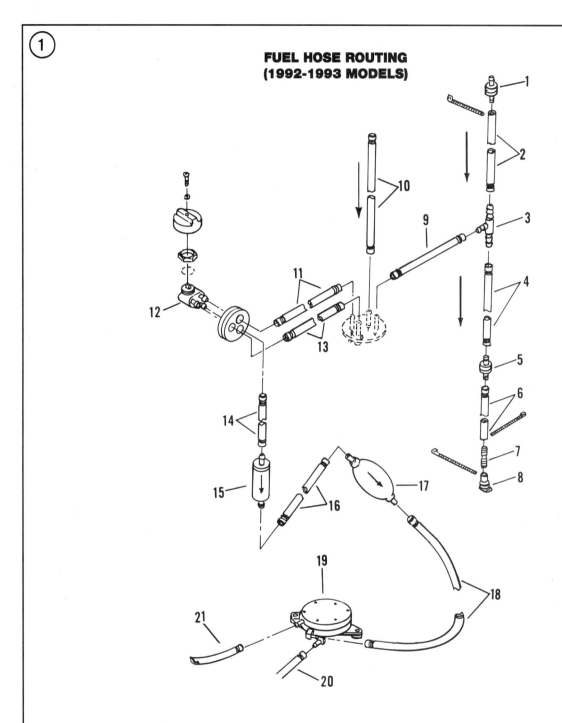

① **FUEL HOSE ROUTING**
(1992-1993 MODELS)

1. Check valve	8. Vent fitting	15. Fuel filter
2. Fuel vent hose	9. Fuel vent hose	16. Fuel hose to pump
3. T fitting	10. Fuel return hose	17. Fuel primer (1992 only)
4. Fuel vent hose	11. Fuel reserve hose	18. Fuel hose to pump
5. Expansion check valve	12. Fuel valve	19. Fuel pump
6. Fuel vent hose	13. Fuel on valve	20. Impulse line to crankcase
7. Fitting	14. Fuel hose to pump	21. Fuel pressure line

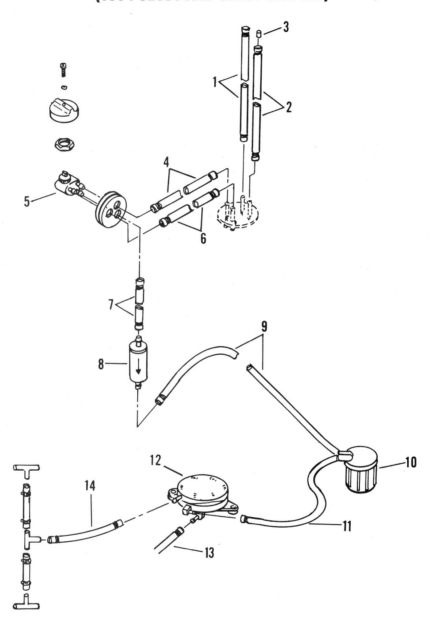

**FUEL HOSE
(1994 SL650 AND SL750 MODELS)**

1. Fuel vent hose
2. Fuel return hose
3. Restrictor orifice
4. Fuel reserve hose
5. Fuel valve
6. Fuel on valve
7. Fuel hose to pump

8. Fuel filter
9. Fuel hose to pump
10. Water/fuel separator
11. Fuel hose to pump
12. Fuel pump
13. Impulse line to crankcase
14. Fuel pressure line to carburetors

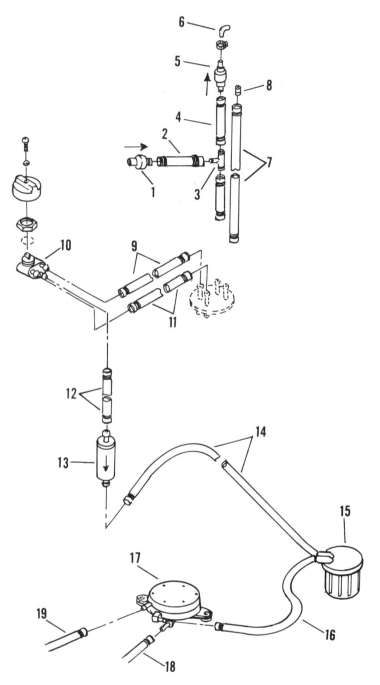

③

**FUEL HOSE
(1994 SLT750 AND ALL 1995 MODELS)**

1. Check valve
2. Fuel vent hose
3. T fitting
4. Fuel vent hose
5. Expansion check valve
6. Hose to vent fitting
7. Fuel return hose
8. Restrictor orifice
9. Fuel reserve hose
10. Fuel valve
11. Fuel on hose
12. Fuel hose to pump
13. Fuel filter
14. Fuel hose to pump
15. Water/fuel separator
16. Fuel hose to pump
17. Fuel pump
18. Impulse line to crankcase
19. Fuel pressure line to carburetors

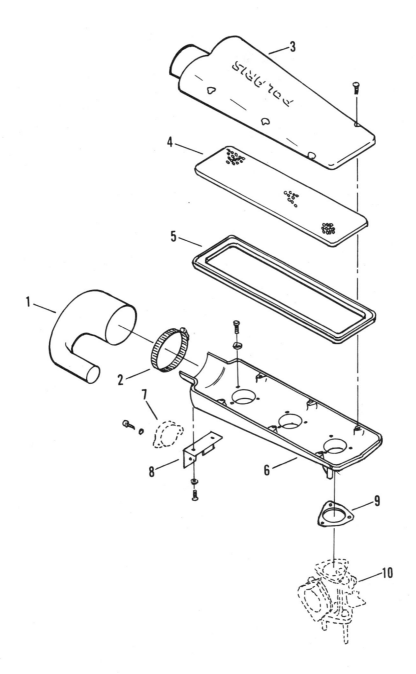

AIR INLET SILENCER AND FLAME ARRESTOR

1. Air inlet
2. Clamp
3. Cover
4. Flame arrestor
5. Gasket
6. Silencer housing
7. Fuel pump
8. Pump mount
9. Carburetor gaskets
10. Carburetors

6

WARNING
Before disconnecting any fuel lines, loosen the fuel filler cap to relieve pressure in the fuel tank.

d. Detach the fuel pressure line (B, **Figure 8**) from the fitting (B, **Figure 9**).

e. Detach the vacuum pulse line from the fuel pump fitting (**Figure 10**). The pulse line is attached to the engine crankcase (C, **Figure 9**).

f. Detach the fuel supply line from the fitting (C, **Figure 8**) on the pump.

g. Remove the 9 screws securing the silencer housing to the carburetors, then lift the housing and the fuel pump from the carburetors.

Cleaning

1. Clean the flame arrestor element (**Figure 6**). Check the flame arrestor for cracks or other damage. Replace if necessary.

2. Clean all sealer residue from the mounting fasteners and from the holder and carburetor mating surfaces.

3. Remove sealer residue from the air silencer cover and housing surfaces.

NOTE
The air intake should not be modified or damaged in any way. Changes to the air intake will change the air/fuel mixture delivered by the carburetors to the engine. Changes will not be uniform and may cause damage to the engine.

Installation

1. Position new gaskets between the silencer housing and the tops of the carburetors.

2. Install the silencer housing and install all 9 of the attaching screws.

3. Remove the screws 1 at a time, coat the threads with Loctite 242, then install the attaching screws, tightening each securely.

4. Attach all of the fuel and vacuum lines.

a. On 1995 and later models, attach the oil injector hoses to the 3 oil injector check valves located in the silencer housing, then secure the hoses with clamps. Refer to **Figure 7**.

NOTE
If the oil has been allowed to drain from the oil injection lines, fill the lines with

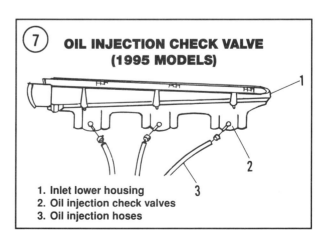

OIL INJECTION CHECK VALVE (1995 MODELS)

1. Inlet lower housing
2. Oil injection check valves
3. Oil injection hoses

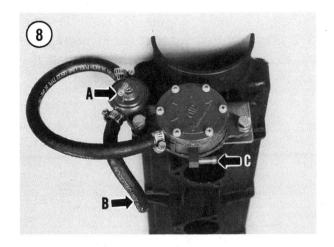

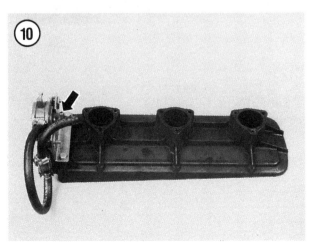

*oil before attaching to the check valves (**Figure 7**) in the silencer housing. Failure to fill the lines with oil can cause serious engine damage. If the lines were properly plugged when disconnected, the lines will remain filled. Refer to Chapter Eight for bleeding air from the oil injection system.*

b. Attach the vacuum line (A, **Figure 9**) to the automatic shut-off valve (A, **Figure 8**). This vacuum line is attached to the reed valve housing.

c. Attach the fuel pressure line (B, **Figure 8**) to the fitting (B, **Figure 9**).

d. Attach the vacuum pulse line for the fuel pump (C, **Figure 9**) to the fitting (**Figure 10**) on the pump. The pulse line is attached to the engine crankcase.

e. Attach the fuel supply line from the tank to the fitting (C, **Figure 8**) of the pump.

CAUTION
Check that all hoses are routed properly and do not have any sharp bends or kinks. Hoses should be positioned away from engine components that could cause damage.

5. Install the gasket around the flame arrestor element and install the silencer housing.

6. Apply a thin, even coat of Loctite Superflex or similar silicone sealer to the surface between the silencer housing and the cover, then position the cover on the housing.

7. Install the cover attaching screws and tighten securely.

8. Slide the air intake over the silencer, then install and tighten the clamp (**Figure 5**). The opening of the air intake should be down, toward the driveshaft.

9. Start the engine and check for fuel leaks. Correct any leaks before proceeding.

6

CARBURETORS

Three Mikuni BN, diaphragm carburetors and a single fuel pump assembly are used on all models.

Removal/Installation

All 3 carburetors must be removed together.
1. Read the WARNING at the beginning of this chapter.
2. Remove the seat and engine cover.
3. Disconnect the negative battery cable.
4. Remove the air intake silencer and flame arrestor as described in this chapter.

> *WARNING*
> *Before disconnecting any fuel lines, loosen the fuel filler cap to relieve any pressure in the fuel tank.*

5. Detach the throttle and choke control cables from the front carburetor.

> *CAUTION*
> *The ends of the oil pump control rod on 1995-on models pop into holes in the control levers and is removed by pulling the rod end straight out. The control rod ends are usually damaged by removing and the manufacturer suggests that a new rod be installed, if removed. The engine may be damaged because of lack of lubrication if the rod becomes detached during operation.*

6. On 1995-on models, disconnect the control rod from the oil injection pump.
7. Remove the 6 nuts (**Figure 11**) and lift the carburetors from the engine.
8A. On 1992-1993 models, remove the gaskets (A, **Figure 12**), the mount plate (B, **Figure 12**) and the second set of gaskets.
8B. On 1994-on models, remove the gaskets located between the carburetor bases and the reed valve manifold.
9. Install new gaskets between the carburetor bases and the reed manifolds. On 1992-1993

models, gaskets (A, **Figure 12**) are located on both sides of the mount plate (B, **Figure 12**).
10. Reinstall the carburetors by reversing the removal procedure.

> *WARNING*
> *Check to make sure there is no fuel leakage.*

> *CAUTION*
> *Check the routing of all hoses. They must be routed properly and without any sharp bends or kinks. Hoses must be positioned away from engine components that could cause damage.*

11. Adjust the throttle and choke cables as described in Chapter Three.

Carburetor Disassembly

Refer to **Figure 13** when servicing the carburetor assembly.

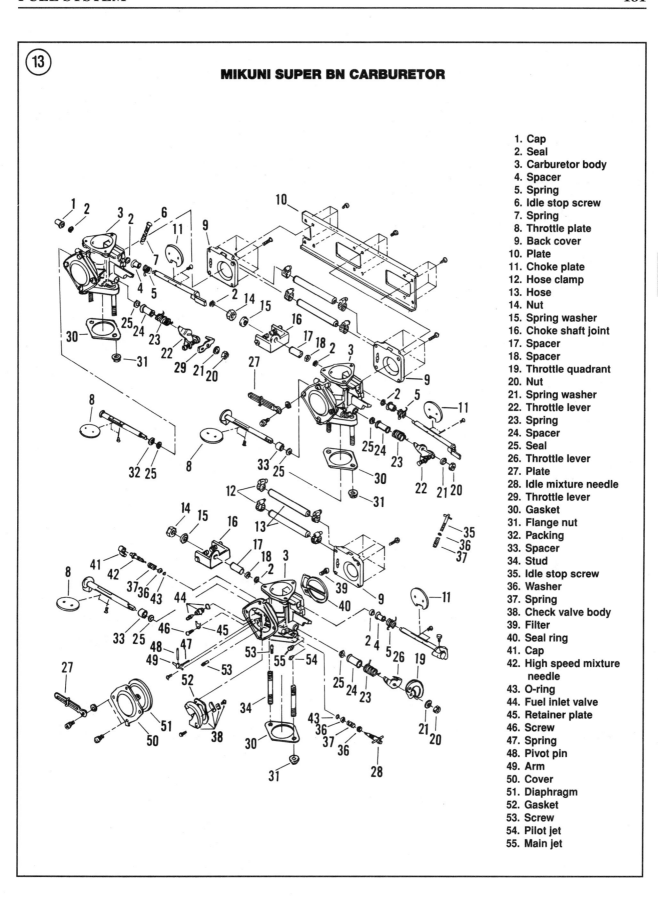

MIKUNI SUPER BN CARBURETOR

1. Cap
2. Seal
3. Carburetor body
4. Spacer
5. Spring
6. Idle stop screw
7. Spring
8. Throttle plate
9. Back cover
10. Plate
11. Choke plate
12. Hose clamp
13. Hose
14. Nut
15. Spring washer
16. Choke shaft joint
17. Spacer
18. Spacer
19. Throttle quadrant
20. Nut
21. Spring washer
22. Throttle lever
23. Spring
24. Spacer
25. Seal
26. Throttle lever
27. Plate
28. Idle mixture needle
29. Throttle lever
30. Gasket
31. Flange nut
32. Packing
33. Spacer
34. Stud
35. Idle stop screw
36. Washer
37. Spring
38. Check valve body
39. Filter
40. Seal ring
41. Cap
42. High speed mixture needle
43. O-ring
44. Fuel inlet valve
45. Retainer plate
46. Screw
47. Spring
48. Pivot pin
49. Arm
50. Cover
51. Diaphragm
52. Gasket
53. Screw
54. Pilot jet
55. Main jet

6

NOTE
Do not relocate the carburetors. Mark each carburetor before disassembling to indicate its cylinder location. The choke and throttle shafts should not be removed from the carburetors. Keep parts from the 3 carburetors separate. Do not mix parts even though they may appear to be identical.

1. Remove the screws (**Figure 14**) attaching the fuel chamber covers to the carburetor bodies. Separate each of the carburetors from the fuel rail and covers.

2. Remove the seal rings (40, **Figure 13**).

3. Remove the filter screen (**Figure 15**) from each carburetor.

4. Remove the screws (**Figure 16**) attaching the covers to the carburetors.

5. Remove the gasket and fuel control diaphragm (**Figure 17**).

6. Remove the pivot pin screw (A, **Figure 18**).

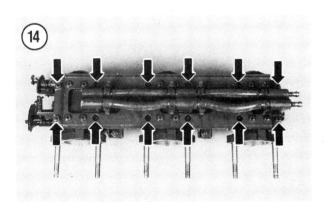

7. Carefully lift the control arm, pivot pin and fuel inlet needle from the carburetor body. Refer to **Figure 19**.

8. Remove the spring (**Figure 20**).

9. Remove screw (B, **Figure 18**) and retaining plate, then lift the fuel inlet valve seat from the carburetor. Refer to **Figure 21**.

10. Remove the screws (A, **Figure 22**) securing the check valve body (B) to the carburetor body.

NOTE
Remove the check valve body if water is suspected to have entered the fuel system. Water can become trapped in this area and will not pass through the jets.

11. Remove the check valve body (B, **Figure 22**) from the carburetor body.

12. Loosen and remove the main jet and its O-ring (**Figure 23**).

13. Loosen and remove the pilot jet (**Figure 24**)

NOTE
*Before removing the low-speed mixture screw (C, **Figure 18**), check **Table 1** for the standard setting for your model.*

14. Turn the low-speed mixture screw (C, **Figure 18**) IN (clockwise) and count the number of turns required to seat the needle lightly. Record the number of turns or part turns to seat the low-speed mixture screw, then remove the screw, spring, washer and O-ring.

6

15. Do not attempt to remove the throttle or choke valves or shafts.

Cleaning and Inspection

Always use new O-rings, gaskets and seals when reassembling.

1. Thoroughly clean and dry all parts. Because seals are used at the choke and throttle shaft positions, use a cleaner that does not damage rubber and plastic parts. Alloy and metal parts removed from the carburetor housing can be soaked in carburetor cleaner. Follow the manufacturer's suggested soak time, then remove and wash parts with hot soapy water and rinse a final time with cold, clear water. If you do not have compressed air, place all of the carburetor parts on a clean lint-free cloth and allow them to air dry.

2. Remove all gasket residue and check that all fuel and vent passages are clear. Clean with compressed air, if necessary. Do not use wire to clean any of the orifices; wire will enlarge them and change fuel flow rates.

3. Check the fuel control diaphragm (**Figure 17**) for flexibility, tearing or pin holes. Replace if necessary.

4. Inspect the fuel control lever (**Figure 19**) and replace if excessively worn.

5. Replace the fuel control spring (**Figure 20**) if damaged or weakened.

6. Check the taper on the fuel inlet valve needle and valve seat (44, **Figure 13**) for wear, scratches or other damage. Replace the seat and needle as a set if either part is defective.

7. Inspect the check valve and check valve body for wear or damage. The check valve must be flat and not distorted to seal properly against the seat. Install a new valve if it is warped or distorted. If the valve does not close properly, the engine may be difficult to start. A cylinder can also be damaged by a lean fuel condition. Always install a new gasket when assembling.

8. Check the tapered end of the low-speed mixture screw (C, **Figure 18**) for wear grooves or a damaged tip. Inspect the O-ring and replace if worn or damaged.

9. Operate the choke and throttle shafts by hand and check the movement and operation of both shafts. Shafts should move smoothly, but should not be loose. Check for damage to the shaft, plates (throttle or choke) and other shaft components. Choke and throttle shaft assemblies should not be removed and components are not available for service.

10. Check the screw thread holes in the carburetor body. Minor thread damage may be repaired with the correct size tap.

11. Check for a loose welch plugs (**Figure 25**). Reseat the plug with a punch and hammer and recheck.

12. On 1994-on models, inspect the small orifice (3, **Figure 2** or 8, **Figure 3**) in the return line. If the orifice is missing or too large, the carburetors may operate too lean. Correct orifice size is 0.4 mm (0.02 in.) diameter.

Assembly

Refer to **Figure 13** when assembling the carburetor.

1. Install the washer, spring, washer and O-ring onto the low-speed mixture screw (C, **Figure 18**) and thread it into the carburetor. Turn the screw clockwise until it seats lightly, then back the screw out the number of turns listed in **Table 1**.

Compare the setting listed in **Table 1** and the original setting recorded during removal. If the original setting is significantly different than listed in **Table 1**, determine the cause before proceeding.

> *CAUTION*
> *Do not seat the low-speed mixture screw too hard or the tip (and probably the seat in the carburetor body) will be damaged and require replacement.*

2. Install a new O-ring onto the main jet and install the main jet (**Figure 23**).

3. Install the pilot jet (**Figure 24**).

4. Install the check valve assembly (B, **Figure 22**) as follows:
   a. Make sure that valve is correctly installed in the valve block and retaining screw is tight.
   b. Position the gasket and install the check valve block assembly.
   c. Coat threads of the retaining screws with Loctite 242 (blue) and secure the block with the 2 screws (A, **Figure 22**).

5. Install the fuel valve assembly as follows:
   a. Check that the fuel valve needle and seat are clean and in good condition.
   b. Install a new O-ring on the fuel valve seat, then install the seat (**Figure 21**). Install the retaining plate and screw. Tighten the retaining screw (B, **Figure 18**) securely.

   c. Install the fuel inlet lever spring in the hole as shown in **Figure 20**.
   d. Insert the pivot pin through the fuel inlet lever.
   e. Hook the wire clip attached to the inlet valve needle to the fuel inlet lever, then position the fuel valve needle and lever as shown in **Figure 19**.
   f. Align the spring (**Figure 20**) with the small bump on the bottom of the fuel inlet lever and position the pivot pin in its groove.
   g. Install and tighten the retaining screw (A, **Figure 18**).

6. Check fuel inlet lever height as follows:
   a. The round end of the control lever must be level with the surrounding chamber wall surface as shown in **Figure 26**.
   b. If the adjustment is incorrect, remove the control arm and bend it carefully. Reinstall the control arm and recheck the adjustment.
   c. If the height of the fuel control lever is too high, the fuel mixture will be too rich throughout the engine speed range. If the fuel control lever is below the surrounding surface, the fuel mixture will be too lean.

7. Install the fuel control diaphragm assembly.
   a. The fuel control diaphragm is directional. The inner side of the diaphragm is equipped with an aluminum support plate (**Figure 17**). The outer side does not have a support plate.
   b. Install the diaphragm so that the outer or plain side faces out. Align the diaphragm tab with the notch in the carburetor housing.
   c. Install the gasket, aligning the gasket tab with the carburetor notch.
   d. Install the cover plate (**Figure 16**) and its mounting screws. Coat the threads of the screws with Loctite 242 (blue) and tighten the screws securely.

8. Install the fuel filter screen (**Figure 15**).

9. Install the gasket, cover and retaining screws (**Figure 14**).

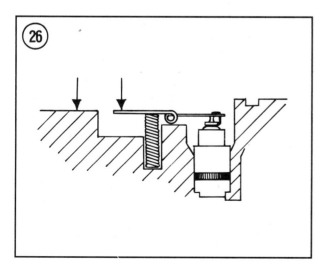
26

NOTE
If the pop off pressure is to be checked as suggested in Step 10, the fuel lines must be detached from the cover for testing. It may be easier to remove 1 of the covers and use this cover to test the pop off pressure on all 3 carburetors.

10. Perform *Carburetor Pop Off Pressure* and *Leak Test* as described in this chapter.

Carburetor Pop Off Pressure

The Mity Vac pump/gauge tester (part No. 2870975) or equivalent is required to perform these test procedures.

1. Remove the carburetors as described in this chapter.

2. Detach the fuel return line (A, **Figure 27**) and the fuel delivery line (B, **Figure 27**) from the fittings located on the carburetor cover.

3. Attach the tester hose to the fitting for the fuel delivery line (B, **Figure 27**).

4. Plug the carburetor return line fitting (A, **Figure 27**).

5. Apply pressure with the tester until there is a sudden pressure drop, indicating that the inlet release pressure (pop off pressure) was reached.

6. Pop off pressure must be within the specification listed in **Table 1**.

7. If the pop off pressure is too low, proceed as follows:

   a. Remove the fuel control diaphragm from the carburetor as described under *Carburetor Disassembly* in this chapter.

   b. Recheck the pop off pressure.

   c. If the pressure is now correct, check the fuel inlet lever height as described under *Carburetor Reassembly* in this chapter.

   d. If the pressure is still too low, position the carburetor so the fuel inlet needle valve assembly faces up.

   e. Pour a small amount of light oil over the needle valve.

   f. Pump the tester until the gauge indicates slightly less than the pop off pressure listed in **Table 1**.

   g. Check for bubbles coming from the needle valve and seat or from the O-ring around the valve seat.

   h. If there are bubbles coming from the needle valve and seat, replace the valve and seat as a set. If there are bubbles coming from around the O-ring, remove the seat and replace the O-ring.

8. If the pop off pressure is too high, proceed as follows:

   a. Check the fuel inlet lever height as described under *Carburetor Reassembly* in this chapter.

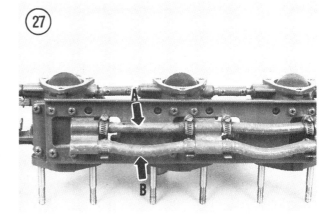

b. If the adjustment is correct, replace the control arm spring (**Figure 21**) and retest.

c. If the inlet lever height is too low, adjust the height of the fuel inlet lever as described under *Carburetor Reassembly* in this chapter.

9. The pop off pressure may be too low because:

a. Foreign material on the fuel inlet needle causing it to leak.

b. Worn, broken or damaged spring (**Figure 20**).

c. Leaking needle seat O-ring.

d. Corrosion on fuel inlet lever, pivot pin and/or spring.

e. Incorrect parts (lever, valve or spring) installed.

10. The pop off pressure may be too high because:

a. Restricted fuel inlet passage.

b. Inlet needle stuck to the seat.

c. Corrosion on fuel inlet lever, pivot pin and/or spring.

d. Incorrect parts (lever, valve or spring) installed.

11. Improper operation similar to low pop off pressure can be caused by a kinked or restricted fuel return hose or a plugged restrictor orifice (3, **Figure 2** or 8, **Figure 3**).

12. Clean, reassemble and reinstall the carburetor(s) as described in this chapter.

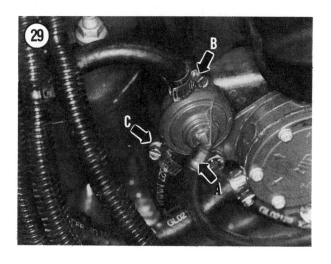

AUTOMATIC SHUTOFF VALVE

Removal/Installation

To prevent engine flooding when the engine is turned off, an automatic shut-off valve is installed in the fuel circuit between the fuel pump and the carburetor fuel inlet fitting (**Figure 28**). The valve is opened by engine vacuum when the engine is running and shuts off when the engine is not running. Vacuum is delivered from the reed valve for the rear cylinder by hose (A, **Figure 9**).

1. Shut the fuel off at the dash mounted valve.

2. Loosen the fuel tank fill cap to relieve pressure from the system.

3. Remove the seat and engine cover.

4. Detach the vacuum pulse line (A, **Figure 29**) from the valve.

NOTE
Be prepared to plug the hose from the pump when it is detached from the fitting.

5. Loosen the clamp (B, **Figure 29**), then detach the hose from the fitting. This is the fuel line from the pump.

6. Loosen the clamp (C, **Figure 29**), then detach the hose from the fitting on the automatic shutoff valve. Plug the disconnected hose to stop fuel from draining and prevent dirt from entering the hose. This is the hose that delivers fuel to the carburetors.

7. Unbolt the automatic fuel shutoff from the fuel mounting bracket.

8. Service to the valve is limited to replacement of the unit. Vacuum at the fitting (A, **Figure 29**) should permit fuel to flow through the valve. Removing vacuum from the fitting should immediately stop the flow of gasoline through the valve.

9. Attach a new valve to the fuel pump bracket and attach the fuel and vacuum hoses as shown in **Figure 28** and **Figure 29**. Make sure the clamps on fuel hoses are tight.

10. Make sure the fuel tank fill cap is tight and turn the fuel valve ON.

11. Clean any spilled fuel and allow the compartment to air out until the fuel odor has dissipated.

12. Start the engine and check for fuel leaks.

> *CAUTION*
> *Do not operate the craft with any sign of spilled or leaking fuel. Allow the engine compartment to air out sufficiently before starting the engine.*

MANUAL SHUTOFF VALVE

A shutoff valve is located on the console (A, **Figure 30**, typical).

Removal/Installation

1. Read the WARNING at the beginning of this chapter.

2. Remove the seat and engine cover.

3. Disconnect the negative battery cable.

4. Loosen the fuel tank fill cap to relieve pressure from the system.

5. Remove the screw attaching the knob (B, **Figure 30**) to the shutoff valve and lift the knob from the valve.

6. Remove the screws attaching the console and pull the console away from the hull. Refer to **Figure 31**.

7. Loosen the clamps (**Figure 31**) and detach the hoses from the valve.

8. Remove the attaching screws and remove the shutoff valve.

9. Install a new shutoff valve by reversing the removal procedure.

   a. Make sure the fuel tank fill cap is tight.

   b. Clean any spilled fuel and allow the compartment to air out until the fuel odor has dissipated.

   c. Turn the fuel valve ON.

   d. Start the engine and check for fuel leaks.

> *CAUTION*
> *Do not operate the craft with any sign of spilled or leaking fuel. Allow the engine compartment to air out sufficiently before starting the engine.*

FUEL PUMP

The fuel pump is mounted on a bracket attached to the intake air silencer lower housing (**Figure 8**). The diaphragm type fuel pump is operated by the vacuum and pressure pulses in the crankcase for the rear cylinder. Pulses from the crankcase are delivered to the pump through the hose (C, **Figure 9**).

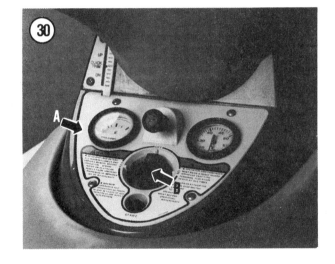

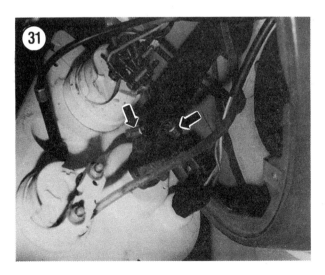

Removal/Installation

1. Read the WARNING at the beginning of this chapter.
2. Remove the seat and engine cover.
3. Disconnect the cable from the negative battery terminal.
4. Shut the fuel off at the dash mounted valve.
5. Loosen the fuel tank fill cap to relieve pressure from the system.
6. Remove the air intake silencer and flame arrestor as described in this chapter. The fuel pump (A, **Figure 32**) is attached to a bracket connected to the silencer lower housing.
7. Detach the necessary hoses and unbolt the fuel pump from the bracket.
8. Attach the fuel pump to the bracket and tighten the bolts securely. Make sure the arrows on the pump are pointing the direction of correct fuel flow. Fuel from the pump (A, **Figure 32**) should flow through the hose to the automatic shutoff valve (B, **Figure 32**).
9. Complete assembly by reversing the removal procedure. Observe the following:

a. On 1995 and later models, attach the oil injector hoses to the 3 oil injector check valves located in the silencer housing, then secure the hoses with clamps. Refer to **Figure 7**.

> *NOTE*
> *If the oil has been allowed to drain from the oil injection lines, fill the lines with oil before attaching to the check valves (**Figure 7**) in the silencer housing. Failure to fill the lines with oil can cause serious engine damage. If the lines were properly plugged when disconnected, the lines will remain filled. Refer to Chapter Eight for bleeding air from the oil injection system.*

b. Make sure the fuel tank fill cap is tight and turn the fuel valve ON.
c. Clean any spilled fuel and allow the compartment to air out until the fuel odor has dissipated.
d. Start the engine and check for fuel leaks.

> *CAUTION*
> *Do not operate the craft with any sign of spilled or leaking fuel. Allow the engine compartment to air out sufficiently before starting the engine.*

Disassembly/Inspection/Assembly

The fuel pump (**Figure 33**) is a pulse-operated diaphragm type. Do not disassemble the fuel pump body unless necessary. Gaskets, valves and diaphragms should be replaced whenever the fuel pump is disassembled. Purchase replacement parts before taking the fuel pump apart. Replacement parts may not be available.

1. Remove the pump as described in this chapter.
2. Mark across the cover, body and pulse chamber (1, 2 and 3, **Figure 33**) so that these 3 parts can be easily aligned when reassembling.
3. Remove the screws (4, **Figure 33**), then separate the parts of the fuel pump.

4. Inspect the diaphragm for damage. Replace the diaphragm if torn, if it is no longer flexible or if it is damaged. Do not attempt to repair a damaged diaphragm.

5. Inspect valves (5 and 6, **Figure 33**). Install new valves if they are leaking or damaged in any way. Do not attempt to repair a damaged valve.

6. Assemble the pump using new gaskets.

REED VALVES

Each cylinder is fitted with its own reed valve assembly. On 1992-1993 models, an individual carburetor adapter (manifold) is installed for each cylinder, while on 1994-on models the adapters for all 3 cylinders are made as 1 piece.

Removal/Inspection/Installation

1. Remove the carburetors as described in this chapter.

> *NOTE*
> *Be prepared to plug the lines and fittings as hoses are detached in the following Step 2. Plugging the openings will prevent fuel or oil from leaking into the hull. It will also prevent dirt from entering the hoses.*

2. On 1992-1993 models, loosen the spring clamps on the hoses to the 3 oil injector check valves located in the carburetor adapter housings, then detach the hoses from the check valves (A, **Figure 34**).

3. Detach the throttle and choke cable housings from the front of carburetor adapter housing.

> *NOTE*
> *The screws and nuts removed in Step 4A or Step 4B are secured using Loctite and may be difficult to remove. Use care to prevent damage when removing these fasteners.*

4A. On 1992-1993 models, remove the 4 screws and 2 nuts attaching each of the carburetor adapt-

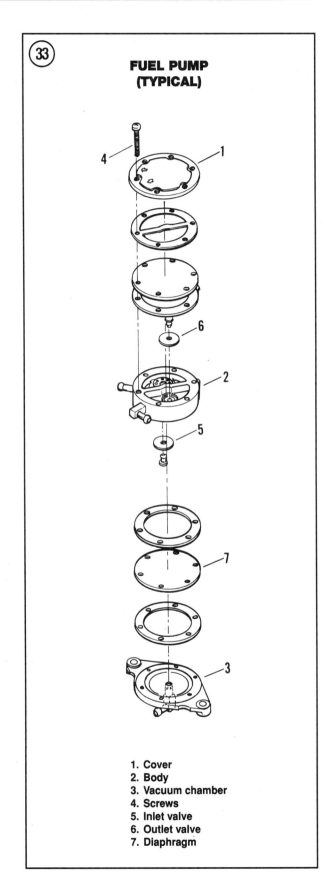

33 **FUEL PUMP (TYPICAL)**

1. Cover
2. Body
3. Vacuum chamber
4. Screws
5. Inlet valve
6. Outlet valve
7. Diaphragm

er housings to the crankcase. Refer to B and C, **Figure 34**.

4B. On 1994-on models, remove the 12 screws and 6 nuts from the adapter housing for the carburetors.

5. Remove the carburetor housing from the crankcase.

6. After the carburetor housing is removed, the reed cage (A, **Figure 35**) and stuffer block (B, **Figure 35**) can be removed from the crankcase.

7. Inspect the reed cages and reed petals for damage.

    a. The reed petals should be very lightly seated against the reed cage (**Figure 36**).

    b. If the clearance between the reed petal and the reed cage exceeds 0.5 mm (0.020 in.), remove the reed and check for some small particle holding the reed away from the cage. If the cage and reed are both clean, install new reed petals.

    c. Inspect the reed petals for damage (**Figure 37**). If a reed petal is damaged, check the seating surface of the cage for damage.

8. Inspect the stuffer block (B, **Figure 35**) for cracks, distortion or other damage.

9. Assemble the reed petals (A, **Figure 38**) and reed stops (B) to the reed cage (C) *without* using any threadlock on the screws (D).

6

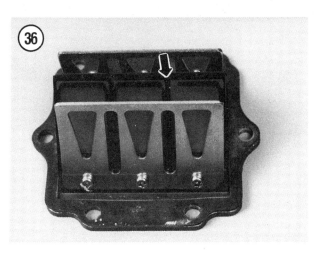

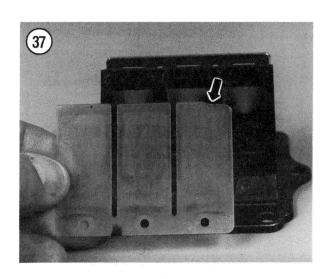

a. Clean the reed petal, cage and stops before assembling.

b. Make sure the petals are centered over the openings in the cage and the stops are centered over the petals before tightening the retaining screws (D, **Figure 38**).

c. After assembling, remove each of the screws (D, **Figure 38**) in turn, coat the threads with Loctite 242 (blue), then install and tighten the screws.

d. Check the reed petals to make sure they are seated properly after the final installation of the retaining screws.

10. Install a new gasket (E, **Figure 38**), install the stuffer block (F) into reedcage (C), then install the assembled reed assembly over the 2 studs.

11. Install the gasket and carburetor adapter housing.

12. Tighten the screws and nuts attaching the carburetor adapters/reed valve assemblies to the crankcase to the torque listed in **Table 2**.

FUEL GAUGE

The fuel gauge consists of a sender unit located in the fuel tank (**Figure 39**, typical) and a gauge unit located in the console or Multi-Function Unit. Refer to Chapter Three for a description of the Multi-Function Unit's operation.

Testing

Refer to Chapter Two checking the resistance of the fuel gauge sender. Refer to Chapter Seven for service to the console mounted instrument.

Fuel Gauge Sender Removal/Installation

The fuel gauge sender, located in the fuel tank (**Figure 39**, typical), should be removed with the fuel tank is empty or nearly empty.

WARNING
Do not use any electric powered tools when working near the fuel tank, even if it is empty. Electrical sparks can ignite the fuel vapors.

1. Lift the front hatch and remove the storage basket (**Figure 40**).

2. Disconnect the wires from the sender unit (**Figure 39**, typical).

NOTE
On some late 1995 models, the fuel gauge sending unit and the fuel pickup are combined in 1 unit. On these models, it is necessary to detach the fuel hoses,

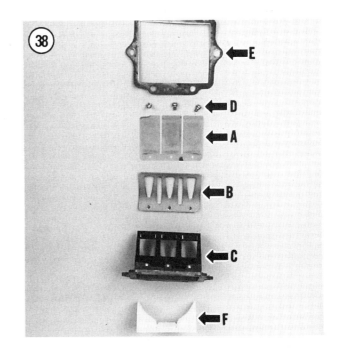

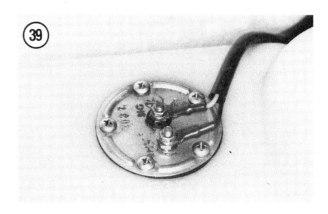

before the unit can be removed. Before detaching any fuel lines, identify the correct attachment location so they can be correctly attached.

3. Remove the screws attaching the sender to the fuel tank, then lift the sender from the tank.

4. Reverse removal procedure to install the fuel gauge sender, observing the following:

a. Use a new gasket when installing the sender unit.

b. Tighten the attaching screws securely.

c. Attach wires from the gauge and tighten nuts securely.

d. Check the installation for fuel leaks.

FUEL TANK

Removal/Installation

WARNING
Fire hazard is always present when servicing any part of the fuel system, so it is important to follow all safety precautions. Refer to the WARNING at the beginning of this chapter.

Various fuel tanks are used and the procedures for removing them may be slightly different than described, but the following provides a guideline for removing the tank.

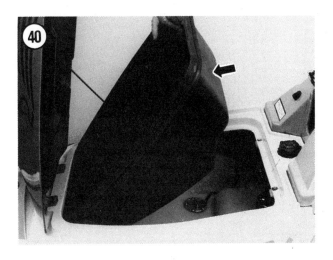

1. Refer to the illustration for your model before removing the fuel tank.

a. **Figure 41**: All 1992-1993 models, 1994 SL 650 and SL 750.

b. **Figure 42**: 1994 SLT 750 and early 1995 models.

c. **Figure 43**: late 1995 models.

WARNING
Before disconnecting any fuel lines, loosen the fuel filler cap to relieve any pressure in the tank.

2. Siphon the contents of the tank into a container approved for gasoline storage.

3. Lift the front hatch and remove the storage basket (**Figure 40**).

4. Disconnect both wires from the fuel level sender unit (**Figure 39**, typical).

5. Mark the fuel hoses (**Figure 44**, typical) to indicate their correct location.

6. Loosen the clamps on the fuel hoses attached to the fuel tank, then detach the hoses.

7. Remove the large connector and fuel pickup hoses (**Figure 45**) from the tank on models so equipped.

8. Loosen the hose clamps located on the filler hose and detach the fill hose from the fuel tank.

9. Remove the oil injection reservoir (tank) as follows:

a. Remove the oil filler cap.

b. Remove the 2 screws (**Figure 46**).

CAUTION
Be prepared to cover all openings as quickly as possible. Plug the detached oil supply hose to stop leakage and prevent the entrance of air into the supply line. If air is allowed to enter this line, it should be filled with oil before starting the engine. Engine damage could result from lack of lubrication if the supply line is not filled with oil upon starting.

c. Move the oil tank out far enough to disconnect the oil supply and vent hoses.

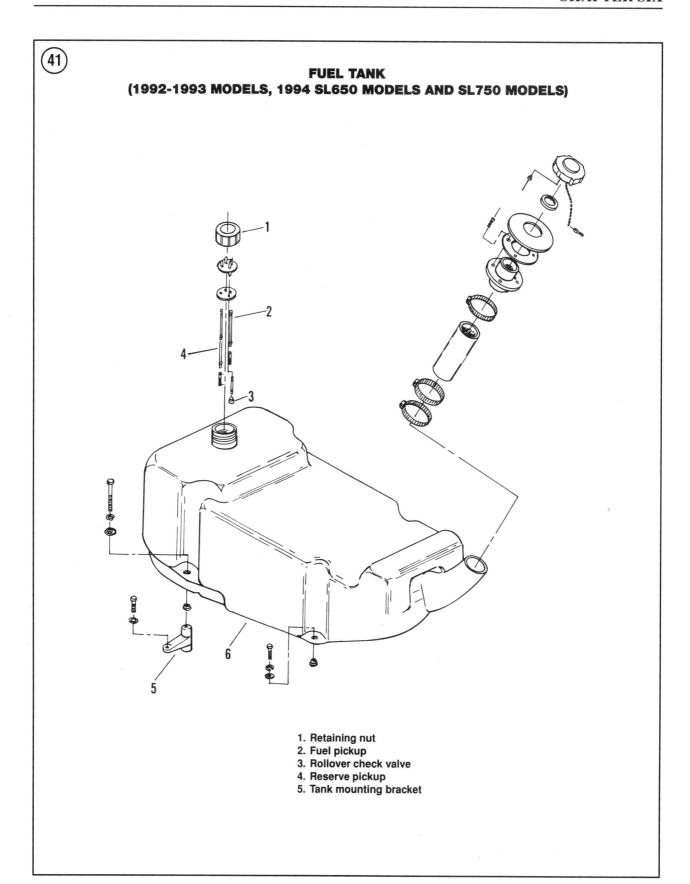

FUEL TANK
(1992-1993 MODELS, 1994 SL650 MODELS AND SL750 MODELS)

1. Retaining nut
2. Fuel pickup
3. Rollover check valve
4. Reserve pickup
5. Tank mounting bracket

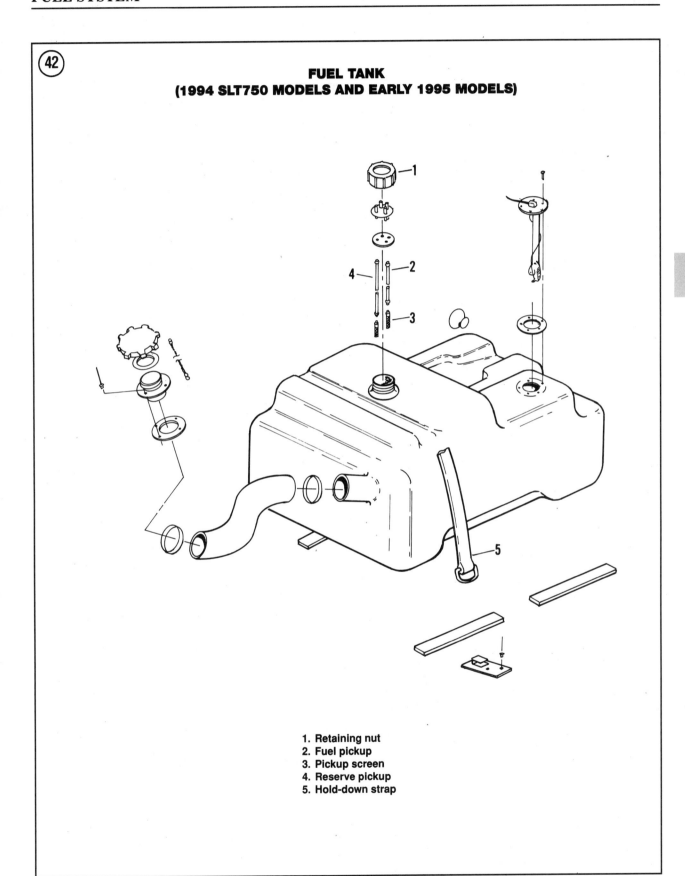

**FUEL TANK
(1994 SLT750 MODELS AND EARLY 1995 MODELS)**

1. Retaining nut
2. Fuel pickup
3. Pickup screen
4. Reserve pickup
5. Hold-down strap

6

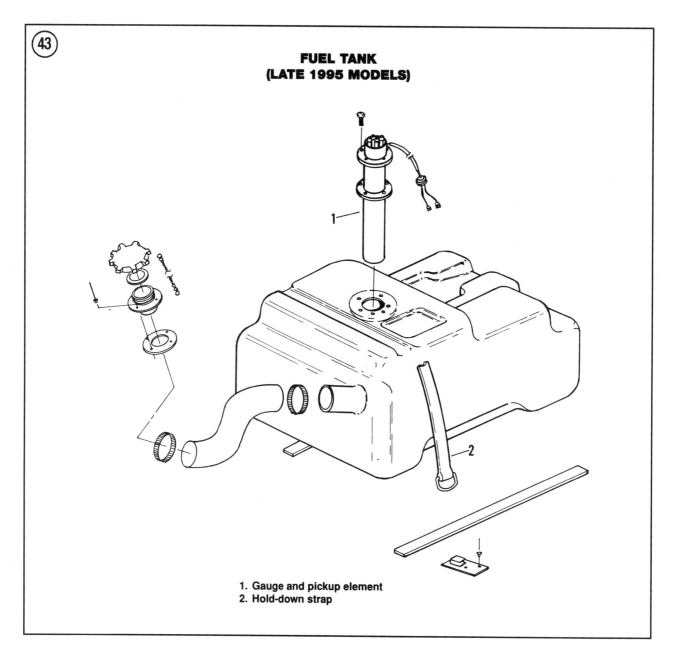

**FUEL TANK
(LATE 1995 MODELS)**

1. Gauge and pickup element
2. Hold-down strap

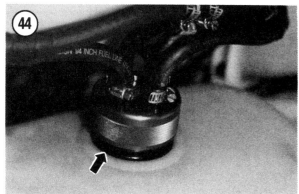

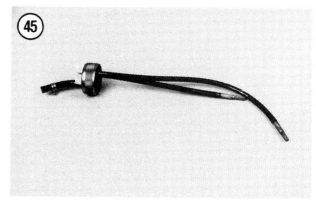

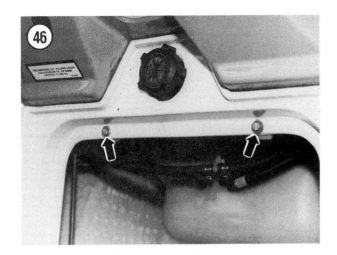

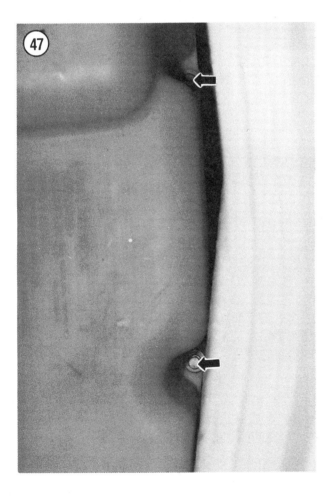

d. Disconnect the wires from the oil level sensor.

e. Cover all openings and store the oil reservoir in such a way that it will not be contaminated while it is removed.

10A. On models with the fuel tank attached by screws (**Figure 41**), first remove the 4 screws that attach the tank to the mounts (**Figure 47**). Remove the 4 screws (**Figure 48**) attaching the mounts to the hull after the tank is loose from the mounts.

10B. On models with the tank attached by a strap (**Figure 42** or **Figure 43**), unhook and release the retaining strap.

11. Lift the fuel tank from the hull.

12. When installing, reverse the removal procedure and observe the following:

a. Make sure the tank is secure.

b. Make sure that all fuel hoses are correctly attached and clamps are tight. The longer pickup hose (**Figure 45**) is for the reserve position. The 2 hose connections that terminate near the top are for the vent and fuel return.

c. Make sure the oil supply hose from the oil reservoir to the oil pump is filled with engine oil.

d. Clean all spilled fuel and oil, then check the system for fuel and oil leaks.

6

Table 1 CARBURETOR SPECIFICATIONS

1992 SL650	Mikuni - Super BN
Size	38 mm with 34 mm venturi
Idle speed in water	1,300 rpm
Low speed screw	1 3/8 turns open
High speed screw	
Magneto end carb.	3/8 turn open
Center carb.	
Early models	1/8 turn open
Later models (June-on)	3/8 turn open
Rear carburetor	1/4 turn open
Pop off pressure	
Early models	25-30 psi (172-207 kPa)
Later models	10-18 psi (69-124 kPa)
Pilot jet	
Early models	#85
Later models (June-on)	#80
Main jet	#80
1993 SL650	Mikuni - Super BN
Size	38 mm with 34 mm venturi
Idle speed in water	1,300 rpm
Low speed screw	1/4 turn open
High speed screw	
Magneto end carburetor	7/8 turn open
Center carburetor	3/8 turn open
Rear carburetor	5/8 turn open
Pop off pressure	10-18 psi (69-124 kPa)
Pilot jet	#77.5
Main jet	#77.5
1993 SL750	Mikuni - Super BN
Size	38 mm with 34 mm venturi
Idle speed in water	1,200-1,300 rpm
Low speed screw	1/2 turn open
High speed screw	
Magneto end carburetor	7/8 turn open
Center carburetor	1/2 turn open
Rear carburetor	5/8 turn open
Pop off pressure	10-18 psi (69-124 kPa)
Pilot jet	#72.5
Main jet	#77.5
1994 SL650 (engine serial No. 94-0001 to 94-02011)	
Carburetor type	Mikuni - Super BN
Size	38 mm with 34 mm venturi
Idle speed in water	1,250-1,350 rpm
Low speed screw	1 1/4 turns open
High speed screw	
Magneto end carburetor	3/4 turn open
Center carburetor	1/4 turn open
Rear carburetor	1/2 turn open
Pop off pressure	10-18 psi (69-124 kPa)
Pilot jet	#75
Main jet	#95

(continued)

Table 1 CARBURETOR SPECIFICATIONS (continued)

1994 SL650 (engine serial No. 94-02011 and up)

Carburetor type	Mikuni - Super BN
Size	38 mm with 34 mm venturi
Idle speed in water	1,250-1,350 rpm
Low speed screw	1 turn open
High speed screw	
Magneto end carburetor	7/8 turn open
Center carburetor	1/2 turn open
Rear carburetor	3/4 turn open
Pop off pressure	10-18 psi (69-124 kPa)
Pilot jet	#75
Main jet	#90

1994 SL750 and SLT750

Carburetor type	Mikuni - Super BN
Size	38 mm with 34 mm venturi
Idle speed in water	1,200-1,300 rpm
Low speed screw	1/2 turn open
High speed screw	
Magneto end carburetor	1 1/4 turns open
Center carburetor	3/8 turn open
Rear carburetor	7/8 turn open
Pop off pressure	10-18 psi (69-124 kPa)
Pilot jet	#75
Main jet	#90

1995 650 STD and SL650

Carburetor type	Mikuni - Super BN
Size	38 mm with 34 mm venturi
Idle speed in water	1,200-1,300 rpm
Low speed screw	1 1/8 turns open
High speed screw	
Magneto end carburetor	1 1/4 turns open
Center carburetor	1/4 turn open
Rear carburetor	7/8 turn open
Pop off pressure	10-18 psi (69-124 kPa)
Pilot jet	#77.5
Main jet	#87.5

1995 650 STD and SL650

Carburetor type	Mikuni - Super BN
Size	38 mm with 34 mm venturi
Idle speed in water	1,200-1,300 rpm
Low speed screw	1 1/8 turns open
High speed screw	
Magneto end carburetor	1 1/4 turns open
Center carburetor	1/4 turn open
Rear carburetor	7/8 turn open
Pop off pressure	10-18 psi (69-124 kPa)
Pilot jet	#77.5
Main jet	#87.5

6

(continued)

Table 1 CARBURETOR SPECIFICATIONS (continued)

1995 750 SL and SLT750	
Carburetor type	Mikuni - Super BN
Size	38 mm with 34 mm venturi
Idle speed in water	1,200-1,300 rpm
Low speed screw	1/2 turn open
High speed screw	
Magneto end carburetor	1 turn open
Center carburetor	1/2 turn open
Rear carburetor	3/4 turn open
Pop off pressure	10-18 psi (69-124 kPa)
Pilot jet	#75
Main jet	#90

Table 2 TIGHTENING TORQUES

	N·m	ft.-lb.
Carburetor adapters/reed valves		
Screws	8.3	6 ft.-lb. (72 in.-lb.)
Nuts	8.6	6 ft.-lb. (72 in.-lb.)

Chapter Seven

Electrical System

BATTERY

All models are equipped with a battery that is required for electric starting. In addition to checking and correcting the electrolyte level, the exterior of the battery should be cleaned. The battery should always remain firmly secured in position and should never be loose in the engine compartment.

> *NOTE*
> *Recycle your old battery. When you replace the old battery, be sure to turn in the old battery. The lead plates and the plastic case can be recycled. Most marine dealers will accept your old battery in trade when you purchase a new one. Never place an old battery in your household trash. It is illegal, in most states, to place any acid or lead (heavy metal) in landfills. There is also the danger of the battery being crushed in the trash truck and spraying acid on the truck or landfill operator.*

Safety Precautions

A battery can be a serious safety hazard, especially if you are careless with it. When working with a battery, use extreme care to avoid spilling or splashing the electrolyte. The electrolyte solution contains sulfuric acid, which can ruin clothing and cause serious chemical burns. If any electrolyte is spilled or splashed on clothing or skin:

1. Immediately neutralize with a solution of baking soda and water.

2. Flush the area with an abundance of clean water.

3. Consult a physician as soon as possible if the electrolyte solution enters your eyes.

WARNING
Electrolyte splashed into the eyes is extremely harmful. Always wear safety glasses while working with batteries. If electrolyte enters eyes, call a physician immediately. Force eyes open and flood them with cool clean water for approximately 15 minutes.

If electrolyte is spilled or splashed onto any surface, it should be neutralized immediately with a baking soda and water solution, then rinsed with clean water.

While batteries are being charged, highly explosive hydrogen gas forms in each cell. Some of this gas escapes through the filler cap openings and may form an explosive atmosphere in and around the battery. This condition can persist for several hours. Sparks, an open flame or a lit cigarette can ignite the gas, causing an explosion and possible personal injury.

Take the following precautions to prevent an explosion:

1. Do not smoke or permit any open flame near any battery being charged or which has been recently charged.

2. Do not disconnect live circuits from the battery terminals since a spark usually occurs when a live circuit is broken.

3. Take care when connecting or disconnecting any battery charger. Be sure its power switch is OFF before making or breaking any connections. Poor connections are a common cause of electrical arcs which cause explosions.

4. Keep children and pets away from charging equipment and batteries.

5. For maximum battery life, check the electrolyte level and state of charge periodically. Also, check the battery and connections for corrosion. In hot, dry climates check the battery more frequently. The electrolyte level should always be between the 2 marks (**Figure 1**). The electrolyte level for each cell can be seen through the battery case. If the electrolyte is below the minimum level, in one or more cells, add distilled water as required.

6. To ensure proper mixing of the water and acid, operate the engine or charge the battery immediately after adding water. *Never* add battery acid instead of water—this will shorten the battery's life.

7. On all models covered in this manual, the negative (–) terminal of the battery is grounded. When removing the battery, disconnect the grounded negative (–) cable before detaching the positive (+) cable. This minimizes the chances of a tool shorting to ground when disconnecting the "hot" positive cable.

Battery Removal

WARNING
When performing the following procedure, protect your eyes, skin and clothing. If electrolyte gets in your eyes, flush

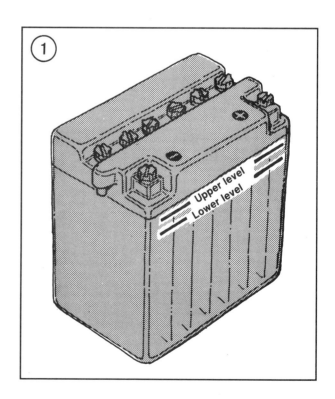

your eyes thoroughly with clean water and get prompt medical attention.

The battery located under the seat in the engine compartment, provides power for electric starting. The electrical box is located above the battery.

1. Remove the battery hold down straps (**Figure 2**) .

2. Lift the electrical box from the top of the battery case and relocate the electrical box out of the way.

3. Clean the battery case. Remove the cover from the battery.

4. Disconnect the ground wire from the negative (–) terminal of the battery before disconnecting the positive (+) lead.

5. Detach the positive (+) lead from the battery terminal.

6. Lift the battery from the battery box (carrier).

7. Clean all dirt and corrosion from the outside of the battery case and from the battery box.

Battery Inspection and Service

The electrolyte level can be checked without removing the battery, but the battery should be removed and cleaned if electrolyte is added or if the specific gravity is checked. The electrolyte level is visible through the battery case. Clean the battery case and observe the height of the fluid level in each cell. Maintain the electrolyte

level between the 2 marks on the case (**Figure 1**). If the electrolyte level is low, remove and clean the battery thoroughly before servicing it.

1. Inspect the pad at the bottom of the battery box (carrier) for contamination or damage. Clean the battery box and pad with a solution of baking soda and water. Dry any bare metal, then repaint to protect surfaces from additional damage.

2. Check the entire battery case for cracks or other damage. If the battery case is warped, discolored or has a raised top, the battery has been overcharged or overheated.

3. Check the battery hold-down straps for acid damage, cracks or other damage. Replace the hold-down if required.

4. Check the electrical box for evidence of battery corrosion or other damage and clean, repair and reseal as required.

5. Check the battery terminal bolts, spacers and nuts for corrosion or other damage. Clean the parts in a solution of baking soda and water. Replace damaged parts.

NOTE
Keep cleaning solution out of the battery cells or the electrolyte will be seriously weakened.

6. Clean the top of the battery with a stiff bristle brush and water. If necessary, a solution of baking soda and water can be used to help clean, but be careful not to contaminate the electrolyte in the battery's cells with either soap or the baking soda solution.

7. Check the battery cable terminal ends for corrosion or other damage. If corrosion is minor, clean the battery cable clamps with a stiff wire brush. Install new cables if terminal ends or cables are severely damaged.

NOTE
Do not overfill the battery cells in Step 8. The electrolyte expands due to the heat of charging and will overflow if the level is above the upper level line.

7

8. Remove the caps from the battery cells and add distilled water, if necessary, to raise the level between the upper and lower level lines on the battery case.

Battery Testing

The best way to check the condition of a battery is to test the specific gravity of the elec-trolyte in each of the battery's cells using a hydrometer. Use a hydrometer that is marked with numbered graduations from 1.100 to 1.300 rather than one with color-coded bands. To use the hydrometer, proceed as follows:

1. Remove the battery.

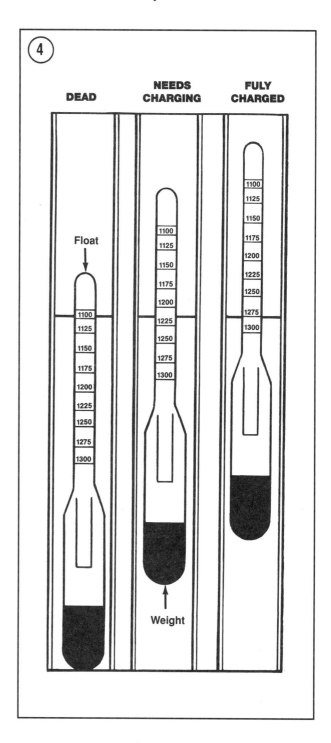

NOTE
Keep any soap, baking soda or other cleaning solution out of the battery cells or the battery will be seriously damaged.

2. Clean the top of the battery with a stiff bristle brush (not metal) and water. If necessary, a solution of baking soda and water can be used to help clean, but be careful not to contaminate the electrolyte in the battery's cells.

NOTE
Do not attempt to test a battery with a hydrometer immediately after adding water to the cells. If possible, wait until after testing the specific gravity to add distilled water. If it is necessary to add water, charge the battery for 15-20 minutes at a rate high enough to cause vigorous gassing before testing.

3. Remove the caps from the battery's cells and check the level of the electrolyte.

NOTE
It is necessary to draw enough electrolyte into the hydrometer to allow the weighted float inside the hydrometer to be suspended in the fluid.

4. Squeeze the rubber ball of the hydrometer, insert the tip into 1 cell and release the ball to draw electrolyte up into the hydrometer. Refer to **Figure 3**. When using a temperature compensat-

ing hydrometer, release the electrolyte and repeat the process several times until the tester has adjusted to the temperature of the electrolyte.

5. Hold the hydrometer vertically and observe the numbered line aligned with the surface of the electrolyte (**Figure 4**). This is the specific gravity of this cell.

6. Return the electrolyte to the cell from which it came.

7. Repeat the test described in Steps 4-6 for the remaining cells.

8. The specific gravity of the electrolyte in each cell is an excellent indication of that cell's condition. Refer to **Figure 5**. The electrolyte in a fully charged cell will have specific gravity of 1.275-1.280, a cell in good condition will have specific gravity of 1.225-1.250 and anything below 1.120 indicates a dead cell.

NOTE
If a temperature compensated hydrometer is not used, add 0.004 to the specific gravity for every 10° above 80° F (25° C). Subtract 0.004 to the specific gravity for every 10° below 80° F (25° C).

Battery Charging

While charging, the battery cells will bubble. If 1 cell does not have gas bubbles or if that cell's

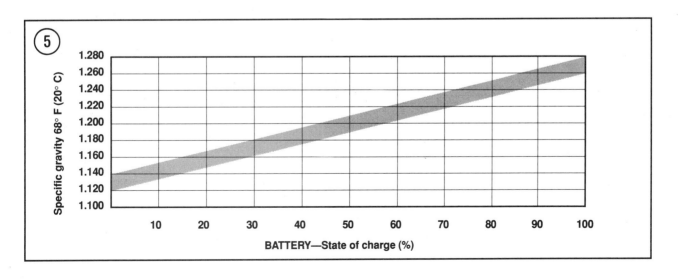

specific gravity is low, the cell is probably defective.

If a battery loses its charge (when not in use) within a week or if the specific gravity drops quickly, the battery is defective. A good battery should only discharge approximately 1 percent each day.

CAUTION
Always remove the battery from the craft before connecting charging equipment.

WARNING
During charging, highly explosive hydrogen gas is released from the battery. Charge the battery only in a well-ventilated area away from any open flames, cigarettes or other ignition sources. Never check the charge of a battery by arcing across the terminals. The resulting spark can ignite the hydrogen gas, causing an explosion.

1. Remove the battery from the craft as described in this chapter.
2. Connect the positive (+) lead from the charger to the battery's positive terminal.
3. Connect the negative (–) lead from the charger to the battery's negative terminal.

CAUTION
The electrolyte level must be maintained at the upper level while charging. Refill with distilled water as necessary.

4. Remove all of the vent caps from the battery and check the electrolyte level. Leave the caps off while charging.
5. Set the charger to 12 volts and turn the charger ON.

NOTE
A battery should be charged at a slow charge rate of 1/10 of its given capacity. The standard charging rate is 1.2 amps.

6. The charging time depends upon the discharged condition of the battery. The chart in **Figure 6** can be used to determine the approxi-

mate charge times at different specific gravity readings. For example, if the specific gravity of your battery is 1.180, the approximate charging time would be 6 hours.

7. After the battery has been charged for the predetermined time, turn the charger OFF, disconnect the leads and check the specific gravity of each cell as described in this chapter.

Battery Installation

1. Make sure the rubber pad for the bottom of the battery is in good condition, clean and correctly positioned in the bottom of the battery box before installing the battery.
2. Install the battery in the battery box (carrier).
3. Connect and route the battery vent tube so that it is not kinked, pinched or plugged. Position the tube so that the hose outlet is located away from all metal components. Install a new vent tube if necessary.
4. Install the top of the battery carrier, then position the electrical box on top of the battery. Make sure the recess in the electrical box is correctly engaged with the battery.

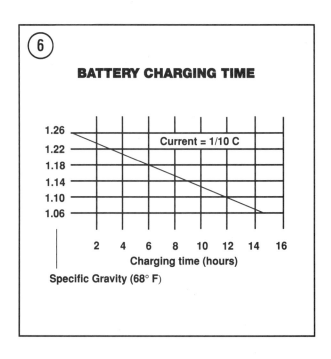

⑥

BATTERY CHARGING TIME

5. Install the battery hold-down straps as shown in **Figure 2**.

> *CAUTION*
> *Be sure the cables are attached to the proper terminals on the battery. Connecting the battery backwards will reverse the polarity and may damage some electrical components, such as the rectifier, CDI ignition and the multi-function display.*

6. Attach the positive (+) battery cable to the positive battery terminal.

7. Attach the negative (–) ground cable to the negative battery terminal.

8. Coat the battery terminals and cable ends with dielectric grease or petroleum jelly.

New Battery Installation

Before installing a new battery remove the cell caps (**Figure 7**), check the electrolyte level and state of charge. Charge the battery as required before installing it, then check the specific gravity of the electrolyte. The specific gravity of the electrolyte in each cell must be 1.260-1.280. A

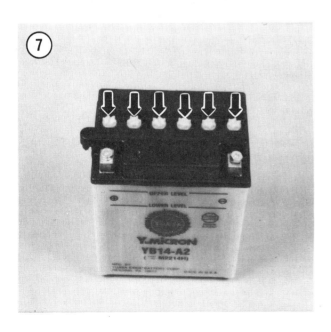

new battery will be permanently damaged if the electrolyte level is too low when it is installed.

IGNITION SYSTEM

Timing

All models are equipped with a sealed capacitor discharge ignition (CDI). Timing with this system is usually not affected by dirt, moisture or wear.

Incorrect ignition timing is difficult to check and nearly impossible to change with the engine installed in the hull.

Usually it is not be necessary to check or change the ignition timing unless the engine is already removed for other repairs or if ignition components are removed. The timing reaches maximum advance at about 3,000 rpm. The flywheel and crankcase are not usually equipped with ignition timing marks. A 2-step procedure that first checks and marks the static timing position, then checks the dynamic ignition timing is recommended.

Static timing requires the use of an accurate dial indicator (part No. 2870459 or equivalent) or degree wheel. Determine the top dead center (TDC) position of the piston, then verify the location of any existing timing marks before making any timing adjustment.

Dynamic ignition timing requires a timing light (part No. 2870630 or equivalent). As the engine is cranked or while it is running, the light flashes each time the spark plug fires. When the light is pointed at the moving flywheel, the mark on the flywheel will appear to stand still. The flywheel mark should align with the stationary timing pointer on the engine. Dynamic timing also requires that the engine be cranked with the starter or running and it is very difficult to see the front of the engine when it is installed in the hull. It is also even more difficult to remove the flywheel and change the position of the stator if timing changes are required with the engine installed.

NOTE
If the timing plug opening in the top of the flywheel cover is used as the stationary pointer (location), the timing mark on the flywheel should align with the center of the timing plug hole. The flywheel may already be marked from a previous timing test. Check the flywheel for previously affixed marks, but be sure to check for proper positioning of these marks.

Static Timing Check

1. Remove the seat and engine cover.

2. Remove all 3 spark plugs as described in this chapter.

3A. If using the timing plug in the top of the flywheel cover located on the front of the engine, remove the plug (**Figure 8**).

3B. If not using the timing port located in the top of the flywheel cover, proceed as follows:

    a. Detach the exhaust support (**Figure 9**) from the engine front cover.

    b. Unbolt and remove the flywheel cover (**Figure 10**).

    c. Attach a timing pointer to a threaded hole (**Figure 11**) or to 1 of the cylinder base studs. The pointer should point toward the flywheel and should be strong enough to remain in place with the engine running.

4. Install and position a dial indicator as follows:

    a. Screw the dial indicator holder into the spark plug hole for the front (magneto end) cylinder. Install the dial indicator into the holder, but do not lock the dial indicator in its adapter at this time.

    b. Rotate the flywheel until the dial indicator rises all the way up in its holder (piston is now approaching TDC). Slide the indicator far enough into the holder to obtain a reading on the dial.

    c. Tighten the set screw on the dial indicator adapter lightly to secure the dial gauge in place.

    d. Rotate the flywheel until the dial indicator on the gauge stops and reverses direction. This is TDC.

    e. Zero the dial gauge by aligning the zero with the indicator needle (**Figure 12**), then

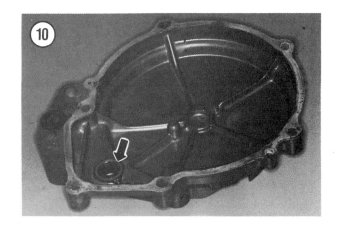

tighten the set screw on the dial indicator adapter securely.

5A. If you are using the timing plug in the top of the flywheel cover, view into the opening for the plug (**Figure 13**). The TDC mark on the flywheel should be centered in the hole.

5B. If a temporary timing pointer is installed (**Figure 11**) install temporary marks as follows:

   a. Clean the flywheel near the timing pointer.

   b. Use paint or a marking pin to place a temporary TDC mark on the flywheel exactly aligned with the timing pointer. Identify this flywheel mark as the TDC mark.

6. Rotate the engine flywheel counterclockwise (viewed from the front of the engine) until the dial indicator is at the ignition timing position (before top dead center) listed in **Table 1**.

7A. If using the timing plug opening (**Figure 13**) in the top of the flywheel cover, view into the opening. Clean the flywheel, then mark the timing position on the flywheel in the center of the hole using chalk, light colored paint and a dark marking pen. This is the advanced timing mark.

7B. If a temporary timing pointer is installed (**Figure 11**), install temporary marks as follows:

   a. Clean the flywheel near the timing pointer.

   b. Use paint or a marking pen to install a temporary mark on the flywheel exactly aligned with the timing pointer. Identify this advanced timing mark so it will not be confused with the TDC mark.

8. After installing the timing marks, rotate the crankshaft and recheck to make sure they align correctly when the piston is at the correct timing position listed in **Table 1**.

9. Remove the dial indicator and install the spark plugs.

10. Perform the *Dynamic Timing Check and Adjustment* as described in this chapter.

Dynamic Timing Check and Adjustment

It is important to identify the correct timing marks as described in the preceding *Static Tim-*

7

ing Check. It is also important to mark them so that you can see them easily when checking with a timing light.

Because ignition components are temperature sensitive, ignition timing should be checked with the engine very near 20° C (68° F). If the temperature is much colder or hotter, timing may be different than when set at the correct temperature.

1. Install timing marks as described in the *Static Timing Check* described in this chapter.

2. Attach a stroboscopic timing light (part No. 2870630 or equivalent) to the spark plug lead for the front (magneto) cylinder. Follow its manufacturer's instructions when attaching the timing light.

3. Connect a tachometer to the engine according to its manufacturer's instructions.

4. Connect a flushing device (Chapter Nine) to provide cooling water to the engine.

> *CAUTION*
> *Prolonged running without coolant will cause serious engine damage. Do not run the engine for more than 10 seconds without cooling water or the rubber parts of the exhaust system will be damaged. Even with the flush kit supplying water to the engine, never operate the engine at maximum speed out of water.*

5. Start the engine, then increase the engine speed to 3,000 rpm.

6. Point the timing light into the timing hole in the flywheel cover or at the stationary timing mark. See **Figure 11** or **Figure 13**.

> *NOTE*
> *If it is difficult to see the flywheel reference mark, turn the engine off, highlight the mark with a grease pencil, chalk or white correction fluid, then recheck.*

7A. If using the timing hole in the flywheel cover, ignition timing is correct when the engine flywheel reference mark is centered in the timing hole (**Figure 13**).

a. If the ignition timing is incorrect, stop the engine, then proceed to Step 8.

b. If the ignition timing is correct, stop the engine, then proceed to Step 12.

7B. If not using the timing hole, ignition timing is correct if the engine flywheel reference mark is aligned with the stationary timing mark (**Figure 11**).

a. If the ignition timing is incorrect, proceed to Step 8.

b. If the ignition timing is correct, proceed to Step 12.

8. If timing is not correct, observe the position of the flywheel mark in relation to the timing pointer (**Figure 11**) or timing hole (**Figure 13**).

a. If the flywheel mark is counterclockwise (when viewed from the front) of the timing

pointer or hole, ignition timing is advanced too much.

b. If the flywheel mark is clockwise (when viewed from the front) of the timing pointer or hole, the ignition timing is retarded.

9. To change ignition timing, proceed as follows:

a. Remove the flywheel cover if not already removed.

NOTE
Be careful not to lose the thrust washer located on the starter shaft. It may stick to the cover as the cover is removed.

b. Remove the flywheel retaining nut and washer.

NOTE
The flywheel retaining nut is secured with threadlock compound and may be difficult to remove.

c. Use puller (part No. 2871043 or equivalent) to pull the flywheel from the crankshaft. Refer to **Figure 14**.

NOTE
*The stator plate has 2 marks that you can use to help adjust the timing. If the lower mark (A, **Figure 15**) is aligned with the crankcase parting line (B, **Figure 15**), the timing will be more retarded (closer to TDC) than if the upper mark is aligned with the crankcase parting line.*

d. Locate the marks (A, **Figure 15**) on the stator plate.

e. Loosen the stator plate retaining screws (C, **Figure 15**). It may be difficult to loosen these screws, because the threads are coated with Loctite.

f. Turn the stator plate counterclockwise (A, **Figure 16**) to advance ignition timing or clockwise (B, **Figure 16**) to retard it.

g. Tighten the retaining screws after repositioning the stator plate.

h. Install the flywheel and tighten the retaining nut to the torque listed in **Table 4**.

NOTE
Allow the engine to cool completely before checking the ignition timing again.

10. Start the engine and recheck ignition timing as described in Steps 5-7. If timing is still not correct, repeat Steps 8-9.

11. After timing is correct, proceed as follows:

a. Remove the flywheel nut and flywheel.

b. Remove the stator plate screws 1 at a time and apply Loctite 242 (blue) to the screw threads.

c. Install and tighten the screw securely.

d. Repeat for each of the remaining screws.

e. Install the flywheel as described in Step 13.

12. Remove the timing light and tachometer.

13. Reinstall all parts previously removed. Observe the following:

NOTE
Do not lubricate the tapered mating surfaces of the crankshaft and flywheel. The assembly should be clean and dry before coating the surface with Loctite 262 (red).

a. Clean the tapered surfaces of the crankshaft and the mating surface of the flywheel.

b. Install the key into the slot of the crankshaft. Make sure the key is seated.

c. Coat the tapered surface of the crankshaft with Loctite 262 (red).

d. Install the flywheel, aligning the slot with the key.

e. Coat the threads of the flywheel retaining nut with Loctite 242 (blue), then install and tighten the flywheel retaining nut to the torque listed in **Table 4**.

f. Clean, then coat the mating surface of the front cover with Loctite 515 (gasket eliminator).

g. Install the front cover and tighten the screws to the torque listed in **Table 4**.

NOTE
Make sure that starter shaft thrust washer is lubricated and installed on the starter shaft before installing the cover. Lubricate the bearing in the front cover before installing the cover.

Stator Assembly Testing

The wires (**Figure 17**) from the stator coils exit the engine under the electric starter motor. The wires are sealed, where they exit the engine housing (**Figure 18**). The wires are contained in a harness that is routed under the engine, then terminate in the electrical box. There are no connectors located between the stator coils and the electrical box.

Resistance of the stator coils can be checked at the ends of the wires in the electrical box, but you must remember that the test will also check the condition of the wires. Any broken or shorted wire between the test point and the stator will indicate a coil failure.

1. Remove the seat and engine cover.

2. Remove the elastic straps (**Figure 19**) that attach the electrical box to the top of the battery.

3. Disconnect the battery ground cable from the negative terminal of the battery.

4. Position the electrical box on top of the engine.

5. Remove the 6 screws attaching the cover to the electrical box.

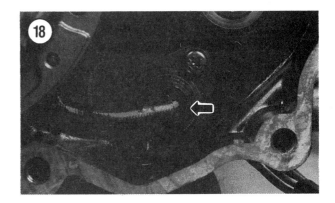

6. Remove the cover from the electrical box. Be careful not to damage the gasket (**Figure 20**).

7. Identify and disconnect the wires from the alternator to the connections in the electrical box. Wires enter the electrical box near the corner (**Figure 21**).

8. Use a precision ohmmeter to measure the resistance of the stator coils. Use the following

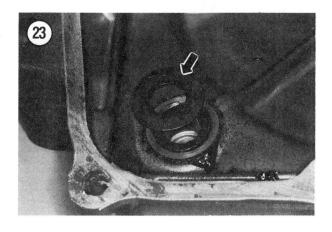

to identify wires. Refer to **Table 3** for recommended resistance.

   a. Wires from the alternator coil are red/purple and yellow.

   b. Wires from the ignition exciter coil are red/white and green/red.

   c. Wires from the ignition pulser coil are blue/red and red/white.

   d. Wires from the ignition Trigger coil are white/yellow and black.

9. If the resistance is more than specified in **Table 3**, first check for an open circuit in the wire to the stator coil.

10. If the resistance is less than specified in **Table 3**, check for a short in the wire to the stator coil.

11. If tests indicate the coil is faulty and not the connecting wire, remove the flywheel and stator (**Figure 22**) as described in this chapter.

12. Reassemble by reversing disassembly procedure. Observe the following:

   a. Be sure that all wires, especially those inside the electrical box, are reconnected.

   b. Make sure the gasket is in good condition and tighten the 6 screws securely. It is important to seal the electrical box.

Flywheel Removal/Inspection/Installation

The flywheel is located at the front of the engine.

1. Remove the engine as described in Chapter Four.

> *CAUTION*
> *Be careful not to lose the thrust washer (**Figure 23**). It may stick to the front cover or may remain on the starter shaft.*

2. Unbolt and remove the front cover.

> *NOTE*
> *The flywheel retaining nut is secured with Loctite threadlock and my be difficult to remove.*

3. Remove the nut securing the flywheel to the engine crankshaft.

4. Attach a puller to the flywheel (**Figure 24**) and pull the flywheel from the tapered end of the crankshaft.

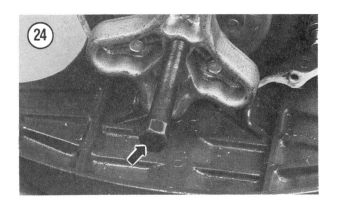

> *CAUTION*
> *It may be necessary to hit the screw (**Figure 24**), located in the center of the puller, to dislodge the flywheel from the tight fit of the crankshaft. Be careful to hit the screw squarely.*

5. Inspect the key and both key slots for damage. Damage to the key slots is usually caused by the flywheel nut not being tightened correctly.

6. Inspect the tapered areas of the crankshaft and flywheel (**Figure 25**) for damage. Fretting damage can usually only be repaired by installing new parts and is caused by the flywheel nut not being tightened correctly or debris on the tapered surfaces when assembling.

> *NOTE*
> *Do not lubricate this tapered surface. Assembly should be clean and dry before coating the surface with Loctite 271 (red).*

7. Clean the tapered surfaces of the crankshaft and the mating surface of the flywheel.

8. Install the key into the slot of the crankshaft. Make sure the key is seated.

9. Coat the tapered surface of the crankshaft with Loctite 271 (red).

10. Install the flywheel, aligning the slot with the key.

11. Coat the threads of the flywheel retaining nut with Loctite 242 (blue), then install and tighten the flywheel retaining nut to the torque listed in **Table 4**.

12. Clean, then coat the mating surface of the front cover with Loctite 515 (gasket eliminator).

13. Install the front cover and tighten the screws to the torque listed in **Table 4**.

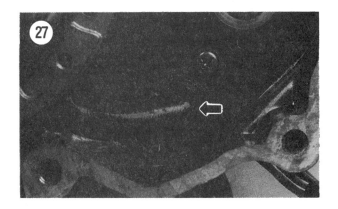

NOTE
*Make sure the thrust washer (**Figure 23**) is lubricated, then installed on the starter shaft before installing the cover. Lubricate the bearing in the front cover before installing the cover.*

Stator Assembly Removal/Installation

1. Remove the engine as described in Chapter Four.

2. Detach the wires leading from the stator assembly inside the electrical box as described in this chapter. Refer to Stator *Assembly Testing* in this chapter.

3. Remove the flywheel as described in this chapter.

4. Remove the starter as described in this chapter.

5. Remove the 7 screws (**Figure 26**) retaining the front housing, then lift the housing from the engine.

6. Carefully lift the starter drive from the housing.

7. Remove the screws attaching the wire seal clamp (**Figure 27**) to the engine.

8. Loosen the seal and withdraw the wires to the front.

9. Check the alignment of timing marks (A & B, **Figure 28**) and note any difference from the alignment shown in **Figure 28**.

10. Remove the screws (C, **Figure 28**) attaching the stator plate, then remove the stator assembly from the engine.

11. If necessary, unbolt and remove the coils from the stator plate.

12. Reassemble by reversing disassembly procedure. Observe the following.

   a. Be sure that all wires, especially those inside the electrical box, are reconnected.

   b. Make sure that all seals and gaskets are in good condition. It is important to seal moisture from the electrical system.

ELECTRICAL BOX

The electrical box is located on top of the battery and contains the CDI ignition module, starter relay, regulator rectifier, 3 ignition coils and the manual reset circuit breaker. Additional components are installed in the electrical box on some models.

Cover Removal/Installation

Internal components of the electrical box are accessible after removing the cover as follows.

1. Remove the seat and engine cover.

2. Remove the elastic straps (**Figure 29**) that attach the electrical box to the top of the battery.

CAUTION
Do not attempt any electrical repair unless the battery ground is first disconnected.

3. Disconnect the battery ground cable from the negative terminal of the battery.

4. Remove the 6 screws attaching the cover to the electrical box.

5. Remove the cover from the electrical box. Be careful not to damage the gasket. Refer to **Figure 30**.

6. Refer to the following sections for service to components located inside the electrical box.

7. Reassemble by reversing the disassembly procedure. Observe the following:

 a. Be sure that all wires, especially those inside the electrical box, are reconnected.

 b. Make sure the gasket is in good condition and tighten the 6 screws securely. It is important to seal the electrical box.

Ignition Coils

The high tension ignition coils (A, B & C, **Figure 30**) are located in the electrical box. Refer to *Cover Removal/Installation* in this chapter for the procedure to open the electrical box for servicing the ignition high tension coils.

1. Detach wires from the coil.

2. Remove the screw attaching the coil to the electrical box.

3. Remove the ignition coil.

4. Check the seal located around the wire to the spark plug. Make sure that the seal prevents moisture from entering the electrical box.

5. Install the coil by reversing the removal procedure.

CDI Module

The CDI module (D, **Figure 30**) is located in the electrical box. Refer to *Cover Removal/Installation* in this chapter for the procedure to

open the electrical box. Service to the CDI module is limited to installing a new similar unit.

1. Unbolt the CDI unit from the electrical box.

NOTE
One of the 2 retaining screws or stud nuts provides a system ground.

2. Detach the wires from the CDI module.

3. Refer to **Table 1** for correct CDI module application for your model. It is important to have the correct unit installed.

Starter Relay

The starter relay (E, **Figure 30**) is located in the electrical box. Refer to *Cover Removal/Installation* in this chapter for procedure to open the electrical box. Refer to the *Starting System* in this chapter for removal of the relay from the electrical box.

CHARGING SYSTEM

The regulator/rectifier unit and the cutoff switch are located in the electrical box. Refer to *Cover Removal/Installation* in this chapter for procedure to open the electrical box for servicing.

1A. On 1992-1993 models, the regulator/rectifier unit (1, **Figure 31**) and the cutoff switch (2, **Figure 31**) are located under the CDI module (3, **Figure 31**). Proceed as follows:

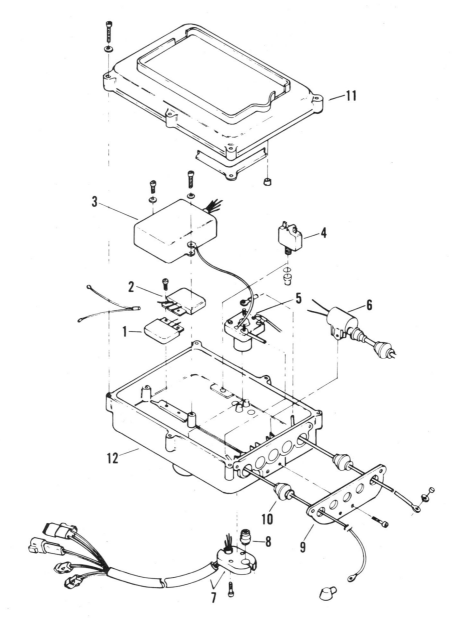

**ELECTRICAL BOX
(1992-1993 MODELS)**

7

1. Regulator/rectifier	7. Wiring harness and clamp
2. Cutoff switch	8. Wire seal
3. CDI module	9. Clamp
4. Manual reset switch	10. Grommet
5. Starter relay	11. Cover
6. Ignition high tension coil (3 used)	12. Electrical box

a. Remove the CDI module as described in this chapter.

b. Lift the CDI module out of the electrical box to expose the regulator/rectifier.

1B. On 1994 SL 650 models, the regulator/rectifier unit (1, **Figure 32**) and the cutoff switch (2, **Figure 32**) are attached to the electrical box cover.

1C. On 1994 SL 750 and SLT 750 models and all 1995 models, the regulator/rectifier unit (1, **Figure 33**) is attached to the electrical box cover.

2. Detach the connecting wires, then unbolt and remove the unit.

3. Make sure the correct unit is installed. Refer to **Table 5**.

STARTING SYSTEM

Starter Relay Removal/Installation

The starter relay (5, **Figure 30**) is located in the electrical box. Refer to *Electrical Box Cover Removal/Installation* in this chapter for procedure to open the electrical box.

1. Detach the battery cable and the starter cable from the relay.

2. Detach the remaining wires from the starter relay.

3. Remove the attaching screws and lift the starter relay from the electrical box.

4. Reverse the removal procedure to install the starter relay. Make sure all connections and fasteners are securely tightened.

Starting Motor Removal/Installation

The starting motor is located on the left side of the engine, below the exhaust manifold.

1. Remove the seat and engine cover.

2. Remove the elastic straps (**Figure 29**) that attach the electrical box to the top of the battery.

CAUTION
Do not attempt any electrical repair unless the battery ground is first disconnected.

3. Disconnect the battery ground cable from the negative terminal of the battery.

4. Refer to Chapter Four and remove the exhaust manifold.

5. Detach the starter cable (A, **Figure 34**).

6. Remove the 2 retaining screws (B, **Figure 34**).

7. Withdraw the starter toward the rear.

8. Check the condition of the O-ring (**Figure 35**). Install a new O-ring if it is damaged.

NOTE
If the gear on the starter shaft is damaged, inspect the starter drive assembly as described in this chapter.

9. Lubricate the O-ring (**Figure 35**) before installing the starter.

10. Insert the starter into the opening. Be careful not to damage the O-ring (**Figure 35**).

11. Coat the threads of the 2 mounting screws with Loctite 242 (blue).

12. Install and tighten the 2 mounting screws (B, **Figure 34**) to the torque listed in **Table 4**.

13. Complete reassembly by reversing the removal procedure. Refer to **Table 4** for the recommended tightening torques.

Starting Motor Disassembly/Reassembly

Refer to **Figure 36**.

1. Remove the 2 through bolts (1, **Figure 36**).

NOTE
*Do not lose or damage the thrust washers (2 and 3, **Figure 36**).*

2. Remove the end cover and seal ring (4 and 5, **Figure 36**).

3. Remove the brushes and holder.

4. Remove the front cover (21, **Figure 36**).

5. Withdraw the armature (15, **Figure 36**) from the housing (14, **Figure 36**).

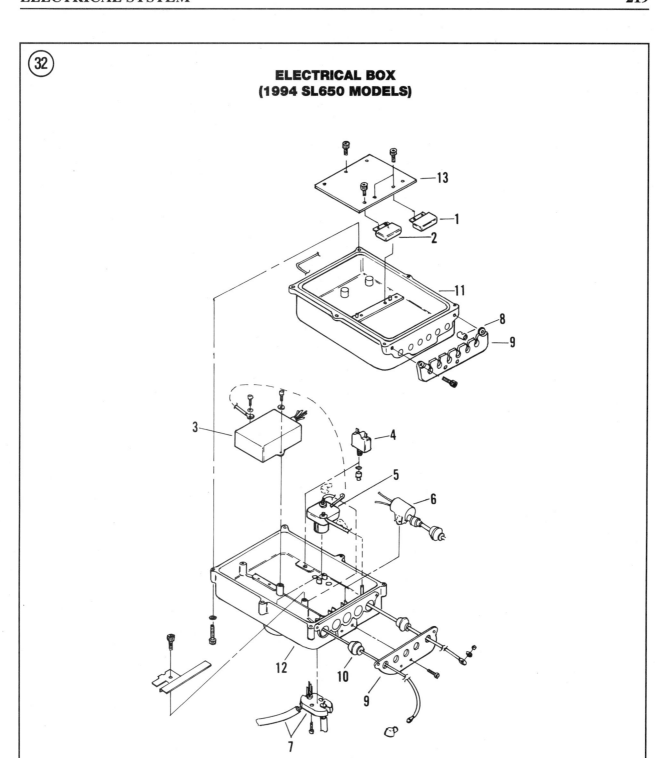

**ELECTRICAL BOX
(1994 SL650 MODELS)**

1. Regulator/rectifier
2. Cutoff switch
3. CDI module
4. Manual reset switch
5. Starter relay
6. Ignition high tension coil (3 used)
7. Wiring harness and clamp
8. Wire seal
9. Clamp
10. Grommet
11. Cover
12. Electrical box
13. Terminal board

7

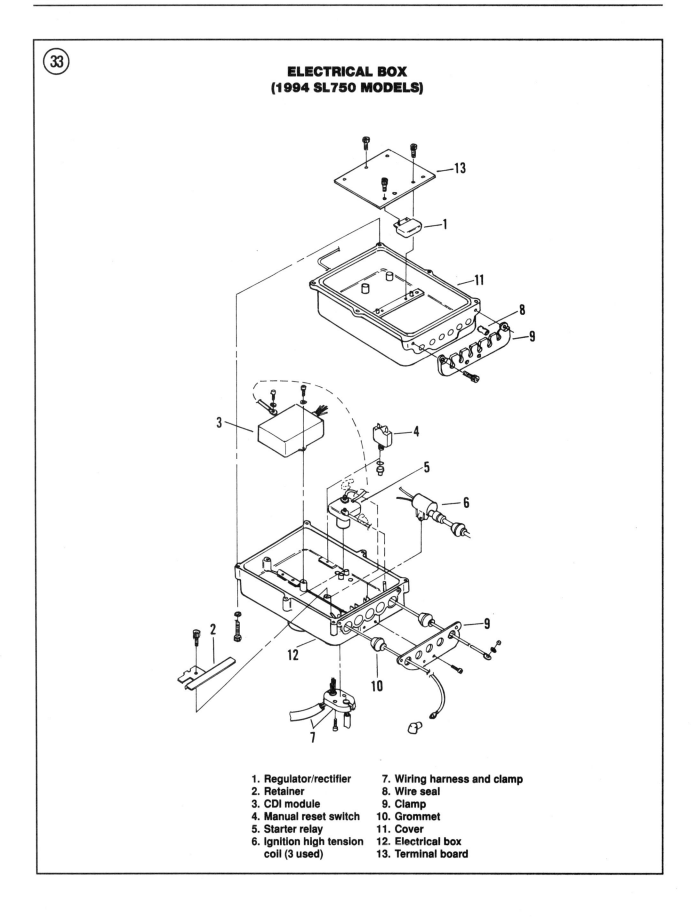

**ELECTRICAL BOX
(1994 SL750 MODELS)**

1. Regulator/rectifier
2. Retainer
3. CDI module
4. Manual reset switch
5. Starter relay
6. Ignition high tension coil (3 used)
7. Wiring harness and clamp
8. Wire seal
9. Clamp
10. Grommet
11. Cover
12. Electrical box
13. Terminal board

6. Replace any part that is damaged or does not meet the minimum specification listed in **Table 6**.

7. Insert the armature (15, **Figure 36**) into the housing (14, **Figure 36**).

8. Position O-ring (16, **Figure 36**) on housing. Lubricate the seal ring lightly to facilitate assembly.

9. Assemble parts (17-20, **Figure 36**). Lubricate the thrust washers and the bearing (20, **Figure 36**) with silicone dielectric grease or equivalent.

10. Install the cover (21, **Figure 36**) over the armature and housing.

11. Install the brushes, holder and springs. Hold brushes away from the commutator while assembling. Make sure that spring(s) are correctly positioned to hold the brushes against the commutator after assembly.

12. Lubricate thrust washers (2 and 3, **Figure 36**) and bearing (6, **Figure 36**) with silicone dielectric grease or equivalent.

13. Install the thrust washers (2 and 3, **Figure 36**) over the end of the armature shaft.

14. Install the O-ring seal (5, **Figure 36**), then install the end cover (4, **Figure 36**).

15. Align covers (4 and 21, **Figure 36**) and install the through bolts (1, **Figure 36**). Check alignment by turning the output shaft. The shaft should turn easily by hand.

16. Test the starter by attaching it to a battery before reinstalling it.

NOTE
If the starter does not operate properly or makes an abnormal noise, it should be disassembled and the problem corrected before reinstalling it.

**Starter Drive Assembly
Removal/Installation**

Refer to **Figure 36**.

1. Remove the engine as described in Chapter Four.

2. Unbolt and remove the front cover (**Figure 37**) from the engine.

3. Remove the flywheel retaining nut, then use a suitable puller to pull the flywheel. Refer to **Figure 38**.

4. Remove the screws (**Figure 39**) attaching the front housing to the front of the engine, then remove the front housing.

5. Withdraw the starter gear (**Figure 40**).

6. Lubricate the bearing (**Figure 41**) in the engine crankcase with grease.

7. Lubricate the thrust washer (**Figure 42**) and install it on the starter gear shaft.

8. Install the starter gear assembly as shown in **Figure 40**.

9. Lubricate the thrust washer (**Figure 43**) and install it on the shaft.

7

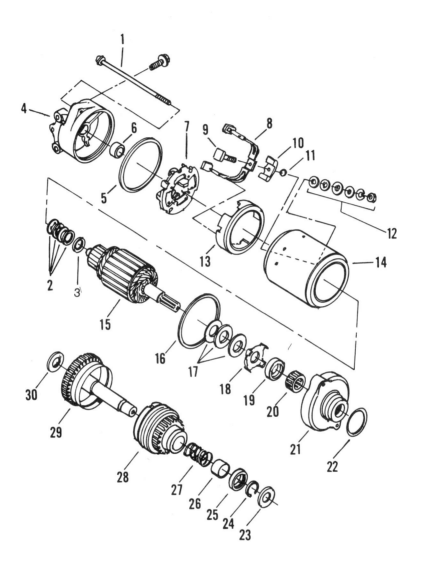

STARTER MOTOR

1. Through bolts
2. Thrust washers
3. Thrust washer
4. End cover
5. O-ring
6. Bearing
7. Brush holder and springs
8. Brushes
9. Terminal bolt
10. Insulator
11. O-ring
12. Insulator washers
13. Cover
14. Housing
15. Armature
16. O-ring
17. Thrust washers
18. Plate
19. Spacer
20. Bearing
21. Cover
22. O-ring
23. Washer
24. Retaining ring
25. Stopper
26. Cover
27. Spring
28. Gear assembly
29. Shaft and gear assembly
30. Washer

10. Clean and dry the sealing surfaces of the front housing and the mating surfaces of the engine and front cover.

11. Coat the sealing surfaces of the front housing and the mating surface of the engine with Loctite 515 Gasket Eliminator (or equivalent).

12. Install the front housing and tighten the retaining screws (**Figure 39**) to the torque specified in **Table 4**.

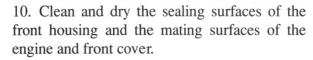

7

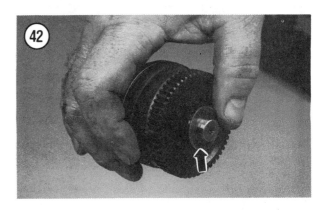

13. Install the flywheel, observing the following:

NOTE
Do not lubricate the tapered mating surfaces of the crankshaft and flywheel. Assembly should be clean and dry before coating the surface with Loctite 262 (red).

a. Clean the tapered surfaces of the crankshaft and the mating surface of the flywheel.
b. Install the key into the slot of the crankshaft. Make sure the key is seated.
c. Coat the tapered surface of the crankshaft with Loctite 262 (red).
d. Install the flywheel, aligning the slot with the key.
e. Coat the threads of the flywheel retaining nut with Loctite 242 (blue), then install and tighten the flywheel retaining nut to the torque listed in **Table 4**.

14. Clean the mating surfaces of the front cover, the front housing and the front of the engine thoroughly.

15. Coat the sealing surfaces of the front of the engine and the mating surfaces of the front housing with Loctite 515 Gasket Eliminator (or equivalent).

16. Install the front housing and tighten the retaining screws to the torque listed in **Table 4**.

17. Coat the mating surfaces of the engine front cover and the front housing with Loctite 515 Gasket Eliminator (or equivalent).

18. Lubricate the bearing (**Figure 44**) in the engine front cover with grease.

19. Install the front cover (**Figure 37**) and tighten the retaining screws to the torque listed in **Table 4**.

ELECTRIC TRIM

The Polaris electric trim (Quick Trim) is controlled by a thumb operated switch (**Figure 45**) located on the left handlebar. Refer to Chapter Five to troubleshoot and repair the electric trim system.

INSTRUMENTS

Multi-Function Panel

Some models are equipped with a multi-function display. Refer to Chapter Three for a description of the multi-function display and

suggested troubleshooting procedures. Service is limited to removing the unit and installing a serviceable similar unit.

Fuel Gauge

On models without a multi-function display, the separate fuel gauge (**Figure 46**) is an electrical devise, controlled by a sender unit located in the fuel tank. Refer to Chapter Two for testing the gauge components. Refer to Chapter Six for safety warnings regarding service to the fuel tank and for removing the sender unit from the tank.

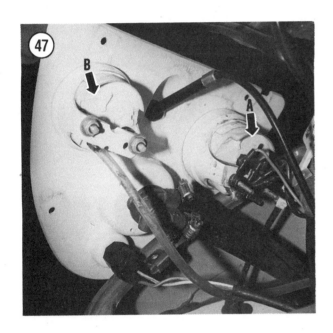

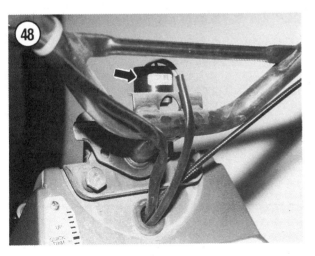

Removal/Installation

To remove the fuel gauge instrument from the console, proceed as follows.

1. Remove the seat and engine cover.
2. Remove the elastic straps that attach the electrical box to the top of the battery.

> *CAUTION*
> *Do not attempt any electrical repair unless the battery ground is first disconnected.*

3. Disconnect the battery ground cable from the negative terminal of the battery.
4. Remove the screws that attach the console and lift the panel up as shown in **Figure 47**.

> *NOTE*
> *Keep the wires that are attached to 1 connector together so they can be easily reattached.*

5. Detach the electrical wires from the gauge (A, **Figure 47**).
6. Remove the 2 nuts that retain the gauge in the panel.
7. Lift the gauge from the panel.
8. Reassemble by reversing the removal procedure. Refer to the wiring diagram for your model to determine the correct wire connections to the gauge.

Warning Buzzer

On models without multi-function display, the high temperature warning buzzer (**Figure 48**) is attached to the center of the handlebar.

1. Remove the screws from the handlebar pad, then remove the pad.
2. Detach the 3 wires leading to the buzzer.
3. Remove the retaining nut from the buzzer and separate the buzzer from the handlebar bracket.
4. Pull the wires up through the grommet in the hull.

7

5. When reinstalling, be sure the wires are properly connected. Refer to the appropriate wiring diagram for your model.

Speedometer

On models without a multi-function display, the speedometer (**Figure 49**) is not an electrical instrument, but is mounted on the panel with the fuel gauge. To remove the gauge, proceed as follows.

1. Remove the screws that attach the console and lift the panel up as shown in **Figure 47**.

2. Detach the tube from the gauge (B, **Figure 47**).

3. Remove the 2 nuts that retain the gauge in the panel.

4. Lift the gauge from the panel.

5. Reassemble by reversing the removal procedure.

Table 1 IGNITION TIMING

Year and model	CDI box identification	Ignition timing @ 3,000 rpm degrees (BTDC)	mm (in.) (BTDC)
1992			
SL 650 B924058			
Early *	F8T16271	22.5-25.5	3.54 (0.139)
Late **	F8T16272	22.5-25.5	3.54 (0.139)
1993			
SL 650 B934058	F8T16273	16.5-19.5	2.01 (0.079)
SL 750 B934070	F8T16273	14.5-17.5	1.59 (0.063)
1994			
SL 650 B944058	F8T16274 (65W95)	16-20	2.01 (0.079)
SL 750 B944070	F8T32071 (75W95)	22-26	3.54 (0.139)
SLT 750 B944170	F8T32071 (75W95)	22-26	3.54 (0.139)
1995			
SL 650 B954058	F8T16274 (65W95)	16-20	2.01 (0.079)
SL650 Std. B954358	F8T16274 (65W95)	16-20	2.01 (0.079)
SL 750 B954070	F8T32071 (75W95)	22-26	3.54 (0.139)
SLT 750 B954170	F8T32071 (75W95)	22-26	3.54 (0.139)
* Early models with large harmonic balancer.			
** Serial No. PLE04039F292 and later models.			

Table 2 SPARK PLUGS

	NGK type	Champion type	Gap mm (in.)
1992-1993 models	BR8ES	RN-3C	0.7 (0.028)
1994-on	BPR7ES	–	0.7 (0.028)

Table 3 CHARGING/IGNITION COILS RESISTANCE

	Resistance
Alternator coil (red/purple to yellow)	0.6 ohms
High tension coils	
Primary winding (black to black/white)	0.6 ohms
Secondary winding (black to spark plug wire)*	3.3 K ohms
Plug cap	5.0 K ohms
Ignition exciter coil (red/white to green/red)	490 ohms
Ignition pulser coil (blue/red to red/white)	90 ohms
Ignition trigger coil (white/yellow to black)	220 ohms

* With the spark plug cap removed. Coil secondary resistance should not be tested with the spark plug cap installed.

Table 4 TIGHTENING TORQUES

	N·m	ft.-lb.
Exhaust manifold	21.7	16
Flywheel cover	8.8	6.5 (78 in.-lb.)
Flywheel housing	8.8	6.5 (78 in.-lb.)
Flywheel nut	74.6	55
Starter mounting screws	7.5-8.1	5.5-6.0
Other fasteners		
5 mm	5.1-5.9	3.8-4.3 (45-52 in.-lb.)
6 mm	7.5-8.8	5.5-6.5 (66-78 in.-lb.)
8 mm	17.6-21.7	13-16
10 mm	35.2-40.7	26-30
12 mm	54.2-59.7	40-44

Table 5 REGULATOR/RECTIFIER AND CUTOFF SWITCH IDENTIFICATION

	Regulator/rectifier unit	Cutoff switch
1992		
SL 650 B924058	LR21	LR50
1993		
SL 650 B934058	LR21	LR50
SL 750 B934070	LR21	LR52

(continued)

Table 5 REGULATOR/RECTIFIER AND CUTOFF SWITCH IDENTIFICATION (continued)

	Regulator/rectifier unit	Cutoff switch
1994		
SL 650 B944058	LR21	LR52
SL 750 B944070	LR23	–
SLT 750 B944170	LR21	–
1995		
SL 650 B954058	LR21	LR52
SL 650 Std. B954358	LR23	–
SL 750 B954070	LR23	–
SLT 750 B954170	LR21	–

Table 6 STARTER MOTOR SPECIFICATIONS

Resistance between	
Commutator segments	less than 0.3 ohms
Input terminal and insulated brushes	less than 0.3 ohms
Brushes	
Minimum length	7.9 mm (5/16 in.)

Chapter Eight

Oil Injection System

Polaris 2-stroke engines are lubricated by oil that is injected into the intake air. The oil circulates through the engine crankcase, and eventually enters the combustion chamber. Components of the engine are lubricated by the oil that clings to the various parts as it passes through the crankcase and cylinders. The oil is burned in the combustion chamber with the fuel and expelled through the exhaust.

The oil is never reused and the amount of oil in the reservoir will diminish as it is used. On 1992-1994 models, a fixed-ratio oil injection system is used. On models so equipped, the injection system delivers oil to the engine at a fixed ratio throughout the entire engine speed range. On 1995 models, a variable ratio oil injection system is used. On these models, the oil pump control lever is connected to the throttle mechanism. The fuel/oil ratio is thereby varied according to engine speed and load cautions.

CAUTION
The engine may be seriously damaged if oil is not constantly being delivered to the engine. Do not allow the oil system to run dry. Bleed the oil injection pump as described in this chapter if the oil lines are disconnected or if air has entered the oil line between the reservoir and the injection pump.

The rider will probably not notice any performance difference if lubrication stops for 1 or more of the 3 cylinders, until the affected cylinder(s) are seriously damaged. It is important to make sure that the engine oil injection system is always properly adjusted and maintained. Oil level in the reservoir (tank) should be checked daily and each time gasoline is added to the fuel tank.

An inline oil filter is installed between the oil tank and the oil pump to prevent contaminants from obstructing oil passages in the oil pump. Inspect the filter for contamination or blockage. If the oil filter is contaminated or blocked, it must be replaced immediately. Refer to Chapter Three for regular maintenance procedures.

CAUTION
A contaminated or plugged oil filter will prevent oil from reaching the engine, causing engine seizure.

SYSTEM COMPONENTS

The plunger type oil pump (**Figure 1**) is driven by the engine crankshaft. The pump draws oil from the reservoir (oil tank), and delivers it to a check valve located in the intake passage of each of the 3 cylinders. The oil reservoir is located in front of the engine (**Figure 2**). On 1992-1994 models, an oil injection check valve is located in each of the carburetor/reed valve adapters as shown in **Figure 3**. On 1995-on models, the oil injection check valves are located in the lower housing of the air intake silencer (**Figure 4**).

The engine will be seriously damaged if the oil system does not deliver oil to each of the 3 cylinders. An oil level sensor is located in the reservoir to warn the operator if the level of oil in the reservoir is low. The low level warning system will not indicate blockage between the reservoir and the pump or other conditions that would stop the delivery of oil, without reducing the amount of oil in the reservoir. The rider will probably not notice any performance difference if lubrication stops for 1 or more of the 3 cylinders, until the affected cylinder(s) are seriously damaged.

OIL PUMP SERVICE

Oil Pump Bleeding

The purpose of bleeding is to remove all air from the oil injection system. The oil pump must be bled whenever one of the following conditions exist.

a. The oil reservoir becomes empty.

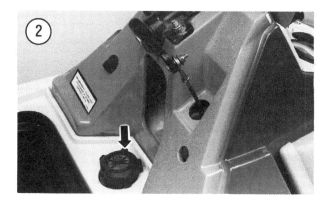

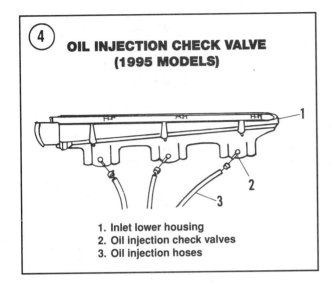

④ **OIL INJECTION CHECK VALVE (1995 MODELS)**

1. Inlet lower housing
2. Oil injection check valves
3. Oil injection hoses

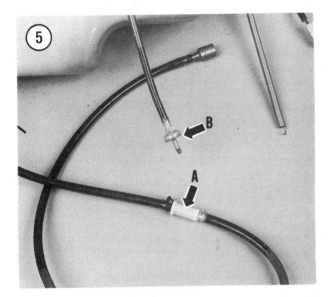

b. Any of the oil injection hoses are disconnected.

c. The craft is turned on its side.

1. Check to be sure the oil reservoir is filled. Refer to Chapter Three for maintenance.

NOTE
*The inline oil filter (A, **Figure 5**) must be installed with the arrow pointing in the direction of oil flow. The oil tank is removed in **Figure 5** for clarity. The vent filter is shown at B, **Figure 5**.*

2. If there is any reason to suspect that the inline oil filter is plugged, refer to Chapter Three and install a new filter.

3. Check that all of the oil hoses are connected properly and not kinked.

4. Place a shop cloth under the oil pump to catch oil discharged from the pump in Step 5.

5. To bleed the main oil hose (between the reservoir and the pump) proceed as follows:

a. Loosen the bleed screw (A, **Figure 6**).

b. Allow oil to flow from the bleed screw port until it is free of air bubbles.

c. If oil does not flow freely from the bleed screw, check for a restriction in the supply line from the reservoir. The restriction could be caused by a kink in the line or a clogged filter (A, **Figure 5**). Make sure the pump has an unrestricted supply of oil before proceeding.

d. Tighten the bleed screw (A, **Figure 6**). Make sure the sealing washer is in place and that the screw is tight.

CAUTION
Do not run the engine without sufficient lubrication to each of the 3 cylinders. If only 1 cylinder is running without lubrication, that cylinder will be damaged in a very short time.

6. Observe the level of the oil in the 3 small injection lines (B, **Figure 6**) to each of the cylinders. Each line should be filled with oil, with

8

no air bubbles. If air is visible in any of the 3 lines, proceed as follows:

    a. Crank the engine with the electric starter and observe the level of the oil in the 3 small injection lines (B, **Figure 6**). The air should be forced out by cranking the engine.

    b. If the injection lines begin to fill with oil when the engine is cranked with the electric starter, continue cranking until the oil reaches the end of the hose.

7. If air is not quickly bled from any of the lines to the individual cylinders as described in Step 6, proceed as follows:

    a. Loosen or remove the clamp from the end of the hose (B, **Figure 6**) which has air in the line, then detach the line from the check valve.

NOTE
Hold the detached oil injection line up so that oil does not drain from the detached line.

    b. Connect a section of clean test hose of the correct size to the check valve.

    c. Test the check valve by first applying pressure to the test hose. The check valve should open when 3-5 psi (21-34 kPa) pressure is applied.

    d. Apply a light vacuum to the test hose. The check valve should be closed.

    e. If the check valve does not operate properly, a new check valve must be installed before proceeding.

    f. Detach the test hose from the check valve, but do not reattach the oil injection hose to the check valve yet.

    g. Crank the engine with the electric starter and observe the level of the oil in the detached injection line.

    h. If the detached line begins to fill with oil when the engine is cranked with the electric starter, continue cranking until the oil reaches the end of the hose, then attach the hose to the check valve.

    i. If the detached oil line does not fill with oil, determine the problem before continuing. First make sure oil is being supplied to the pump, then make sure the pump is operating properly.

Oil Pump Functional Test

If you suspect oil pump failure, perform the following tests.

Oil pump mounted on the engine

The oil pump must be installed on the engine and the engine must be installed in the hull when performing this test.

1. Make sure the oil injection reservoir is full.

2. Check that the main supply line to the pump is attached to the pump and filled with oil. If there is any question, proceed as follows:

    a. Detach the line from the pump and make sure oil flows freely from the hose.

    b. Refer to *Oil Pump Bleeding* in this chapter for suggested causes of reduced oil flow.

    c. Reconnect the main supply line to the pump fitting (C, **Figure 6**).

    d. Bleed the main supply line after attaching it to the pump.

3. Disconnect the oil injection lines from all 3 check valves (**Figure 3** or **Figure 4**). Keep the oil lines pointed up and do not let oil drain from the lines.

4. Crank the engine with the electric starter and observe the level of the oil in the detached injection lines.

5. If the detached lines begin to fill with oil when the engine is cranked with the electric starter, continue cranking until the oil reaches the ends of all of the hoses.

6. If the oil level in 1 or more of the lines does not raise when cranking the engine with the starter, continue testing to determine the cause. Some possible causes are:

    a. Kinked line or lines.

b. Air leak in the supply line to the pump.

c. Damaged oil injection pump or pump drive.

7. Reattach the oil injection hoses to the check valves.

Oil pump removed from the engine

If oil pump failure is suspected, the pump can be checked for proper operation when removed.

1. Remove the oil pump from the engine as described in this chapter.

2. Attach an oil hose the same size as the oil supply hose to the oil pump inlet fitting (C, **Figure 6**).

3. Raise the oil supply hose and fill it with injection oil, then insert the open end into a container of injection oil. Do not allow the oil supply line to come out of the container of oil.

NOTE
It is important to turn the pump in a counterclockwise direction. The pump will not operate properly if the driveshaft is turned the wrong direction.

4. Chuck the oil pump shaft driveshaft with a reversible hand drill and set the drill to rotate the shaft counterclockwise (reverse direction).

5. Hold the pump and operate the hand drill.

6. Observe the oil leaving the pump through the hose fittings (B, **Figure 6**).

7. If oil does not pump from the outlet fittings (B, **Figure 6**), the pump is not operating properly and should be replaced. Individual repair parts of the pump are not available.

8. Remove the pump from the drill and detach the temporary supply hose.

9. If the pump operates satisfactorily, but does not operate when installed, check the following possible causes:

a. Damaged oil pump driveshaft or drive gears in the engine.

b. Oil is not being properly supplied to the pump.

COMPONENT REPLACEMENT

Oil Filter and Vent Filter Removal/Installation

The inline oil filter (A, **Figure 5**) is located in the hose between the oil reservoir and the oil injection pump. The oil filter is directional and must be installed correctly. An arrow indicating the correct direction of oil flow is on the side of the filter. Note the placement of the oil filter in the oil system, drawing a diagram, if necessary, for reassembly. Refer to Chapter Three for regular maintenance of the oil filter.

The inline vent filter (B, **Figure 5**) is located on the vent line for the oil injection pump. If clogged, install a new vent filter.

CAUTION
A contaminated or plugged oil filter will prevent oil from reaching the engine, causing engine seizure.

Oil Reservoir Removal/Installation

The oil reservoir is located between the front storage compartment and the front of the engine.

WARNING
Fire hazard is always present when working on any part of the fuel system, so it is important to follow all safety precautions. Refer to the WARNING at the beginning of Chapter Six.

1. Loosen the fuel filler cap to relieve any pressure in the tank.

2. Lift the front hatch and remove the storage basket (**Figure 7**).

3. Mark the fuel hoses (**Figure 8**, typical) to indicate their position.

4. Loosen the clamps on the fuel hoses attached to the fuel tank, then detach the hoses.

5. Remove the large connector and fuel pickup hoses (**Figure 9**) from the tank on models so equipped.

8

6. Remove the oil injection reservoir (tank) filler cap.

7. Remove the 2 screws (**Figure 10**).

CAUTION
Be prepared to cover all openings as quickly as possible. Plug the detached oil supply hose to stop leakage and prevent the entrance of air into the supply line. If air is allowed to enter this line, it should be filled with oil before starting the engine. Engine damage could result from lack of lubrication if the supply line is not filled with oil prior to starting.

8. Move the oil tank out far enough to disconnect the oil supply and vent hoses (A and B, **Figure 5**).

9. Disconnect the wires from the oil level sensor (**Figure 11**).

10. Cover all openings and store the oil reservoir in such a way that it will not be contaminated while it is removed.

11. When installing, reverse the removal procedure and observe the following:

   a. Make sure the tank is secure.

   b. Make sure that all fuel hoses are attached to the correct places and clamps are tight. The longer pickup hose (**Figure 9**) is for the reserve position. The 2 hose connections that terminate near the top are for the vent and fuel return.

   c. Make sure the oil supply hose from the oil reservoir to the oil pump is filled with injection oil. Bleed the system as described in this chapter if necessary.

   d. Clean all spilled fuel and oil, then check the system for fuel and oil leaks.

Oil Level Gauge

On models with the multi-function display, the warning light will glow when the level of oil in the reservoir becomes low. On models without multi-function display, the alarm buzzer will sound when the oil becomes low. The low oil

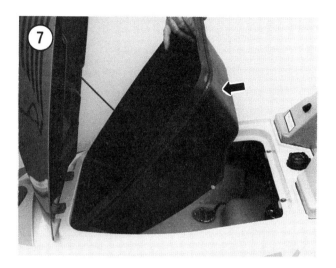

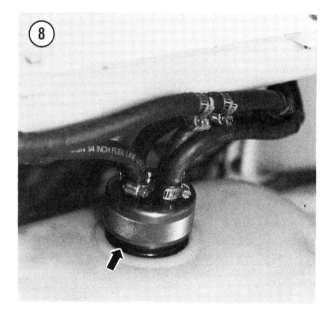

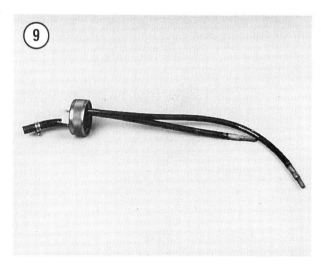

level sending unit is located in the oil tank. Refer to **Figure 11**. Refer to Chapter Seven for testing the sending unit. Refer also to Chapter Seven for service to the multi-function display and the alarm buzzer.

Oil Pump Control Lever and Link Rod (1995-on Models)

On 1995 and later models, a control lever (1, **Figure 12**) is attached to the pump (2, **Figure 12**) to vary the amount of oil delivery. Because the oil pump on late models controls oil flow to the engine, the pump delivery must be matched to the carburetor throttle setting. A rod (3, **Figure 12**) connects the pump control lever to the carburetor throttle linkage (4, **Figure 12**), so the carburetor throttle and the oil pump control move simultaneously.

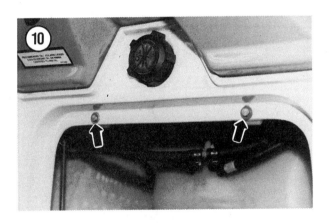

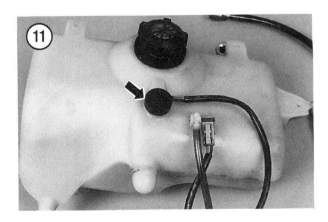

Minimum oil pump output corresponds to idle speed opening of the throttle valve and the wide-open throttle position will move the pump control to its nearly maximum position. The oil pump control lever on 1995 models is spring loaded to the maximum delivery position. Therefore if the rod becomes detached the engine will not be damaged because of insufficient oil. The preload spring (5, **Figure 12**) should turn the pump control to its maximum delivery position.

The amount of oil delivered by the oil pump on 1992-1994 models is fixed and changed only by changing the engine speed.

CAUTION
The engine will be seriously damaged if the oil system is allowed to run dry. If the oil lines are disconnected or if air has entered the oil line between the reservoir and the injection pump, refer to the Oil Injection Pump Bleeding procedure in this chapter. The rider will probably not notice any performance difference if lubrication stops for 1 or more of the 3 cylinders, until the affected cylinder(s) is seriously damaged. It is important to make sure that the engine oil injection system is always properly adjusted and maintained. Check the oil level in the reservoir (tank) daily and each time gasoline is added to the fuel tank.

Oil Pump Removal/Installation

The oil pump is located on the right side of the engine. It is driven by a gear located on the crankshaft. Refer to **Figure 13**.

1. Prepare to plug the oil hoses attached to the pump fittings (A and B, **Figure 14**) as they are disconnected. The supply hose connected to the fitting (A, **Figure 14**) is larger than the outlet hoses attached to the fittings (B, **Figure 14**).

2. Loosen the hose clamp, then detach the supply hose from fitting (A, **Figure 14**). Plug the supply hose quickly to stop the oil from running out.

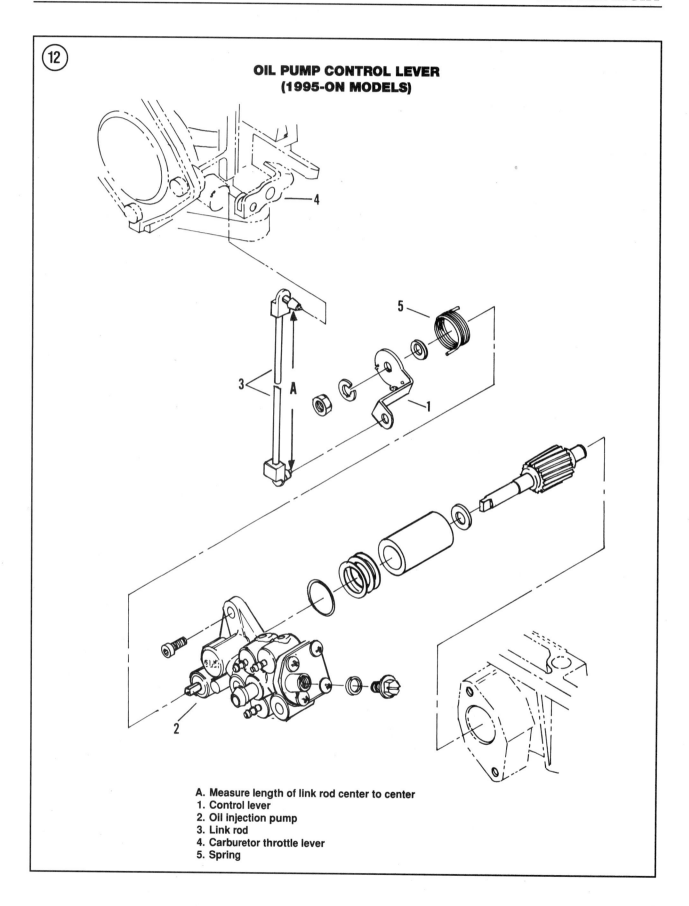

⑫

**OIL PUMP CONTROL LEVER
(1995-ON MODELS)**

A. Measure length of link rod center to center
1. Control lever
2. Oil injection pump
3. Link rod
4. Carburetor throttle lever
5. Spring

(13)

OIL INJECTION PUMP

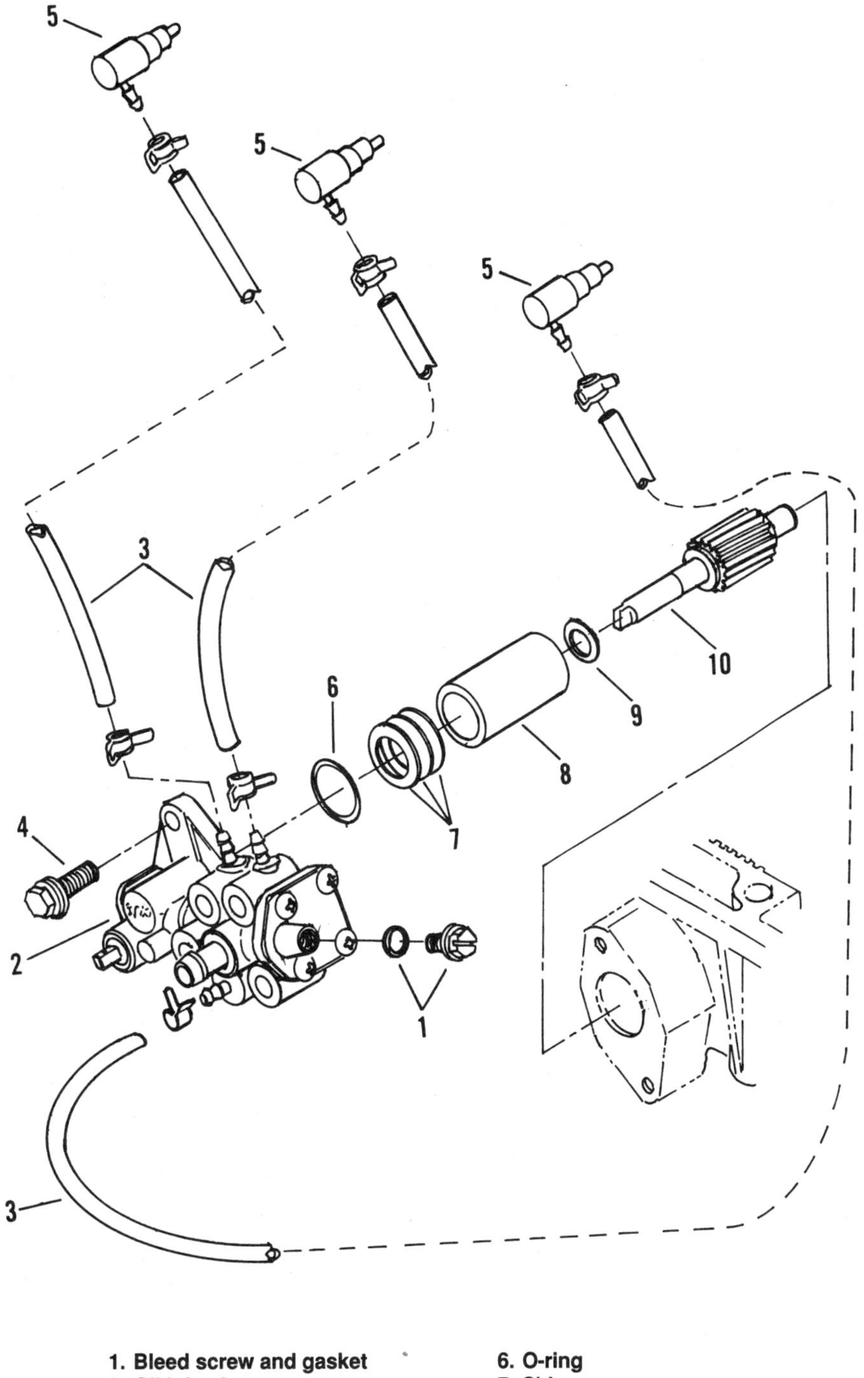

1. Bleed screw and gasket
2. Oil injection pump
3. Oil outlet hoses
4. Screws
5. Check valves
6. O-ring
7. Shims
8. Bushing
9. Spacer
10. Gear and shaft

8

3. Loosen the hose clamps on the outlet hoses attached to the 3 fittings (B, **Figure 14**). Detach and plug the hoses.

4. On 1995-on models, detach the link rod (3, **Figure 12**) from the control lever (1, **Figure 12**).

NOTE
A new control rod must be installed if the link rod is detached from the lever. The attaching clip will be damaged by removing it from the lever.

5. Remove the 2 attaching screws (C, **Figure 14**).

NOTE
*The lower screw (C, **Figure 14**) may be difficult to remove unless the engine is removed and separated from the mounting plate. If it is necessary to remove the engine, refer to Chapter Four.*

6. Pull the pump from the mounting boss. Be careful not to lose the O-ring (6, **Figure 13**) or shims (7, **Figure 13**).

7. The gear and shaft (10, **Figure 13**), bushing (8) and related parts can be removed if necessary for inspection.

8. When installing, observe the following:

   a. Measure how far the oil pump housing extends from the base of the oil pump.

   b. Measure the depth from the pump mounting flange of the crankcase to the bushing (8, **Figure 13**) or installed shims (7).

   c. Subtract the height of the pump extension (measured in substep a) from the depth (measured in substep b). The difference is the end play of the shaft (10, **Figure 13**).

   d. The shaft end play should be limited to the value listed in **Table 1**, by adding or removing shims (7, **Figure 13**).

   e. Install a new O-ring (6, **Figure 13**) on the extension of the oil pump.

   f. Install the oil pump and tighten the retaining screws securely.

   g. Attach the oil lines and bleed the system as described in this chapter.

NOTE
*On 1995-on models, the fittings at the ends of the oil pump control link rod (3, **Figure 12**) are damaged by removing. Install a new rod if it was removed. The length (A, **Figure 12**) of the link rod should be the same as listed in **Table 1**. The link rod should not be bent or otherwise damaged.*

   h. On 1995-on models, attach the link rod (3, **Figure 12**) to the carburetor and the pump control lever.

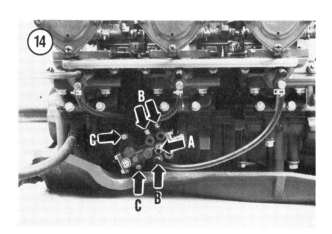

Table 1 OIL INJECTION PUMP SPECIFICATIONS	
Oil pump driveshaft end play	0.3-0.6 mm (0.012-0.024 in.)
Oil reservoir capacity	
All SL 650 and SL 750 models	3.3 L (3.5 qt.)
SLT 750 models	4.7 L (5 qt.)
Oil control link rod	
Length, 1995-on	162.6-164.1 mm (6.40-6.46 in.)

Chapter Nine

Cooling System

This chapter describes inspection and flushing procedures for the engine cooling system. If you are going to store your water craft for an extended length of time, flush the cooling system as described in Chapter Eleven.

HOSES

Routing

The jet pump provides cooling water to the engine and the exhaust for all models. Some models may have upgrade kits installed and the routing of hoses (and water) may be different than shown in the cooling system flow chart. Note any differences between the flow chart and the routing of hoses on your craft.

a. 1992 models: **Figure 1**.
b. 1993 models: **Figure 2**.
c. 1994 and 1995: models **Figure 3**.

Hose and Fitting Replacement

Hoses and fittings are measured by their inside diameters. Always replace hoses and fittings with exact duplicates to ensure proper water flow, cooling and drainage. On some models for example, the upper fitting on the exhaust pipe is also a screen. The attached hose connects the upper and lower chambers of the exhaust pipe and the screen in the upper fitting should not be removed. Cleaning the screen in this fitting should be included in regular maintenance as described in Chapter Three. If replacing a hose

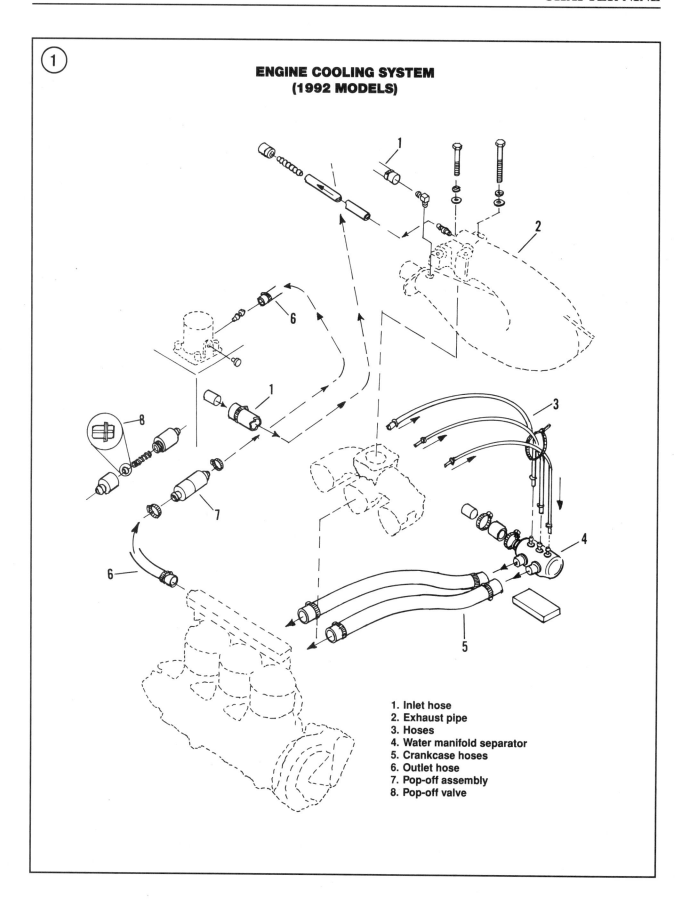

① **ENGINE COOLING SYSTEM
(1992 MODELS)**

1. Inlet hose
2. Exhaust pipe
3. Hoses
4. Water manifold separator
5. Crankcase hoses
6. Outlet hose
7. Pop-off assembly
8. Pop-off valve

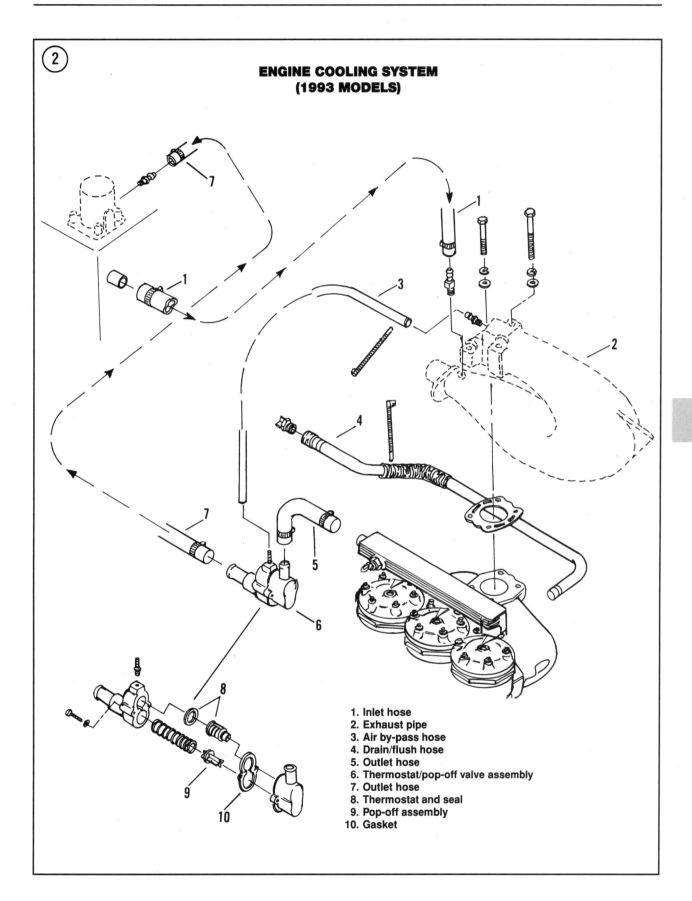

**ENGINE COOLING SYSTEM
(1993 MODELS)**

9

1. Inlet hose
2. Exhaust pipe
3. Air by-pass hose
4. Drain/flush hose
5. Outlet hose
6. Thermostat/pop-off valve assembly
7. Outlet hose
8. Thermostat and seal
9. Pop-off assembly
10. Gasket

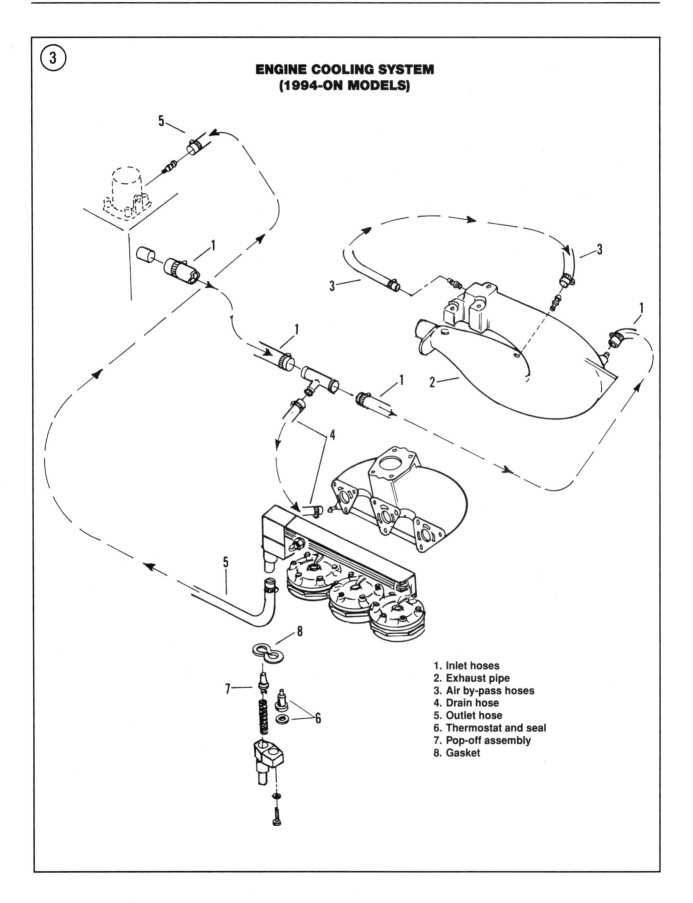

③

**ENGINE COOLING SYSTEM
(1994-ON MODELS)**

1. Inlet hoses
2. Exhaust pipe
3. Air by-pass hoses
4. Drain hose
5. Outlet hose
6. Thermostat and seal
7. Pop-off assembly
8. Gasket

or fitting, take the old part with you to a Polaris dealership. If the new part is different, have the dealer explain the difference to you.

Models produced for 1992 are not equipped with a thermostat. The engine temperature is controlled by a balance of fitting and hose sizes. Any changes in the cooling system on 1992 models (**Figure 1**) is especially critical and can result in serious damage.

Hose Clamps

If the hose is retained by plastic tie wraps, it is necessary to cut the old clamp to remove it. If the old hose is reattached, it may be difficult to tighten a new tie wrap enough to prevent leakage. The hose may slide from the fitting when under pressure and cause engine damage if the clamp is not installed properly. Screw clamps can be substituted and a new hose can be installed. Do not tighten screw type hose clamps enough to cut through the hose.

MAINTENANCE

Flushing the System

Flush the cooling system as part of the regular maintenance outlined in Chapter Three. More

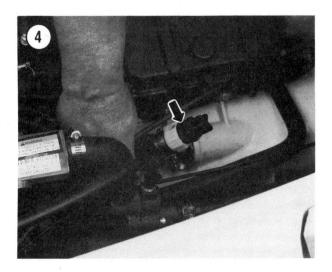

frequent flushing is recommended if the craft is operated in muddy, silty or salty water. Flushing will help prevent the cooling system from becoming blocked by sand and salt deposits.

The following procedure can be used for flushing the cooling system as well as supplying water to the engine when running it out of the water. When storing, use the flushing procedure described in Chapter Eleven; do not use the following procedure.

Read this procedure through before flushing the cooling system. If you have any questions, ask your Polaris dealer before beginning.

> *CAUTION*
> *Never flush a hot engine. The engine may be damaged if it is not allowed to cool before flushing. Also, never attempt to flush an engine that is not running, because water will enter the engine's cylinders and cause extensive damage.*

> *NOTE*
> *A flush kit is available for models not originally equipped. It is recommended that the flush kit be installed to make the flushing procedure easier.*

1. Remove the seat and engine cover.

2A. On 1992 and 1993 models, locate the drain and flush hose and fitting (**Figure 4**).

2B. On 1994-on models, locate the flushing adapter (**Figure 5**).

> *NOTE*
> *It may be necessary to attach an adapter before the hose can be attached.*

3. Remove the plug from the flush hose (**Figure 4**) or flush adapter (**Figure 5**) and attach a garden hose.

> *NOTE*
> *The engine can be damaged if the water is turned on too soon. It is possible that water from the cooling system can enter the engine cylinders if the engine is not yet running.*

4. Attach the hose to a faucet that can supply a steady supply of clean freshwater, but *do not turn the water on.*

5. Turn the fuel valve ON.

> *WARNING*
> *The exhaust gasses are poisonous. Do not run the engine in a closed area. Make sure there is plenty of ventilation.*

6. Press the starter button and start the engine.

7. Turn the water faucet ON as soon as the engine starts.

> *CAUTION*
> *The engine can be damaged if it runs for longer than a few seconds without a supply of cooling water. Also, do not operate the engine at high speed or for very long (no more than about 3 minutes) with the craft out of the water. The flushing attachment and water supply is not sufficient to cool the engine under these conditions.*

8. Increase the engine speed slightly. The engine should be completely flushed in about 1 minute.

9. When stopping the engine, first turn OFF the water to the flushing attachment.

10. Stop the engine within about 10 seconds. Water should be expelled from the cooling system within this time.

11. Disconnect the garden hose from the flushing adapter or hose and install the plug (**Figure 4** or **Figure 5**). Be careful not to drain water from the flushing hose into the engine after the engine is stopped.

12. Wipe any water from the engine and engine compartment.

Draining the Engine Cooling System (1992-1993)

The procedure for draining 1992-1993 models is different from later models. Refer to the correct procedure for your model.

1. Remove the seat and engine cover.

2. Remove the exhaust/water box and drain water from the unit.

3. Detach the lower hoses from the left side of the crankcase.

4. Disconnect the water inlet hose from the exhaust pipe. This hose begins at the water connection located at the right rear of the hull, but the hose should be detached from the exhaust pipe.

5. Raise the right side of the craft and allow water to drain from the engine.

6. Remove the plug from the end of the drain/flush hose.

7. If the system is to be filled with antifreeze, refer to the *Off Season Storage* described in Chapter Eleven.

8. Install the plug when water has stopped draining.

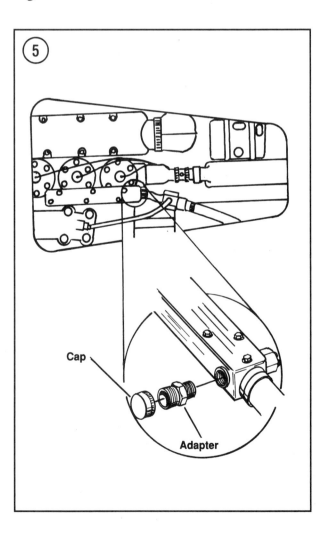

9. Attach the hose that was detached from the exhaust pipe in Step 4.

Draining the Engine Cooling System (1994-on)

On 1994-on models, the engine cooling system is drained automatically. Draining is accomplished by starting the engine after the craft is removed from the water and accelerating the engine slightly before stopping it.

The procedure for draining 1992-1993 models is different. Refer to the preceeding description in this chapter for the earlier models.

COMPONENT REPLACEMENT

Internal Pop-Off Valve (1992)

A pop-off valve is located in the coolant exit hose on 1992 models (**Figure 1**). The pop-off valve (1, **Figure 6**) can be disassembled, but it is important to assemble the unit correctly. The shorter end of the valve (1, **Figure 6**) must be toward the spring (2, **Figure 6**). The assembly must be installed in the hose as shown so the valve will allow cooling water to pass from the engine.

Thermostat and Pop-Off Valve (1993)

The thermostat and pop-off valve assembly is located in the coolant exit hose on 1993 models (**Figure 2**). The pop-off valve should open when the engine speed is increased to 3,000-3,200 rpm and the thermostat should open when the temperature reaches 61.7° C (143° F).

The assembly (1, **Figure 7**) can be disassembled for inspection and cleaning, but it is important to assemble the unit correctly. The thermostat and gasket (2, **Figure 7**) should be installed as shown. The small end of the pop-off valve (3, **Figure 7**) must be in the spring (4, **Figure 7**) as shown. Make sure that the gasket (5, **Figure 7**) does not leak when the unit is assembled and installed. The fitting (6, **Figure 7**) connects to the air bypass hose that is also connected to the fitting (7, **Figure 7**) on the exhaust pipe.

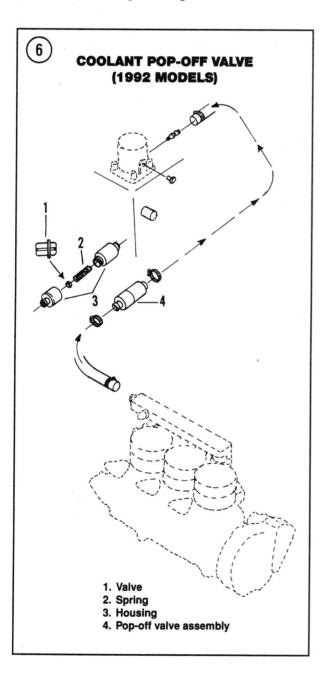

(6)

COOLANT POP-OFF VALVE (1992 MODELS)

1. Valve
2. Spring
3. Housing
4. Pop-off valve assembly

9

Thermostat and Pop-Off Valve (1994-on)

The thermostat and pop-off valve assembly is located in a housing attached to the coolant outlet manifold on 1994-on models (1, **Figure 8**). The pop-off valve should open when the engine speed is increased to 3,000-3,200 rpm and the thermostat should open when the temperature reaches 61.7° C (143° F).

The housing can be separated from the outlet manifold for inspection and cleaning, but it is important to assemble the unit correctly. The thermostat and gasket (2, **Figure 8**) should be installed as shown. The small end of the pop-off valve (3, **Figure 8**) must be in the spring (4, **Figure 8**) as shown. Make sure that the gasket (5, **Figure 8**) does not leak when the unit is assembled and installed. A hose connects the fittings (6 and 7, **Figure 8**) to provide an air bypass on the exhaust pipe.

Exhaust Coolant Filter (1994-on)

A filter screen is attached to the upper fitting (6, **Figure 8**) for the air bypass hose on 1995 models and some 1994 models. The filter traps debris that is circulated with the cooling water, helping to ensure an adequate supply for proper cooling. The filter should be removed and cleaned as required to make sure the exhaust is cooled properly.

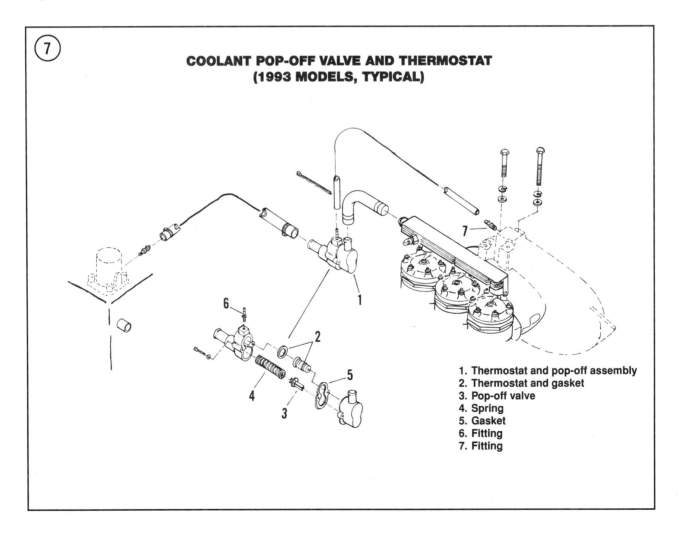

⑦

**COOLANT POP-OFF VALVE AND THERMOSTAT
(1993 MODELS, TYPICAL)**

1. Thermostat and pop-off assembly
2. Thermostat and gasket
3. Pop-off valve
4. Spring
5. Gasket
6. Fitting
7. Fitting

1. Loosen the clamp and detach the hose from the top fitting (6, **Figure 8**).

2. Use a deep 9/16 in. 6 point socket or a flare nut wrench to unscrew the fitting from the exhaust manifold.

3. Carefully withdraw the fitting and filter from the exhaust. The filter extends into the manifold and may catch slightly.

4. Clean any debris from the filter and inspect the condition of the filter screen. Install a new fitting and screen if it is damaged. Leaving the filter out may reduce performance and can cause damage.

5. Reinstall the fitting and filter. Tighten the fitting securely.

6. Attach the air bypass hose and secure the hose to the fitting with a clamp.

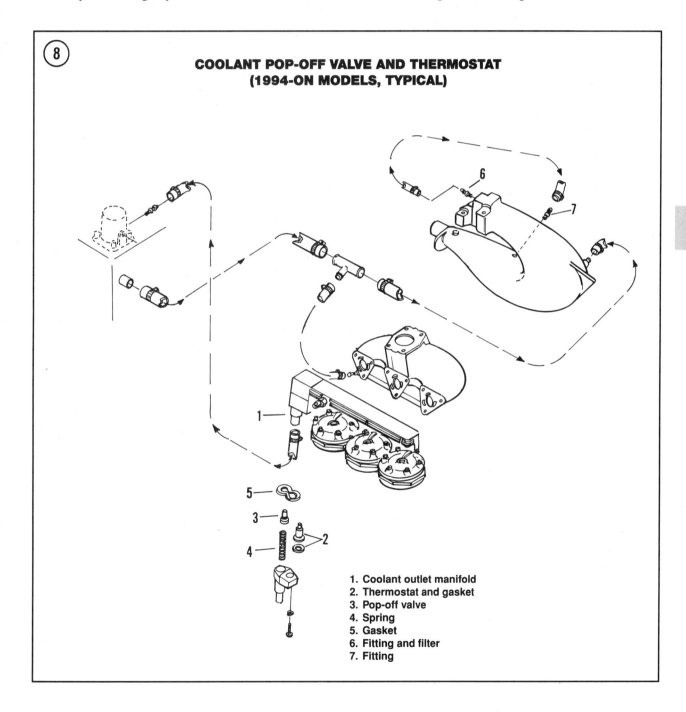

(8)

**COOLANT POP-OFF VALVE AND THERMOSTAT
(1994-ON MODELS, TYPICAL)**

9

1. Coolant outlet manifold
2. Thermostat and gasket
3. Pop-off valve
4. Spring
5. Gasket
6. Fitting and filter
7. Fitting

Chapter Ten

Steering System

The main components of the steering system are the handlebar assembly (1, **Figure 1** or **Figure 2**), lever 3, **Figure 1** or **Figure 2**), steering cable (3, **Figure 1** or **Figure 2**) and steering nozzle (4, **Figure 1** or **Figure 2**). Adjustment of the steering cable is described in Chapter Three. All models are similar, but the steering cable (3, **Figure 2**) is adjusted at the front on 1995-on models. The cable (3, **Figure 1**) on 1992-1994 models is adjusted at the rear, where it exits the hull.

COMPONENT REPLACEMENT

Handlebar Cover

The foam handlebar cover (5, **Figure 1** or **Figure 2**) is wrapped around the handlebar and brace rod. The pad affords protection to the rider and should be maintained in good condition. Remove the screws attaching the upper part of the pad to the lower part, then pull the pad from the handlebar. On some models, the multi-function display (6, **Figure 2**) is located in the center of the pad.

> *WARNING*
> *Do not operate the craft with the handlebar cover damaged or removed. Serious injury could result.*

Handlebar Grips

A loose or damaged grip can cause the rider to lose control. Replace or reglue grips when required.

1A. To remove the grip without damaging it, proceed as follows:

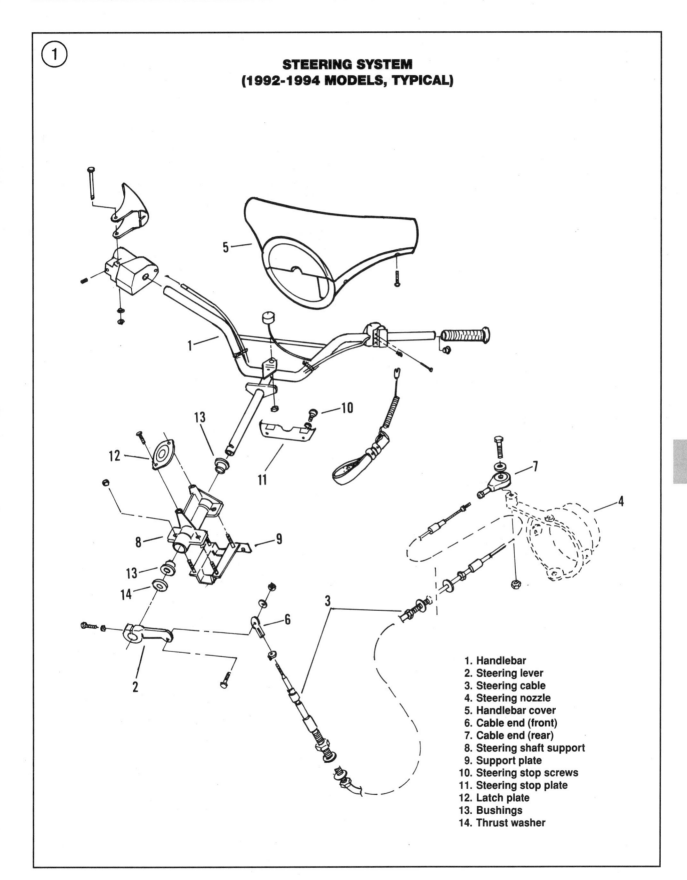

① **STEERING SYSTEM
(1992-1994 MODELS, TYPICAL)**

10

1. Handlebar
2. Steering lever
3. Steering cable
4. Steering nozzle
5. Handlebar cover
6. Cable end (front)
7. Cable end (rear)
8. Steering shaft support
9. Support plate
10. Steering stop screws
11. Steering stop plate
12. Latch plate
13. Bushings
14. Thrust washer

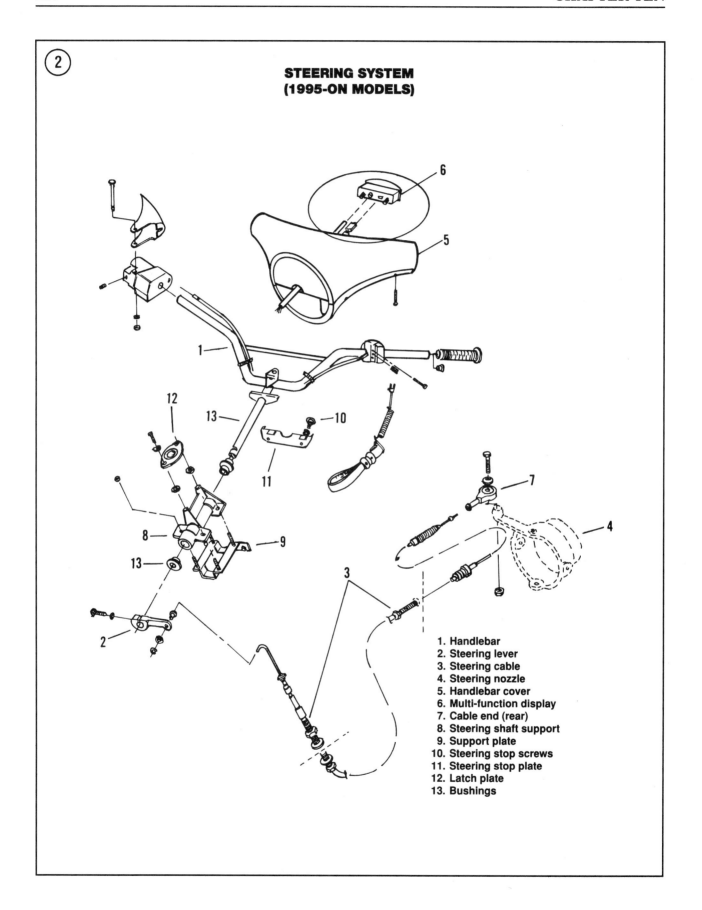

**STEERING SYSTEM
(1995-ON MODELS)**

1. Handlebar
2. Steering lever
3. Steering cable
4. Steering nozzle
5. Handlebar cover
6. Multi-function display
7. Cable end (rear)
8. Steering shaft support
9. Support plate
10. Steering stop screws
11. Steering stop plate
12. Latch plate
13. Bushings

a. Insert a long, thin screwdriver blade between the grip and the handlebar.

b. With the screwdriver in place, squirt some electrical contact cleaner between the grip and the handlebar.

c. Remove the screwdriver quickly and twist the grip, then slide the grip from the handlebar.

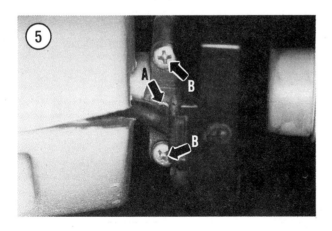

1B. To remove a damaged grip, carefully cut the grip lengthwise and peel the grip from the handlebar.

2. Remove all sealer residue from the handlebar.

3. If you are reinstalling the used grips, remove as mush sealer as possible from inside the grip.

NOTE
It is important to seal the grips to the handlebar. Loose grips will not become tighter with use.

4. Install the handlebar grip using an approved sealant. Follow the sealant manufacturer's instructions.

Handlebar and Stem

The steering stem is welded to the handlebar. Refer to **Figure 1** or **Figure 2**.

1. Open the front compartment.

2. Remove the handlebar cover and handlebar grips as described in this chapter.

3. Remove hand throttle control from the right side as follows:

a. Loosen the cable adjuster (**Figure 3**), align the cable with slot in housing, then pull the cable from the housing.

b. Detach the end of the cable from the throttle lever. If necessary, remove the E-ring (A, **Figure 4**) and the pivot pin (B, **Figure 4**).

NOTE
It is important that all sealer is removed from the handlebar before attempting to remove the throttle lever housing.

c. Loosen the set screw (C, **Figure 4**) and pull the housing from the handlebar.

4. Remove the switch assembly from the left side of the handlebar as follows.

a. Loosen the set screw (A, **Figure 5**).

b. Loosen screws (B and C, **Figure 5**).

10

NOTE
It is important that all sealer is removed from the handlebar before attempting to remove the switch assembly.

c. Pull the switch assembly from the handlebar. It may be necessary to detach the wires before the switch can be removed.

5. Detach the steering cable (A, **Figure 6**) from the lever.

6. Loosen clamp screw (B, **Figure 6**), then pull the steering lever from the steering shaft.

7. Remove the thrust washers and pull steering shaft from the bracket and bushings.

8. Coat the steering shaft and bearings with Polaris marine grease part No. 2871066 or equivalent.

9. Install the steering shaft through the support housing and bearings.

10. Install the thrust washers at the lower end of the steering shaft.

NOTE
Apply Loctite 242 (blue) to the threads of all fasteners of the steering system.

11. Slide the steering lever onto the lower end of the steering shaft, then tighten the clamp screw to the torque listed in **Table 1**.

12. Attach the forward end of the steering cable to the steering lever. Tighten the retaining screw on 1992-1994 models to the torque listed in **Table 1**.

13. Turn the steering first to the right, then to the left and check for free movement.

14. Check the steering center adjustment and adjust the cable as described in Chapter Three if necessary.

15. When installing the switch on the left handlebar, tighten the screws (**Figure 5**) as follows:

a. Loosen the set screw (A, **Figure 5**), then install the switch assembly loosely.

b. Position the switch where it can be easily activated.

c. Tighten the lower screw (C, **Figure 5**) to 2.5 N•m (22 in.-lb.) torque.

d. Tighten the upper screw (B, **Figure 5**) to 2.5 N•m (22 in.-lb.) torque.

e. Tighten the set screw (A, **Figure 5**) to 1.1-1.4 N•m (10-12 in.-lb.) torque.

f. Tighten the lower screw (C, **Figure 5**) to 2.8-4.5 N•m (25-40 in.-lb.) torque.

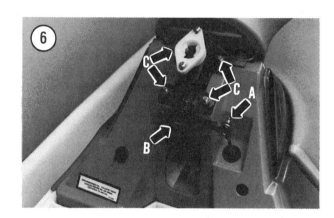

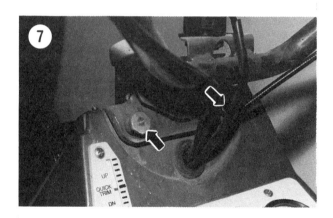

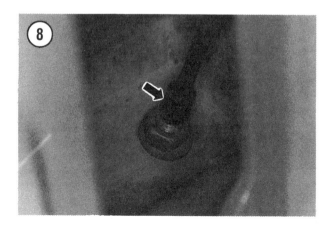

g. Tighten the upper screw (B, **Figure 5**) to 2.8-4.5 N.m (25-40 in.-lb.) torque.

h. Tighten the set screw (A, **Figure 5**) to 16.3 N.m (30 in.-lb.) torque.

16. Install the throttle lever on the right handlebar as follows.

a. Slide the lever housing onto the right handlebar and position it so the throttle can be operated easily.

b. Tighten the set screw (C, **Figure 4**) to the torque listed in **Table 1**.

c. Attach the throttle cable to the lever and adjust the cable free play as described in Chapter Three.

17. Install the grips using the appropriate sealer.

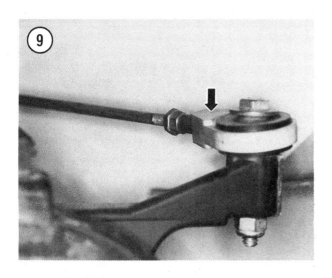

Steering Shaft Support

Refer to **Figure 1** for 1992-1994 models or **Figure 2** for 1995 models.

1. Remove the handlebar as described in this chapter.

2. Remove the 4 nuts (C, **Figure 6**) and lift the steering shaft support from the hull.

3. Withdraw the support plate (9, **Figure 1** or **Figure 2**) after removing the stop screws (**Figure 7**) and the stop plate (11, **Figure 1** or **Figure 2**).

Steering Cable

The front of the steering cable on 1992-1994 models is provided with a cable end (6, **Figure 1**) that is attached to the steering lever with a bolt as shown. The front of 1995 models is attached directly to the steering lever and retained with a clip as shown in **Figure 2**. The cable is provided with a cable end (7, **Figure 1** or **Figure 2**) at the rear of all models and the cable end is attached to the steering nozzle (4, **Figure 1** or **Figure 2**) with a bolt as shown. Remove the cable and cable housing as follows.

1. Open the front compartment and remove the seat.

2. Detach the front of the cable from the steering arm (2, **Figure 1** or **Figure 2**).

3. On 1992-1994 models, loosen the locknut, then remove the rod end (6, **Figure 1**) from the end of the cable.

4. Remove the nut (**Figure 8**) from the front end of the cable housing.

5. Detach rod end at the rear of the cable (**Figure 9**) from the steering nozzle.

6. Loosen the locknut, then remove the rod end (7, **Figure 1** or **Figure 2**) from the rear of the cable.

7. Remove the nut (**Figure 10**) from the end of the cable housing.

10

8. Withdraw the cable from the hull at both ends. Check the cable for attachments inside the engine compartment, when removing it.

9. Install the cable by reversing the removal procedure. The color band on the cable housing should be toward the rear (pump). Refer to **Table 1** for the recommended torque values. Be sure the cable is properly routed through the engine compartment and does not interfere with other components.

10. Adjust the cable to center the steering as described in Chapter Three. Adjustment is accomplished at the front of the cable (**Figure 8**) on early models or at the rear of the cable (**Figure 10**) on later models. Refer to **Table 1** for the recommended tightening torque for the nuts that clamp the cable housing at the rear of the hull.

11. Turn the steering first to the right, then to the left and check for free movement.

Table 1 TORQUE VALUES

	N·m	ft.-lb.
Front compartment latch to steering		
support bracket	19	14
Steering cable front rod end to steering lever		
1992-1994	4.5	40 in.-lb.
Steering cable rear rod end to jet nozzle		
All models*	10.8	8
Steering cable housing nut at the rear of the hull		
1992-1994	40.7	30
1995-on	5.9	52 in.-lb.
Steering lever clamp screw	24.4	18
Steering shaft support bracket	19	14
Steering stop screws	19	14
Throttle housing right handlebar		
Set screw	1.4-1.5	12-14 in.-lb.
Switch housing left handlebar		
Set screw	Refer to text	
Clamp screw	Refer to text	
* Do not overtighten this bolt.		

Chapter Eleven

Off-Season Storage

STORAGE

One of the most critical aspects of maintaining a personal watercraft is off-season storage. If your watercraft is stored improperly for several months, serious problems and a general deterioration of the craft's condition is a nearly certain result. To minimize the damage, prepare the craft for storage and service as described in this chapter.

Selecting a Storage Area

Many people store their watercraft in home garages; however, facilities for long term boat storage are readily available for rent or lease.

Consider the following points when selecting a building for storage.

1. The storage area must be dry. Heating is not necessary (even in cold temperatures) but the building should be well insulated to minimize extreme variations in temperature.

2. Avoid buildings with large windows or cover the windows to prevent direct sunlight from falling upon the craft. Covering windows is also a good security measure.

Preparing Craft for Storage

Careful preparation will minimize deterioration and make it easier to return the craft to service later. The following is one satisfactory storage procedure.

1. Repair any service problems that were known before storing the craft.

2. Remove the seat and engine cover.

3. Flush the cooling system as described in this chapter.

4. Drain water from the cooling system. Fill the cooling system with antifreeze as described in this chapter if there is any possibility (no matter how remote) that the watercraft may be exposed to temperatures below 0° C (32° F).

> *WARNING*
> *Serious fire hazards always exist around gasoline. Do not allow any smoking in areas where fuel is being mixed or while refueling your machine. Always have a sufficiently large fire extinguisher, rated for gasoline and electrical fires, within reach.*

5. Either drain the fuel tank completely or service the fuel tank with STA-BIL or equivalent fuel conditioner/stabilizer as directed by the manufacturer. Refer to **Table 1** for fuel tank capacity for your model.

6A. Fog the engine with Polaris fogging oil (part No. 2870791 or equivalent) as described in this chapter. The fogging procedure should be sufficient to use the gasoline remaining in the carburetors.

6B. If the fogging procedure described in Step 6A is *not used*, proceed as follows:

> *CAUTION*
> *Blow away any dirt that has accumulated around the spark plug base before removing the spark plugs. Dirt could fall into the cylinder when a plug is removed, causing serious engine damage.*

  a. Remove the 3 spark plugs (**Figure 1**).

  b. Pour about 1 teaspoon of engine oil into each cylinder.

  c. Apply antiseize compound to the spark plug threads, then reinstall the spark plugs.

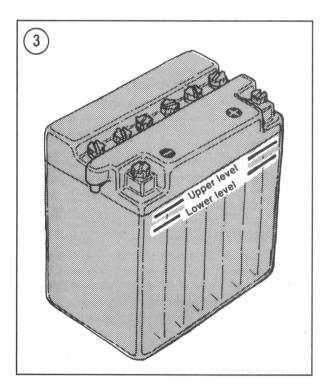

d. Crank the engine to distribute the oil in the cylinders.

7. Lubricate the throttle and choke cables as described in Chapter Three.

8. Lubricate the steering cable as described in Chapter Three.

9. Wash the craft completely with mild (dish) soap and warm freshwater. Make certain to remove dirt from the hard to clean parts.

10. Rinse the craft thoroughly with clean freshwater and dry with clean cloths. Allow the craft to air dry completely if possible.

11. Remove the straps (**Figure 2**) holding the electrical box to the top of the battery, then lift the electrical box and battery cover from the battery.

12. Disconnect the ground cable from the negative terminal of the battery.

13. Disconnect the positive cable from the battery.

14. Remove the battery.

15. Clean the battery cables and battery terminals, then coat the terminals and cable ends with petroleum jelly.

16. Check the electrolyte level in the battery (**Figure 3**) and if necessary, fill with distilled water. Refer to Chapter Seven for battery service.

17. If necessary, charge the battery. The battery should be recharged about once each month.

18. Store the battery in a cool, dry place out of direct sunlight and in a location that will not freeze.

19. Refer to the procedure in the *Pre-Season Service* section of Chapter Three and grease the driveshaft couplings and bearing housing.

20. Spray the engine and other metal parts with Polaris metal protectant part No. 2871064 (WD-40, JB-80, CRC 5-56, LPS or equivalent) to prevent corrosion.

21. Reposition the covers on the craft, but do not latch the covers. Allow room for air to circulate freely throughout the engine compartment.

22. Cover the entire craft with a tarp or heavy drop cloth. This cover serves mainly as a dust cover and must not hold moisture inside. Do not wrap this cover tightly, because it may trap condensed moisture. Leave room for air to circulate around the craft.

Engine Fogging

This procedure coats the internal parts of the engine including the crankshaft, main bearings, connecting rod bearings, pistons and rings. with oil to prevent rust or corrosion during storage. The manufacturer recommends the use of Engine Storage Fogging Oil (part No. 2870791) that is available from a Polaris dealership.

1. Remove the seat and engine cover.

2. Loosen the large clamp (**Figure 4**) from the air intake silencer.

3. Remove the 6 screws attaching the cover of the air intake silencer, then remove the cover.

4. Remove the air intake screen (**Figure 5**).

11

WARNING
The exhaust gases are poisonous. Do not run the engine in a closed area. Make sure there is plenty of ventilation.

CAUTION
Prolonged running without coolant will cause serious engine damage. Even with freshwater supplied to the engine by the flushing attachment, do not run the engine for more than 10 seconds or the rubber parts of the exhaust system will be damaged. Never operate the engine at maximum speed out of the water.

5. Make the fogging oil spray ready, then start the engine.

6. Quickly spray the fogging oil into the carburetors for about 2-3 seconds each, then quickly stop the engine.

NOTE
Do not crank the engine or otherwise turn the engine crankshaft after fogging until you are ready to remove the engine from storage.

7. Assemble the gasket (A, **Figure 6**) around the air intake screen (B, **Figure 6**), then position the screen assembly in the lower part of the air intake silencer (**Figure 5**).

8. Apply Loctite 242 (blue) to the mating surface between the lower part of the silencer housing and the upper cover (C, **Figure 6**), then install the upper cover.

9. Install the cover attaching screws and tighten securely.

10. Slide the air intake over the silencer, then install and tighten the clamp (**Figure 4**). The opening of the air intake should be down, toward the driveshaft.

Cooling System Flushing

The engine on 1992 models is not equipped with a flush kit. If not already fitted, install the optional flush kit (part No. 2871034) on these early models. The engine on 1993 models is

fitted with a flush attachment. The engine on 1994-on models is fitted with a cooling system flush attachment kit (part No. 2871193).

CAUTION
Be careful when flushing the engine cooling system. Improper use of the flushing attachment can result in severe engine damage. Observe the following:

a. Do not flush a hot engine, because the sudden change in temperature may cause severe engine damage.

b. Do not attempt to flush the cooling system unless the engine is running. If the cooling system is flushed without the engine running, water will fill the engine and result in damage.

c. The flush kit can be used to supply engine coolant when the craft is out of the water, but only for running a very short time.

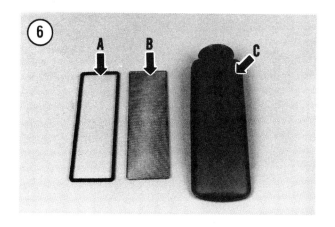

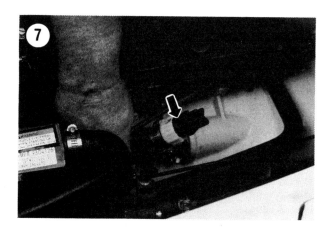

Running the engine for more than about 10 seconds without water will damage the rubber parts of the exhaust system and may damage other engine parts.

   d. Never operate the engine at maximum speed out of the water, even with the flush kit attached.

1. Remove the seat and engine cover.
2. Locate the flush adapter plug.

   a. The plug on 1992-1993 models is in the end of the drain/flush hose (**Figure 7**), which is usually at the bottom of the craft near the driveshaft.

   b. The plug on models from 1994-on is located in the left side of the water outlet manifold near the rear (A, **Figure 8**, typical).

3. Remove the plug from the flushing adapter.

CAUTION
Do not turn the water on until after the engine starts. However, be prepared to turn it on immediately upon starting.

4. Attach a garden hose to the flushing adapter.
5. Start the engine, then immediately turn the water to the flushing adapter ON.
6. Increase the engine speed slightly, then vary the engine speed for about 1 minute to completely flush the cooling system.
7. Turn the water OFF to the flushing adapter.

8. Stop the engine after all water has been expelled. Do not run the engine for more than a few seconds after turning the water OFF.

CAUTION
Running the engine for more than about 10 seconds without water will damage the rubber parts of the exhaust system and may also damage other engine parts.

9. Detach the hose from the flushing attachment.

10A. On 1992-1993 models (**Figure 9** or **Figure 10**), drain water from the engine as follows.

   a. Detach the hose connecting the pump to the exhaust manifold.

CAUTION
Do not raise the left side of the watercraft, or water can drain into the engine through the exhaust port. The engine can be easily damaged by water inside the cylinder and crankcase.

   b. Lower the exhaust manifold by tipping the right side of the craft up. The exhaust (left) side will be lower.

   c. Allow water to drain from the engine into the manifold, then drain from the manifold.

   d. Reattach the hose to the exhaust manifold.

   e. Reinstall the plug in the flushing adapter.

10B. On 1994-on models, draining is automatic. It is important to run the engine for a short time (10 seconds or less) after detaching the flushing hose, to make sure that all water is drained from the exhaust manifold.

11. The cooling system should be filled with antifreeze if there is any possibility of temperatures near 0° C (32° F). Refer to the following section in this chapter for filling the cooling system with antifreeze.

Filling the Cooling System with Antifreeze

If there is any possibility the craft will be subjected to temperatures near 0° C (32° F), the

11

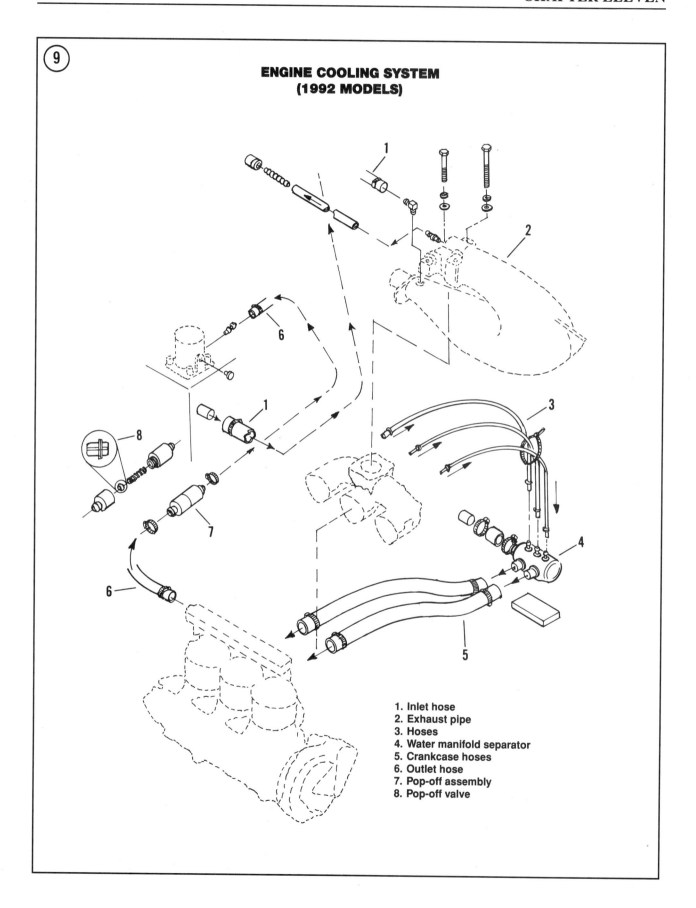

**ENGINE COOLING SYSTEM
(1992 MODELS)**

1. Inlet hose
2. Exhaust pipe
3. Hoses
4. Water manifold separator
5. Crankcase hoses
6. Outlet hose
7. Pop-off assembly
8. Pop-off valve

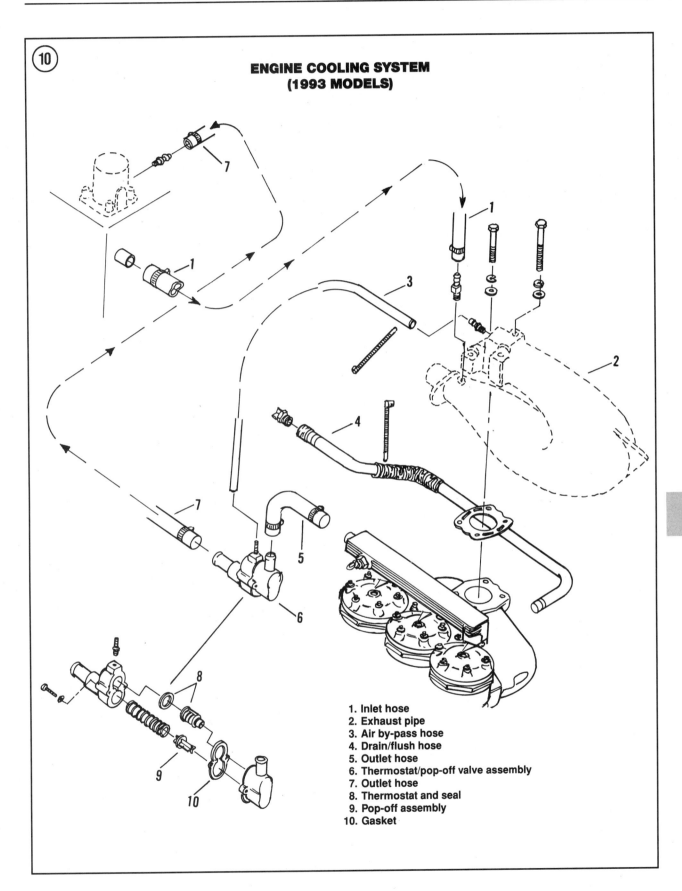

**ENGINE COOLING SYSTEM
(1993 MODELS)**

10

1. Inlet hose
2. Exhaust pipe
3. Air by-pass hose
4. Drain/flush hose
5. Outlet hose
6. Thermostat/pop-off valve assembly
7. Outlet hose
8. Thermostat and seal
9. Pop-off assembly
10. Gasket

11

cooling system should be drained and the system should be filled with antifreeze. Environmentally safe, biodegradable antifreeze designed for recreational vehicle water systems is recommended.

1. Flush the cooling system and drain all water as described in this chapter.

2. Allow the engine to run for a short time after disconnecting the flushing hose to blow some water from the system.

3A. On 1992-1993 models, detach the flushing hose, then proceed as follows.

    a. Leave the plug (**Figure 7**) out of the flushing adapter.

    b. Loosen the clamp (**Figure 2**, **Figure 8**) and the similar lower clamp on the same hose.

    c. Detach the lower end of the hose from the thermostat and pop-off housing.

    d. Turn the lower end of the disconnected hose up, so antifreeze can be poured into the hose, then tighten the upper clamp (B, **Figure 8**) temporarily.

    e. Pour about 2 L (1/2 gal.) of environmentally safe antifreeze into the open end of the 3/4 in. hose. While antifreeze is being poured into the hose, water will drain from the open drain/flush hose. The engine is sufficiently filled with antifreeze when antifreeze begins to flow from the drain/flush hose.

    f. Install the plug in the drain/flush hose.

    g. Loosen the clamp (B, **Figure 8**), turn the hose down and attach the end to the thermostat and pop-off housing. Tighten both clamps on the hose.

    h. Loosen the clamp and detach the coolant inlet hose from the lower end of the exhaust pipe.

    i. Temporarily attach a 5/8 in. hose to the fitting in the lower end of the exhaust pipe and pour about 2 L (1/2 gal.) of environmentally safe antifreeze into the upper end of the hose.

    j. Remove the hose that was temporarily attached to the exhaust pipe fitting and reattach the coolant inlet hose. Make sure the hose clamp is tightened securely.

3B. On 1994-on models (**Figure 11**), detach the flushing hose, then proceed as follows:

    a. Attach a short 1/2-1 M (2-3 ft.) section of garden hose to the flushing adapter and hold the free end of the hose up.

    b. Pour about 1/2 gal. of environmentally safe antifreeze into the engine, through the open end of the attached hose.

    c. Remove the short hose that was temporarily installed and install the plug securely in the flushing adapter.

Inspection During Storage

Inspect the craft frequently while in storage. Correct any deterioration as soon as possible. For example, if corrosion is observed, coat it lightly with grease or silicone spray.

CAUTION
Do not start the engine while it is in storage.

Restoring Craft to Service

A personal watercraft that has been properly prepared and stored in a suitable building should require only light maintenance before returning it to service. In addition to the following, it is advisable to perform a *Pre-Season Check-Up* as described in Chapter Three.

1. Remove the cover from the craft and check for visible signs of damage. Mice and other animals sometimes select a boat as a homesite. Check all rubber hoses and wiring for damage. Install new parts or repair all noticeable damage.

2. Make sure the on board fire extinguisher is fully charged.

3. Inspect your life jacket for condition.

4. Check the boat registration and make sure that your craft meets current local laws.

5. Fill the fuel tank with fresh gasoline.

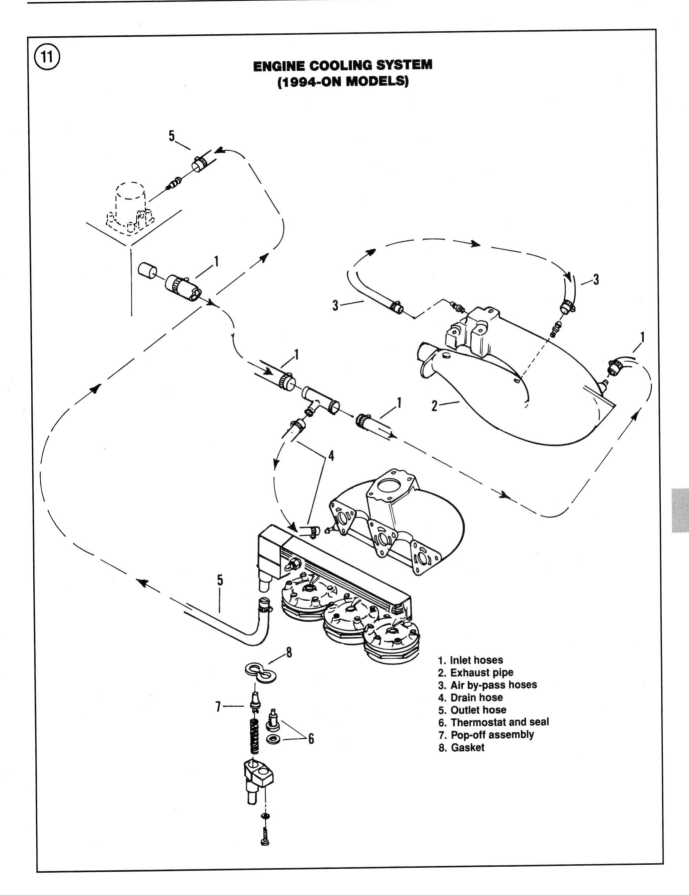

**ENGINE COOLING SYSTEM
(1994-ON MODELS)**

1. Inlet hoses
2. Exhaust pipe
3. Air by-pass hoses
4. Drain hose
5. Outlet hose
6. Thermostat and seal
7. Pop-off assembly
8. Gasket

11

6. Fill the oil tank with fresh 2-stroke engine oil.

7. Remove the spark plugs and install new or cleaned and regapped ones of the correct type and heat range.

8. Perform the standard tune-up as described in Chapter Three.

9. Start the engine and check the operation of the engine stop switch and tether switch. Oxidation may have occurred during storage that makes a switch inoperative. Do not operate the engine it can not be stopped by activating both of the stop switches.

10. Clean and test ride the craft.

Table 1 APPROXIMATE REFILL CAPACITY

Oil injection reservoir		
SL650 & SL750	3.3 L	3.5 qt.
SLT750	4.7 L	5 qt.
Fuel tank		
SL650 & SL750	37.1 L	9.8 gal.
SLT750	41.6 L	11 gal.

Index

12

1992 SL650

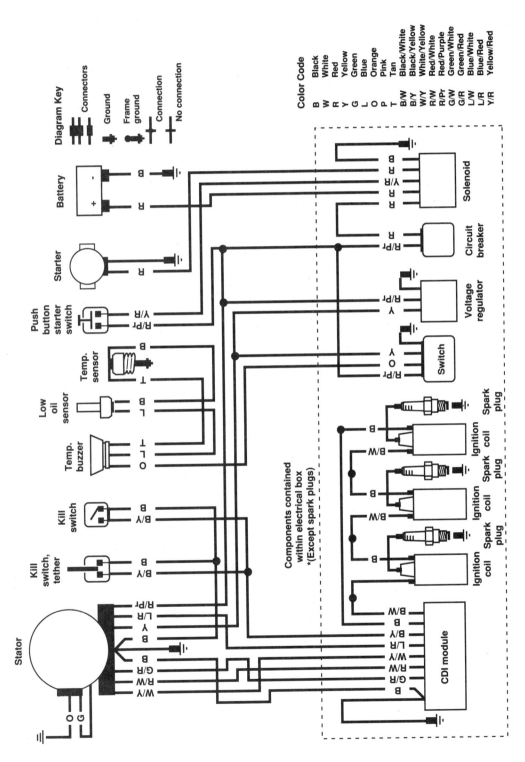

13

1993 SL650

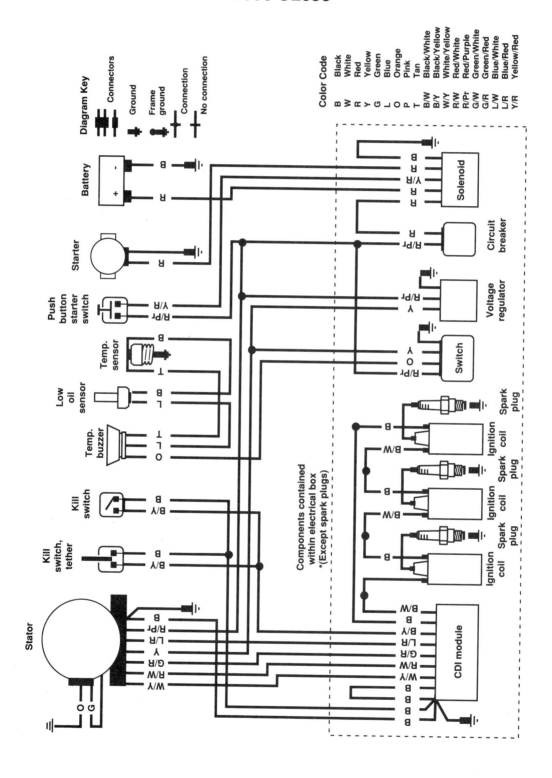

1993 SL750

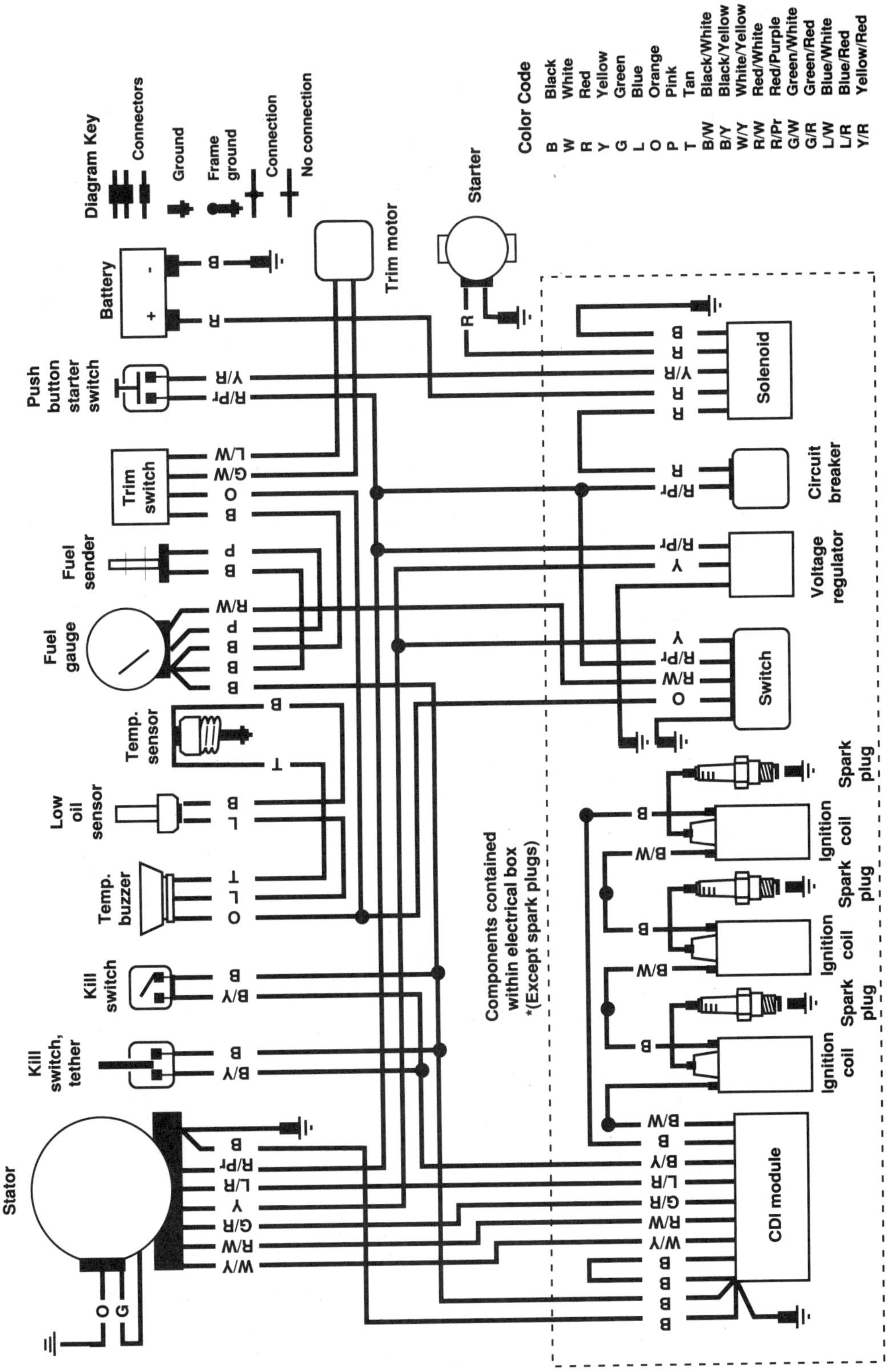

Diagram Key

Connectors

Ground

Frame ground

Connection

No connection

Color Code

B	Black	B/W	Black/White
W	White	B/Y	Black/Yellow
R	Red	W/Y	White/Yellow
Y	Yellow	R/W	Red/White
G	Green	R/Pr	Red/Purple
L	Blue	G/W	Green/White
O	Orange	G/R	Green/Red
P	Pink	L/W	Blue/White
T	Tan	L/R	Blue/Red
		Y/R	Yellow/Red

Battery

Push button starter switch

Trim switch

Fuel sender

Fuel gauge

Temp. sensor

Low oil sensor

Temp. buzzer

Kill switch

Kill switch, tether

Stator

Trim motor

Starter

Solenoid

Circuit breaker

Voltage regulator

Switch

Spark plug

Ignition coil

CDI module

Components contained within electrical box
*(Except spark plugs)

13

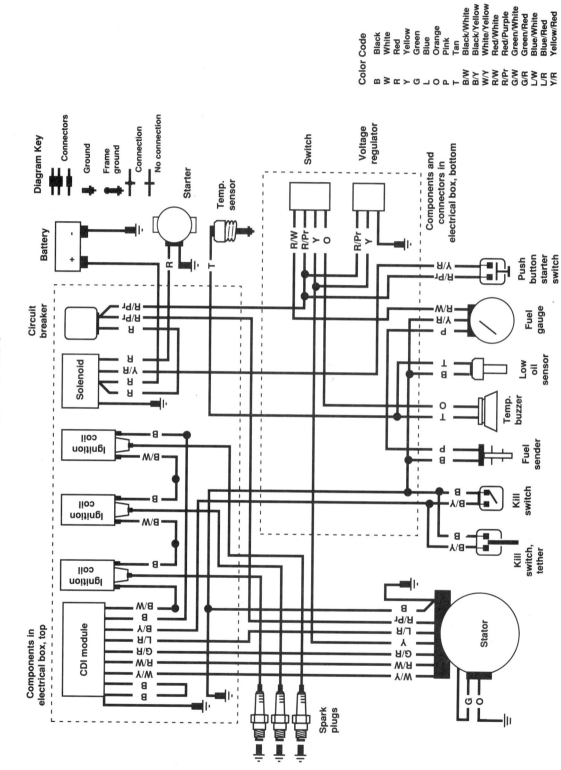

1994 SL650

Color Code
B — Black
W — White
R — Red
Y — Yellow
G — Green
L — Blue
O — Orange
P — Pink
T — Tan
B/W — Black/White
B/Y — Black/Yellow
W/Y — White/Yellow
R/W — Red/White
R/Pr — Red/Purple
G/W — Green/White
G/R — Green/Red
L/W — Blue/White
L/R — Blue/Red
Y/R — Yellow/Red

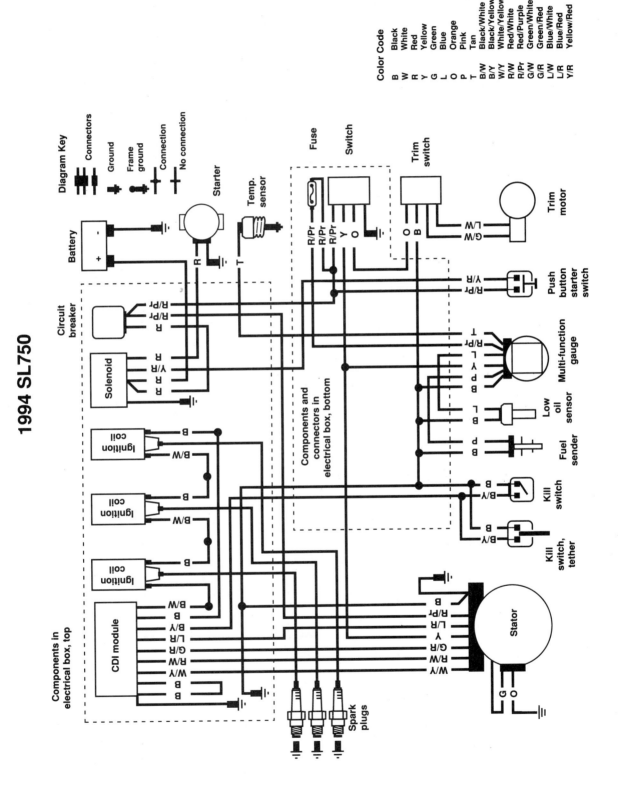

1994 SL750

13

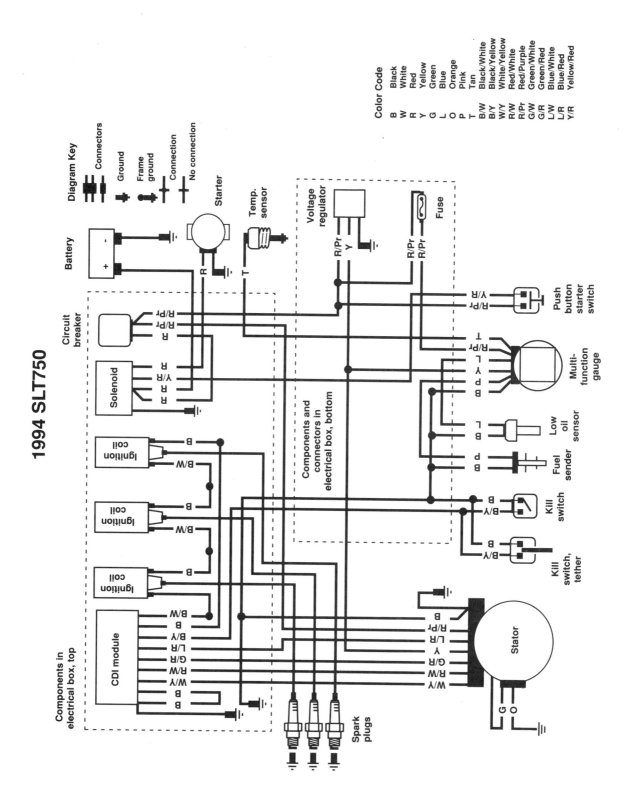

1994 SLT750

Color Code

B	Black	
W	White	
R	Red	
Y	Yellow	
G	Green	
L	Blue	
O	Orange	
P	Pink	
T	Tan	
B/W	Black/White	
B/Y	Black/Yellow	
W/Y	White/Yellow	
R/W	Red/White	
R/Pr	Red/Purple	
G/W	Green/White	
G/R	Green/Red	
L/W	Blue/White	
L/R	Blue/Red	
Y/R	Yellow/Red	

Diagram Key

Connectors

Ground

Frame ground

Connection

No connection

Battery

Starter

Temp. sensor

Voltage regulator

Fuse

Circuit breaker

Solenoid

Ignition coil

Ignition coil

Ignition coil

CDI module

Components in electrical box, top

Components and connectors in electrical box, bottom

Push button starter switch

Multi-function gauge

Low oil sensor

Fuel sender

Kill switch

Kill switch, tether

Spark plugs

Stator

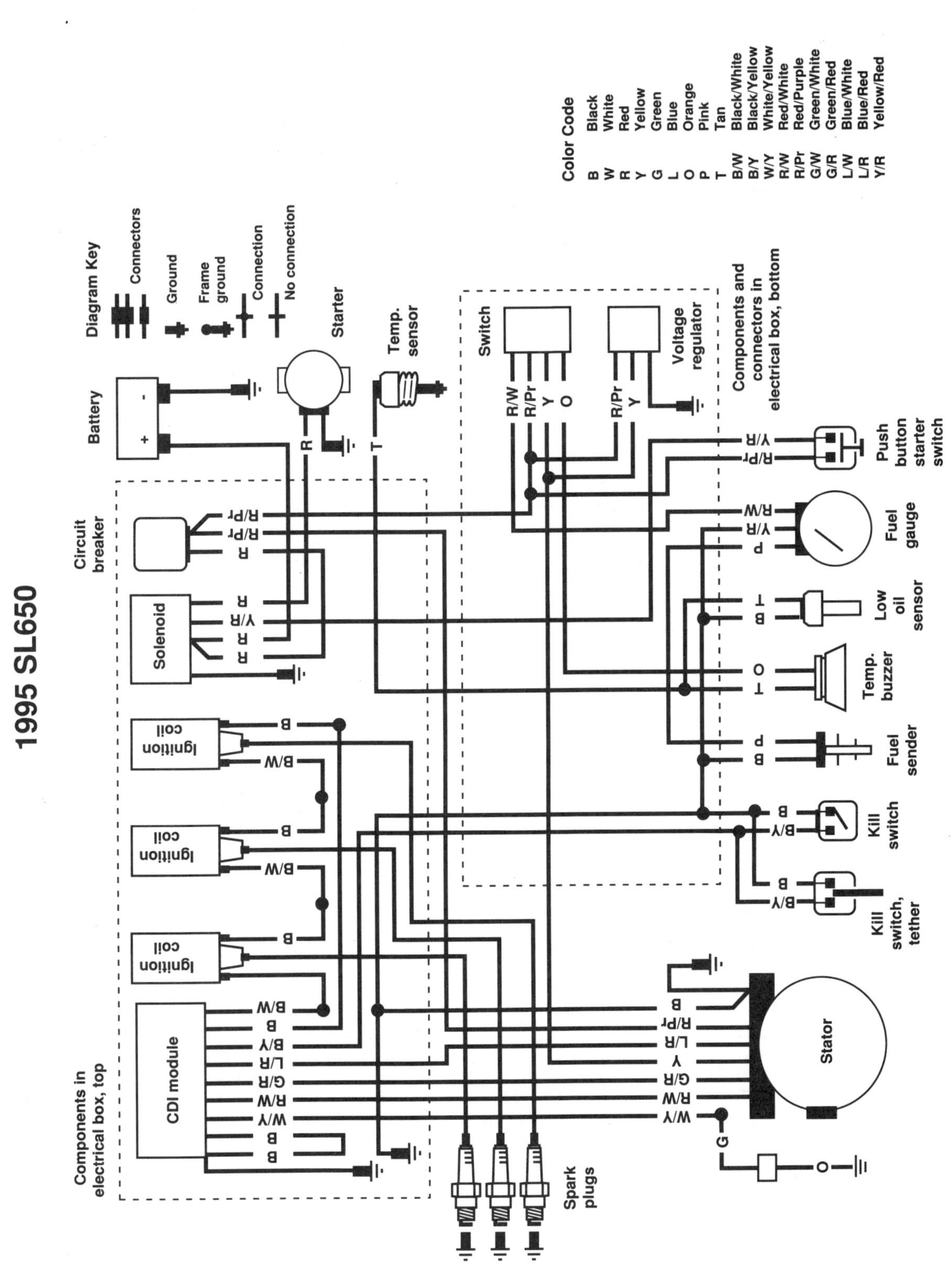

1995 SL650

Color Code

B	Black	B/W	Black/White
W	White	B/Y	Black/Yellow
R	Red	W/Y	White/Yellow
Y	Yellow	R/W	Red/White
G	Green	R/Pr	Red/Purple
L	Blue	G/W	Green/White
O	Orange	G/R	Green/Red
P	Pink	L/W	Blue/White
T	Tan	L/R	Blue/Red
		Y/R	Yellow/Red

Diagram Key

Connectors
Ground
Frame ground
Connection
No connection

Battery
Starter
Temp. sensor
Switch
Voltage regulator
Components and connectors in electrical box, bottom

Circuit breaker
Solenoid
Ignition coil
CDI module
Components in electrical box, top

Push button starter switch
Fuel gauge
Low oil sensor
Temp. buzzer
Fuel sender
Kill switch
Kill switch, tether
Stator
Spark plugs

R/W
R/Pr
Y
O

R/Pr
R/Pr
R
R
Y/R
R
R

B/W
B
B/Y
L/R
Y
G/R
R/W
W/Y
B

B
R/Pr
L/R
Y
G/R
R/W
W/Y

Y/R
R/Pr
R/W
Y/R
P
T
B
O
T
P
B
B
B/Y
B
B/Y
G

13

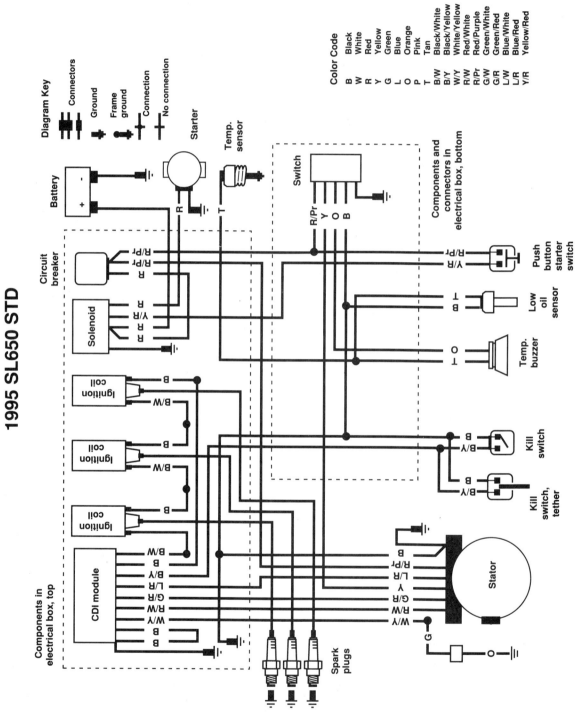

1995 SL650 STD

Diagram Key

Connectors
Ground
Frame ground
Connection
No connection

Color Code

B	Black
W	White
R	Red
Y	Yellow
G	Green
L	Blue
O	Orange
P	Pink
T	Tan
B/W	Black/White
B/Y	Black/Yellow
W/Y	White/Yellow
R/W	Red/White
R/Pr	Red/Purple
G/W	Green/White
G/R	Green/Red
L/W	Blue/White
L/R	Blue/Red
Y/R	Yellow/Red

Battery

Starter

Temp. sensor

Switch

Components and connectors in electrical box, bottom

Circuit breaker

Solenoid

Ignition coil

Ignition coil

Ignition coil

CDI module

Components in electrical box, top

Spark plugs

Push button starter switch

Low oil sensor

Temp. buzzer

Kill switch

Kill switch, tether

Stator

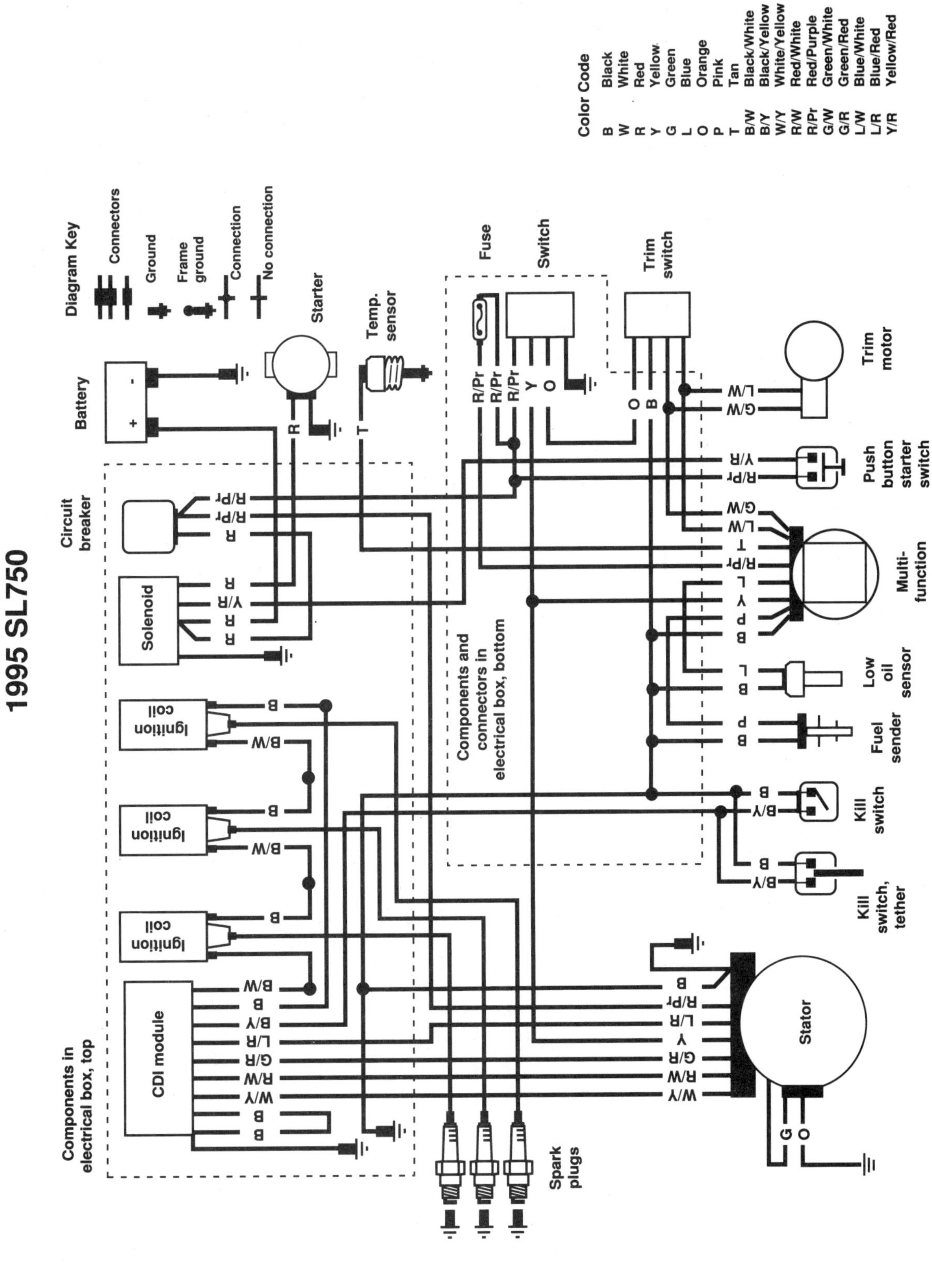

1995 SL750

Color Code

B	Black
W	White
R	Red
Y	Yellow
G	Green
L	Blue
O	Orange
P	Pink
T	Tan
B/W	Black/White
B/Y	Black/Yellow
W/Y	White/Yellow
R/W	Red/White
R/Pr	Red/Purple
G/W	Green/White
G/R	Green/Red
L/W	Blue/White
L/R	Blue/Red
Y/R	Yellow/Red

13

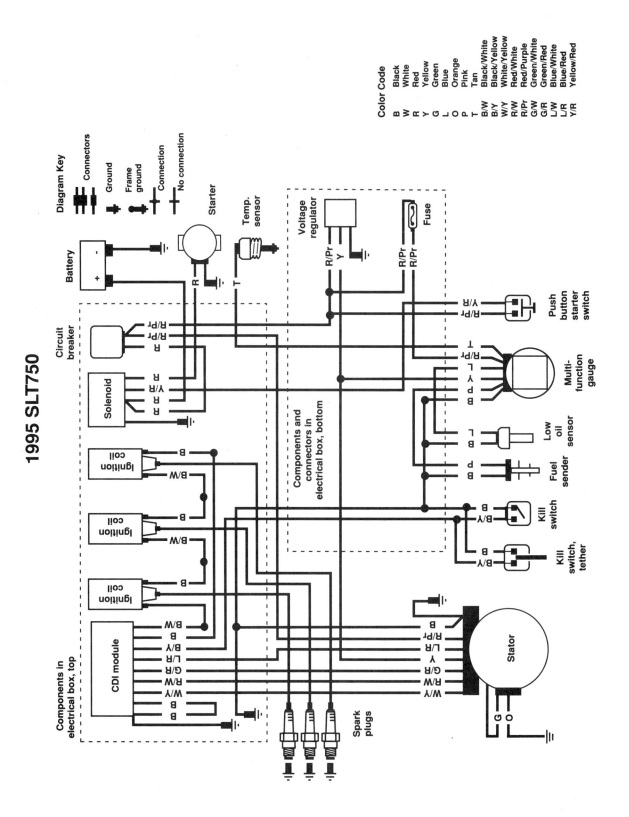

1995 SLT750

Color Code

B	Black
W	White
R	Red
Y	Yellow
G	Green
L	Blue
O	Orange
P	Pink
T	Tan
B/W	Black/White
B/Y	Black/Yellow
W/Y	White/Yellow
R/W	Red/White
R/Pr	Red/Purple
G/W	Green/White
G/R	Green/Red
L/W	Blue/White
L/R	Blue/Red
Y/R	Yellow/Red

Diagram Key

Connectors
Ground
Frame ground
Connection
No connection

NOTES

NOTES

NOTES

MAINTENANCE LOG

Service Performed   **Mileage Reading**

Oil change (example)	2,836	5,782	8,601		